A FOREMOST NATION

CANADIAN FOREIGN POLICY
AND A CHANGING WORLD

Edited by
Norman Hillmer
and
Garth Stevenson

McClelland and Stewart

Carleton Contemporaries

A series of books designed to stimulate
informed discussion of current and
controversial issues in Canada, and to
improve the two-way flow of ideas
between people and government.

ISSUED UNDER THE EDITORIAL
SUPERVISION OF THE INSTITUTE OF
CANADIAN STUDIES, CARLETON
UNIVERSITY, OTTAWA.
DIRECTOR OF THE INSTITUTE,
DAVIDSON DUNTON

Copyright © 1977 by McClelland & Stewart

0-7710-9911-8

The Canadian Publishers
McClelland and Stewart Limited
25 Hollinger Road, Toronto

PRINTED AND BOUND IN CANADA

For
Pat
and
Carol

TABLE OF CONTENTS

FOREWORD

There is no shortage of literature on recent Canadian foreign policy. The events of the last few years, however, have rendered much of this literature obsolete. Traditional controversies, such as the validity of Canada's membership in NATO, have largely been forgotten or superseded. New concerns have arisen: energy resources, the collapse of consensus on the Law of the Sea, and the international implications of industrial strategy, to name only a few.

At the same time, apparently, Canada's star has risen. John Holmes, it is true, has written of the nation's sad fate — "middle-powered, middle class and now middle-aged" — but Peter Dobell has recently elevated Canada's status from that of a "middle power" to that of a "minor great power." For James Eayrs, writing in the May-June (1975) issue of *International Perspectives*, such terms have lost their significance and meaning. Canada, he argues, has become a "foremost power" — foremost in the sense of being a "most notable or prominent" nation "in a world where the substance, and hence the distribution of power has undergone a swift and radical change." There are three major "new realities" in the international environment: the emergence of *le défi opec*; the increasing importance of resources; and the relative decline of the superpowers, the United States and the Soviet Union. Eayrs suggests that all these factors accrue particularly to Canada's benefit. "Compared to the ordeals," he has concluded elsewhere, "of so many peoples — destruction and occupation in war, civil strife, scouring tyranny, grinding poverty — our lot is singularly fortunate. By any of the indices of influence — food, land, minerals, oil, hydro-electricity, industrial capacity, high technology, to say nothing of what gifted immigrants can help us make of all of these — we are inordinately favoured."

Eayrs, as always, is controversial. We have adopted his terminology (without the characteristically Canadian question mark) for two reasons. First of all, the phrase "foremost nation" illustrates graphically the rapid changes which the world in general and Canadian foreign policy in particular have recently undergone. Certainly most of the contributors to this volume would agree that, at the very least, Canada is not a small and fragile nation, the "modest power" of which Prime Minister Trudeau spoke in 1968. Secondly, Eayrs' formulation of the problem points to the challenges which some of our contributors have issued to the Canadian foreign policy community, and the questions which others have raised about the conduct, nature and direction of our foreign policy. Many, although by no means all of our authors, are saying, with Eayrs, that we need a foreign policy to match our rhetoric and our endowments.

A major theme of this volume is the complexity and diversity of a Canadian foreign policy which for so long seemed merely one or two dimensional. We have sought to maintain a balance between essays mainly focussing on economic aspects of our external relations and those dealing with the diplomatic, security-oriented, or "voluntaristic" aspects, although a number of our papers testify to the increasing element of artificiality in these distinctions. We have avoided giving disproportionate weight to Canadian-American relations, since a considerable literature has recently been published in that field. Nonetheless, some of the essays inevitably deal with selected aspects of Canadian-American relations, and all of course make reference to the subject.

This volume has been written under the sponsorship, and with the financial assistance, of the School of International Affairs and the Institute of Canadian Studies of Carleton University. We gratefully acknowledge the advice, support, and encouragement of Michael G. Fry, Deputy Director of the School of International Affairs, Davidson Dunton, Director of the Institute of Canadian Studies and James Marsh, the Executive Editor of the Carleton Library Series and editor of the Carleton Contemporary series. The editors — one in particular — would also like to thank Pat Hillmer for her careful attention to matters of both substance and detail.

Carleton University   N.H.
October 15, 1975   G.S.

CHAPTER 1

THE IMPLICATIONS
OF AMERICAN ECONOMIC
NATIONALISM

Ian M. Drummond

Canadians brood on foreign trade with an intensity that is certainly excessive. Journalists and politicians think they understand the issues but, while expounding, they systematically misinform and mislead the public. As sources of public enlightenment, academic political scientists and historians have not been much better. These facts should not surprise us. Canadians are inheritors of a mercantilist tradition that we rediscover every generation. We all like to watch a good fight. And we can all enjoy the spurious drama of an international "confrontation" from which no blood will flow. Better a battle on beef or car parts than an anti-Communist crusade.

In recent years, Canadians in and out of office have begun to suspect that the United States is showing signs of "economic nationalism". In Canadian usage, this phrase is always a synonym for "protectionism", and I shall interpret it in that sense. Since we tend to think that American protectionism has hurt us in the past, we naturally worry at its reappearance. In the first part of this paper I shall sketch the historical background against which we can place the recent changes in American commercial policy. I do not think that the United States is suffering from a simple outbreak of economic nationalism. But in the 1960s she did have balance-of-payments problems, which finally demanded drastic surgical measures. Further, she has had to respond to protectionist initiatives in other countries — especially in Canada. These circumstances, not a wave of economic nationalism, have caused the actions that since 1971 have annoyed Canadians so much. In the second part of the essay, I shall canvass the strengths and weaknesses of our negotiating posture vis-a-vis the

3

United States. I conclude that our position is inherently far stronger than we usually think, and that we need not change our traditional trade orientations. Our commercial diplomacy, too, can continue with little fundamental change, though possibly we should defend our national interests more vigorously.

From the end of the War until the early 1960s, Canadian policy could be pursued in an extraordinarily self-regarding way. The reason for this was simple. We could count on a remarkably complaisant American government. The United States put no barriers in the way when its citizens wanted to export capital funds. It supplied Europe and other areas with the monetary aid that they needed in order, first, to reconstruct and then to resume economic progress. It happily watched its own gold reserves dwindle, and its short-term liabilities accumulate, because America's current-account surplus was not large enough to finance all of America's foreign lending and giving. The United States took the lead in helping to free world trade from the many tariff and non-tariff barriers that had accumulated in the thirties and forties. For Canada, all these American policies were extremely convenient. We wanted to expand our exports, both to the United States and to other countries. We wanted to import capital funds to prevent our development programmes from pressing too heavily on our own standards of living. By allowing capital exportation on so large a scale, by reducing trade barriers, and by flooding the world with dollars, the United States created an environment in which we could pursue our own national policies with relative ease.

We need not ask whether the United States' motives were or were not self-interested. Many years ago, Richard Gardner explained how mixed had been the motives of the Roosevelt administration when it extended lend-lease and reconstruction aid to Britain; with respect to America's post-war initiatives, other scholars and publicists have more recently trodden the same path. But international trade and investment do not constitute a zero-sum game. Whatever America's intentions, and whatever the results for the United States, other states could and did gain as well. We cannot, indeed, understand Canada's remarkable record of growth, expansion, and structural change, unless we place this record against its appropriate background: complaisant American policy.

Admittedly, things were not entirely smooth sailing even

before 1960. After the Second World War, the Canadian government faced an extremely difficult trading situation. Britain and Europe were eager for our goods, but could not supply us with what we wanted. The United States was eager to sell us what we wanted, but was much less eager to buy enough from us. Hence we had a chronic deficit with the United States and a chronic surplus with Britain and Europe. Before the war, we could convert our overseas surplus into dollars, and use these American dollars to pay for our imports from the United States. After the war, sterling and the continental currencies were not convertible; the overseas governments had no confidence in their abilities to earn enough dollars to pay for their own American purchases, much less ours. The Canadian government saw one solution in freer trade through which Britain and Europe, and perhaps Canada, could sell more to the United States. Canada's overseas earnings, plus our own American earnings, might then cover our American purchases. If American tariffs could be reduced, overseas currencies would become convertible, and we would be saved. Meanwhile, we would have to cover our deficits with the United States by importing capital funds and by drawing on our reserves.

In the 1940s, the United States appeared eager to co-operate in the creation of a new international order in which tariff barriers would be low and falling, and in which currencies would be freely convertible. It would seem that the Canadian government deliberately decided to handle our balance of payments problem by encouraging Americans to invest in Canada, and by trying to stimulate the development of industries that could export to the American market. Given our disadvantages in manufacturing, and given American tariff policies, these could only be resource industries. Hence it is hardly surprising that when the Eisenhower government showed signs of renewed protectionism, especially in the resource industries, our protests were so long and pained. It must have seemed that the Americans would not let us win, under any circumstances. When the Eisenhower regime also began to subsidize agricultural exports, damaging our traditional overseas earnings, our plaints were even longer and louder. Fortunately, the United States did not try to control capital exports during the fifties. Indeed, after 1956 our own central bank took steps that actively encouraged our import of American capital.

In the end, although American subsidies and protectionism were cause for international discussion and for journalistic disquisition, they did not hurt us very much. Through 1956, we shared in the worldwide boom, and our living standards rose dramatically. In the late 1950s we suffered from recession, and we certainly caught this recession from the United States. The basic problem was not American protectionism or American economic nationalism; it was, rather, that the United States itself was having a slump. A fall in American economic activity meant a weaker demand for Canadian exports, regardless of the minor protectionist steps that the American Government was taking.[1]

In the early 1960s the skies grew slightly more cloudy. The United States, in sponsoring the Kennedy Round of trade talks, was still pursuing world-wide tariff reduction through GATT. But in 1959 Washington had imposed quotas on her imports of overseas oil. More serious, the American Treasury had become worried about its national balance of payments. The United States was still exporting far more than she was importing, but her foreign aid, lending, and direct investing had so far exceeded her current-account surplus as to reduce her gold reserves from $24 billion in 1948 to $16 billion in 1962. Meanwhile, foreigners had built up their short-term claims from $7 billion to $24-billion, and all these liabilities were payable in gold. By keeping interest rates relatively high at home, the Americans could have discouraged new capital exports, while encouraging the foreigners to retain these enormous short-term claims not in gold but in interest-bearing forms. However, the American government wanted lower interest rates, in order to encourage domestic investment, especially in housing. Thus for the first time in many years the United States authorities faced a conflict between the imperatives of domestic monetary policy and the external pressures of the national external assets and liabilities. To escape the dilemma, in 1963 the United States invented an "interest equalization tax". This was meant to ensure that when foreigners borrowed in the United States they would pay more than American borrowers. The tax would allow the authorities to lower domestic interest rates without provoking a capital flight.[2]

Canada responded with squeals of outrage. We "depended" on American capital! We were America's best friend, and her best customer! We had pegged our exchange rate! We had a special relationship! How could they do this to us? Our representatives trotted off to Washington and returned with an exemption. As long as we did not borrow to increase our reserves of gold and foreign exchange, our new borrowings would not pay the new tax; that is, so long as we used our borrowings to finance our overall current-account deficit, and not to build up gold and foreign exchange by borrowing in the United States capital market, we were to be allowed preferential access to that market.

We did not really need the exemption. If our monetary authorities had been willing to force our interest rates sufficiently higher, we could have attracted the necessary flow of American dollars, even if our borrowings had been subject to the tax. Or if we had been prepared to devalue our dollar relative to the American, our export receipts would have risen and our import payments fallen in a fashion that would have reduced our need for external funds. But the Canadian government was prepared neither to change our exchange rate nor to force our interest rates upward. In effect, we wanted the exemption only because we were unwilling to use the macro-economic weapons that were already present in our own armoury. Only because of this reluctance did American economic nationalism impinge on us; only because of this reluctance did we need to ask for an exemption, and to accept the limitations on our freedom that were attached thereto.

Similar problems arose when, in 1968, the United States Government proposed "guidelines" for multi-national corporations. These guidelines were widely interpreted as an evil attempt to manipulate other countries in the American national interest, but they were simply a reflection of America's peculiar and growing balance-of-payments problem. Having noticed that multi-national corporations exported a good deal of finance from the United States to their external subsidiaries, and that they did not always transfer their foreign profits back home, the Americans proposed that in future such companies should bring back more profit and export less finance. Again Canadians wailed about our balance of payments, and our ministers were quick to reiterate their own 1966 guidelines: if a multi-national company was operating in Canada, it should continue to bring funds from its home country, and it should not send too much

7

back! Like the row over the interest-equalization tax, this disturbance reflected our unwillingness to employ our own macroeconomic weapons — in particular, to use interest rates and exchange rates in an equilibrating way.

Perhaps, in the long years of calm, our weapons had rusted with disuse, or perhaps we had begun to forget that they existed. During the later sixties, our politicians and officials liked to pretend that we would never again change our exchange rate. Since they had promised the United States that they would not allow our foreign-exchange reserves to increase, they had to manage our domestic monetary and financial system in accordance with that promise; that is, they had to make sure that Canadian interest rates and credit flows would attract only enough American capital funds to finance our current-account deficit. In this situation, therefore, we had willingly surrendered our power to use monetary policy or exchange-rate policy. The result was convenient for professors of economics. It is much simpler to teach macro-economics when exchange rates do not move and when a country has no independent monetary policy, but if we had persevered in this self-abnegation, we should have seriously damaged our ability to manage our own price and employment levels, and even our balance of payments itself. Fortunately, it appears that within the offices of Ottawa there must have been some officials who remembered how well we had managed a floating exchange rate in the early 1950s, and who understood that neither exchange rates nor exchange reserves can stay pegged forever. In 1968, faced with an inflow of European capital funds, the Canadian government persuaded the Americans to agree that we could add to our reserves as long as we were not borrowing the extra reserves in New York. In May 1970, we floated the Canadian dollar.

Thereafter, though the American guidelines and the interest equalization tax lingered on, we could ignore them. Whatever American policy might be, we could rely on the foreign exchange market to avert balance-of-payments problems, because the price of foreign exchange would automatically react to any untoward movements of American capital funds. In the event, during 1970 and for two years thereafter, our balance of payments was extraordinarily strong. Running current-account surpluses for the first time in twenty years, we no longer needed to rely on American capital funds, and our government was able to increase its own foreign-exchange reserves. Furthermore, by floating our dollar in 1970 we prepared ourselves psychologically for the international excursions and alarums that President Nixon provoked with his "New Economic Policy".

In 1970, we worried about a congressional measure that would have allowed Nixon to impose import quotas. Fortunately, that measure died on Capitol Hill, but on August 15, 1971, President Nixon torpedoed the international monetary system which we had helped to erect at Bretton Woods in 1944, and within which we had prospered so mightily throughout the 1950s and 1960s. Further, by devising import surcharges and export subsidies, Nixon and Connally appeared to drag the United States back into the protectionism from which Cordell Hull had so painfully extracted it in the 1930s.

Nixon broke the link between gold and the U.S. dollar. Since August 15, 1971, the Treasury has been free from its old obligation to sell gold at the official price. In other words, the Treasury is no longer required to sell gold for dollars. Nixon also announced that the American authorities would no longer intervene in foreign exchange markets to support or manipulate exchange rates. Other countries quickly abandoned the attempt to peg their currencies. Mr. Nixon had introduced a system of "general floating" that is with us still. Though there have been spasmodic attempts to reconstruct the Bretton Woods regime of fixed exchange rates, these attempts have been in part short-lived, and in part failures.

Connally and Nixon also wanted to "improve the American balance of payments". Though the United States had been running a current-account surplus for decades, by 1971 the mass of foreign claims had reached $68 billion — an embarrassingly large amount relative to Treasury gold reserves, which had shrunk to $11 billion. The United States could not, or would not, take further measures to restrict the private capital-exports that had largely caused the problem. However, by protectionism she might restrict her imports of goods, or encourage foreign countries to reduce their trade barriers and to choose more realistic exchange rates. Further, by subsidy she might increase her exports of goods, further strengthening her current account for the sake of her capital-exports.

Nixon did not tell Canada of his plans. The "special relationship" had ended. Canadian publicists and public figures were inclined to see his initiatives as an evil piece of economic nationalism, and as a major threat to our own prosperity. Of course the American president was trying to advance his own country's interests. In so doing he was serving notice that the days of American complaisance were gone, perhaps forever. Aside from this, it is certainly true that by summer 1971 the Bretton Woods system was rotten at the core. Since 1968 it had been kept going only by a series of rescue operations, and it had generated a series of international monetary crises from which only currency speculators had gained. Further, by 1970 everyone knew that the great capitalist powers would never agree on reform. Indeed, even to bandage the old system they had to spend weeks and months on excruciating negotiation. Since the United States dollar was at the centre not only of the Bretton Woods agreements themselves, but of the international financial system that had grown up around the Bretton Woods regime, at any time the United States could have acted to destroy or modify the system. For instance, in 1968 or in 1971, as in 1944, she could have compelled the other countries to acquiesce in American desires. That is what President Nixon did in August 1971. He did not usher in an "era of chaos". In Canada, as elsewhere, real output and employment rose extremely rapidly from mid-1970 to early 1974. Admittedly, we have had some monetary disturbances, and the press has called them "crises" but these ripples did not interrupt the wave of inflationary expansion that spread around the world.

Because exchange rates have been floating or frequently changing all over the world, things have been easier for our own government. Ottawa has been able to preserve the "right to float" far more easily than it could have done in a "fixed-rate" environment, and we have been able to "manage the float" for the sake of domestic objectives, without attracting the unfortunate notice that so discomfited Finance Minister Donald Fleming when, in 1961-2, he was experimenting with a managed float.

As for Connally's DISCs and import surcharges, the latter were gone by December 1971, and no one knows how important the former may have been. The DISC problem is quite complicated. The law allows an American corporation to set up a special export subsidiary — a DISC. The DISC's profits are partially exempt from tax so long as they are not distributed to the parent corporation. Thus the DISC will keep more of its profits than if the concession did not exist. But the concession cannot create profits. And it works only on American exports. Hence no DISC could affect the profitability of exporting from a Canadian branch plant to the American market. Only where Canadian and American plants are competing within Canada and in third countries could the DISC cost us sales or jobs. Further, even in these markets the DISC affects competitiveness only in rather special circumstances. First of all, the firms must be selling in particular marketing conditions (technically, monopolistic competition or differentiated oligopoly). Second, the firms must be fixing their prices by applying a target rate of return after tax to their production costs. Finally, American production costs must be sufficiently higher than Canadian for this pricing convention to produce a lower selling price. Many DISCs have been set up since 1971. But in practice one or more of these conditions is often violated. In such cases, the DISC raises after-tax profit but it does not affect the international distribution of orders, production, or jobs. Our fear of the DISC was understandable but not creditable. It is another paper tiger.

After Nixon introduced his programme, the American current account did not improve. It worsened substantially, moving into deficit for the first time in this century.[3] Thereafter it again improved, and the usual surpluses have now reappeared. In so far as the DISCs contributed to this improvement, they may have captured some business from Canadian factories, but two other things probably deserve most of the credit. One is the explosion of food prices. Since the United States is a massive exporter of foods and fibres, whose prices rose especially high, the terms of trade have turned in America's favour, and the effect is shown on her balance of payments. The other is the new constellation of exchange rates. If we compare 1975 with 1970, we see that the American dollar is now substantially cheaper relative to the yen or the mark, while American inflation has been less rapid than the Japanese and no more rapid than the German. Hence many American manufacturers, must have recaptured some of the competitive edge, both at home and abroad, that they had enjoyed in the fifties and earlier sixties. Further, these price changes have discouraged the ubiquitous American tourist.

So far we have been examining those aspects of American economic nationalism that we can handle, or live with, by employing the ordinary tools of macro-economic policy. However, there are many problems that cannot be handled in this way. Recently, the most important have arisen in connection with automobiles, water, oil, and food. We shall glance at these in turn. As other papers in this volume treat some of them in greater detail, our comments are brief.[4]

Canadian government actions have made our car industry sensitive to American protectionism. In the early sixties, our government was worried about the future of the industry. Overseas competitors — first British, then German, and at length Japanese — were taking more and more of the Canadian domestic market. Before 1939 our car industry had exported both cars and parts, largely to Britain and to certain Commonwealth countries that granted preferential duties. The Second World War ended this trade. During the fighting and for some years thereafter, our former export markets were closed by high duties and import controls. As these barriers fell during the 1950s, it became clear that the North American car, in which Canadian factories specialized, had little future overseas. Our cars had become too large, flimsy, ugly, and thirsty for some markets, while in others, such as Australia and India, local governments were determined to promote their own car factories.

In short, though preferential duties often survived within the Commonwealth, the market was dead by 1960, while outside the Commonwealth where our goods enjoyed no tariff concessions our factories could not compete with the American. Canadians sometimes suspected that the multinational car companies discriminated against their Canadian plants in the allocation of export orders, but it is now reasonably clear that the problem was profitability, not nationalism. Canadian costs were so high relative to American costs that no rational, profit-maximizing car firm would supply an overseas non-Commonwealth market from its Canadian plant.

The Canadian government first tried to revive our car industry with tariff devices that were thinly disguised subsidies. Then it determined on a bold stroke. It would negotiate a continental free-trade agreement for cars and parts. Canada's plants would specialize, thus lowering their costs. We would buy more cars from the United States, but sell even more to the United States. Our current-account balance would improve — no small matter during the period when our exchange rate was pegged. There would be more jobs in the car works, and more votes from them. The American automobile producers would probably expand their Canadian works, because Canadian wage rates were lower than American.

To the Pearson government the Auto Pact of 1965 was a victory. Nevertheless, in negotiating the agreement our ministers gave hostages to fortune. Sooner or later some American was bound to suspect the awful truth. In the United States the Pact could not expand car sales because it would not lower car prices. In Canada, where the car firms had not promised to lower prices, and where government did not force them to do so, the same thing was true. Hence Canadian output and employment could rise only at the expense of American. The Pact, in other words, is a classic example of the "beggar-my-neighbour" solution to unemployment. The automobile manufacturers are presumably indifferent, or actively in favour of the Pact. Having plants on both sides of the border, they can adjust to whatever legal framework the two governments may devise. Indeed, they should favour the Pact, since it has certainly increased their profits. On the other hand, considering the overall effects of the Pact, it is hardly surprising that American critics, especially unionists, began to lobby against it almost as soon as it had been published.

Meanwhile, on the Canadian side the Pact has created a series of commitments that future Canadian governments will ignore only at their peril. New factories have been built, new jobs created, new municipal revenues generated. For the indefinite future our governments will feel obliged to protect these commitments against American "economic nationalism". They may convince the American Government that it should continue to let us export some unemployment via the Auto Pact. If so, we are not likely to get away scot-free. From another area — perhaps a more dangerous and painful one — we shall certainly have to yield up a pound of flesh.

Some years ago, we all learned in *Doctor Strangelove* that we must safeguard our vital bodily fluids. Canadians seem to have taken this advice to heart. Some parts of the United States want to use our water for hydro-power. Some want to drink from our crystal springs. Others want our gas and our oil. Vital fluids, certainly. The United States, outgrowing its own resource base, has begun to look for cheap and reliable supplies elsewhere. For fifteen years or more, our own politics and our own federal-provincial relations have been conditioned by this American desire — not only by its existence but also by its changing nature and content.

The United States does not have a national water policy, but American politicians, like Canadian, have begun to notice that it is politically dangerous to raise the prices of the basic utilities — especially water, electricity, and gas. Further, in the future as in the recent past, the environmentalists' lobby will try to prevent the construction of new generating capacity — expecially thermal or nuclear plants. Hence the vital-fluids problem will not go away. Wherever it is politically possible to dam a river and flood a border valley, we should expect that the American authorities will want to do so. Faced with such proposals, we should do our best to respond rationally. Artificial lakes can be beautiful and useful. Nor should we object merely because some Canadians have to move. The right questions are so obvious that it is rather embarrassing to have to underline them. Will the Americans pay enough to compensate the displaced Canadians? Once proper compensation is paid, will our governments get anything, and will they get enough? Our governments should certainly try to exact the maximum payment. Often they have a great deal of leverage. In the past, particularly in British Columbia, it seems they have not used it. In future we should not let our provincial and national governments repeat such errors. The Columbia fiasco stands as a terrible warning.

If we generate the hydro power and then export it, the same general argument applies. So long as the power is badly needed, and so long as other sources are costly or unavailable, our bargaining position is inherently strong, and we should recognize this fact. Fortunately, in exporting hydro power we are not depleting an exhaustible resource, but we should make sure that we retain control. Contracts should be for relatively short periods, and there should be plentiful provision for re-negotiation of the price and for termination after due notice. There is, I think, no general case for simply refusing to export hydro power. It used to be said that if we kept the power the industry would come to Canada and use it here, but as we become less enamoured of massive capital inflows, and more interested in the preservation of the environment, the force of this argument has weakened greatly.

As for food, Canada can seldom expect much access to the American market, where a variety of import-controls are needed to support farm incomes. Farmers are influential in both countries, and our own protectionist devices are paralleled south of the border. This agrarian protectionism should not be seen as some new kind of economic nationalism. Consider the recent "beef war". In excluding Canadian beef, the United States was trying in part to offset the fall in domestic beef prices. This fall, in turn, reflected Mr. Nixon's inept manipulation of domestic price controls, and it also echoed the extremely high beef prices of preceding years. But the United States was also reacting to our own protectionist measures, by which we too were trying to shelter our farmers against their own overproduction.

The petroleum perplex is the most puzzling of all. For many years, American economic nationalism and national security determined the United States petroleum policy. By quotas and tariffs American high-cost wells were protected from cheaper Arab and Venezuelan oil. Though it did not aim at complete self-sufficiency, the American Government was reluctant to depend on overseas oil. The Government retained certain reserves, and by its tariff, quota, and tax policies it deliberately encouraged domestic exploration and production. Canadian oil was considered a special case. It was fairly safe, since the pipelines came overland and since we could be trusted politically and militarily. Therefore, until 1970 we were exempted from the oil quotas, thanks not to American benevolence but to American self-interest. However, as so often occurred in the fifties and early sixties, American self-interest coincided with Canadian. We had plenty of Alberta oil. Eastern Canada could be supplied more cheaply from overseas. By building a fence at the Ottawa River, the Canadian government had generated an artificial and protected market for the Alberta crude. How fortunate that in the Middle West and Far West the Americans were eager to buy more of the stuff!

In the "energy crisis" atmosphere of 1974-75, it is hard to recall how angry we were when President Nixon tried to regulate our oil exports. Of course we should now be grateful. He prevented us from selling our oil at $2.50 or less; we can now sell the same oil for $10.50 or more. This is not to say that we were wrong to export so much oil in the 1960s. During those years, world oil prices were relatively depressed by the vast flow of Arab oil, and few people suspected that the Arabs would ever manage to create a strong cartel. Even now, their success may prove temporary. In the past, no cartel has long managed to control world trade in any raw material. In the sixties, OPEC twice tried to raise oil prices, and twice the price fell back to the old level, but the Arabs' action has frightened Canadians so thoroughly that we shall not find it easy to be rational about our past oil sales and about any future exports. On the one hand, so long as OPEC is fractious, American fright makes Canadian oil a potent weapon. On the other hand, our publicists and politicians seem likely to opt for a high-cost self-sufficiency, turning off the oil tap rather firmly and rather rapidly. It is easy to construct the following scenario. First, we reduce our oil exports, annoying the Americans and causing them to retaliate on some other front, while we frantically develop extra high cost oil production from tar sands or ice floes. Next, OPEC collapses once more, and world oil prices fall sharply. Third, we find ourselves with the worst of all possible worlds: an overexpanded, high cost oil industry, an unco-operative American administration, and an unreceptive export market.

It would be wrong to construe from the "beef war", the energy crisis, Connally's adventures, and the famous "eleven grievances", that the United States is embarked on a protectionist course. It would be even more silly to assert that this rather scattered group of incidents justifies or requires any fundamental change in Canada's trading patterns or in our economic policy. In the future, as in the past, our best course is to extract sizeable gains from the international specialization and division of labour, to which we have long committed ourselves, while we use diplomacy — quiet or noisy as the occasion demands — to protect our national interests. In so doing, we are more likely to get full value if we recognize how strong our position really is.

By 1975, we had recovered the power to use not only tax policy and monetary policy but also exchange-rate policy. We had begun to realize that as long as our exchange rate was floating we need not worry about our balance of payments. We could, instead, apply all the weapons of macro-economic policy in the service of our domestic objectives. In so far as American

16

economic nationalism has a macro-economic impact, our government can deal with that impact by employing the right weapons from our own armoury. It need not run to Washington and ask for special treatment; it need not behave as if Canada's fate is in the hands of the United States president. Admittedly, macro-economic weapons do not always work perfectly, and we cannot always predict exactly how potent they may be. But the same can be said of the traditional responses: protectionist retaliation and autarchy. Furthermore, in Canada the science of econometric forecasting is now well-developed. We can now work out the probable effects of various American actions and Canadian counter-actions in some detail. If our publicists and intellectuals ever trouble to recognize this fact, they may gradually learn to avoid the more paranoid responses with which they all too frequently greet any self-serving American action.

If macro-economic weapons are too slow or too broad in their effect, we can, and often should, subsidize the industries that American policy has injured. In 1971, fearing the worst from the Nixon-Connally adventures, our government did exactly this. Because we had exaggerated the damage, the programme proved to be larger and more generous than it really had to be. Nevertheless the action was sensible in principle, and we should remember it.

In responding to American actions, we should try to remember that what is good for some single country is sometimes good for others as well. This was true of American largesse in the immediate post-war years. In large part it was true of Nixon's New Economic Policy. Perhaps it will be true of Washington's next policy initiative, whatever that may be.

We are accustomed to moan and groan about the multi-national corporations to which we are hosts, but these companies can perhaps strengthen our hand when we must counter or prevent some American protectionist idea. It used to be argued that if foreign firms were obliged to choose between their domestic and their external operations they would systematically favour their domestic plants. Few economists ever believed this. We should expect, instead, that capitalists would allocate production and jobs in accordance with profitability, not nationality. Safarian's work has tended to confirm this deduction with a mass of factual information. We should not expect foreign capitalists to worry about Canadian jobs unless we make

17

it worth their while. However, they will certainly worry about the use of their Canadian plants. In so far as these plants are designed to service American markets, the foreign firm has an interest in opposing American protectionism. Surely it is easier for Congress or the executive to gore a Canadian-owned company than an American firm.

If the American firms were a substantial burden to our economy, we might reject this line of thought, arguing that the insurance premium was too high. In fact, however, the burden is remarkably small.

In 1973, Canada had a surplus of $2.1 billion on merchandise trade, but on services we had a deficit of $2.8 billion. Thus our current account was in deficit to the amount of $0.7 billion. Among the "services" entries are all our international payments of interest and dividends, and all such receipts. We received $653-million in interest and dividends from abroad, but we paid out $1905 million, of which $1246 million was dividends. The ordinary citizen is bound to think that these figures are frighteningly large. But they are small relative to the total size of the Canadian economy. In 1973, our gross national product was $119 billion. Thus our current-account deficit was 0.6 percent of GNP, and our remittances of interest and dividends were 1.6 percent of GNE, and 6 percent of our current export receipts. If we deduct our receipts of interest and dividends from our payments, in order to measure the net burden of our foreign indebtedness, of course the percentages are even less: 1.1 percent of GNE, and 4 percent of export receipts.[5]

Not only is the burden small; it has been falling for a decade, and it is far less than it was in the 1920s. In 1926, debt service absorbed 4.6 percent of our GNP, and 14.5 percent of our export receipts. The percentages fell sharply in the forties, but then they rose again. In 1963, after Mr. Coyne's nationalist extravaganza, but before Mr. Gordon's, they were 2 percent and 9.3 percent. Since that time they have fallen, to the point where no rational and well-informed person should now regard them as a serious macro-economic problem.

We may take further comfort from the recent changes in the international monetary system. Since the U.S. dollar is now a floating currency, and is no longer convertible into gold, America's balance of payments can no longer provide any objective justification for her protectionism. This is not to say that we have nothing to fear. Just as Ottawa might spawn another Coyne or Gordon, so Washington might attract another Nixon or Connally. But since Mr. Connally left office, and since the logic of floating has gradually permeated the official Washington mind, Canada, like other countries, has found American trade policy far more accommodating than anyone would have predicted in the fall of 1971.

Nevertheless, in so far as we trade with the United States we do run the risk that American domestic pressures will now and then force the American authorities to restrict or exclude some of our goods. I do not think that this risk is great enough, or that the damage would be great enough, to justify us in trying to change the pattern of Canadian-American trade. In particular, I think we should be most unwise if we let the events of 1971 drive us farther toward that protectionism from which we have been so lately and incompletely weaned. So far as I can see, the usual economists' argument still applies: there are gains from trade, and in our own national interest we should seize them so far as we can. To capture them, of course we must engage in trade, and in particular we must import as well as export.

On the other hand, we should certainly refrain from giving unnecessary hostages to fortune. Here I find real difficulty with the Auto Pact, and real perplexity about continental energy flows. We gain leverage in so far as we make Americans depend on our power, gas, and oil; we lose leverage in so far as Canadian jobs and political successes come to depend on the continuation or extension of special deals which we obtained only because of our "special relationship". Deduction cannot tell us where the balance lies. Indeed, we may never know until long after some agreement has been reached. Only then can we hope to detect the actual impact, not only on our prosperity but on our autonomy.

To many readers, this sort of prescription is insufficiently dramatic. We are used to strident calls that summon us to action. Is genuine dramatic action impossible? Of course it is not. Our government could wrench Canada away from the American market. In time, we would export less to the United States, and import less from her. The process, however, would be neither quick nor easy. We export over 25 percent of our output and import over 25 percent of our needs. Our economy is closely integrated with the world economy in general, and with the

American economy in particular. We have developed whole industries, especially extractive industries, on an export basis. If we decide to abstain from exportation because this is a risky sort of dependent relationship, these industries will have to shrink. Our manufacturing depends heavily on imports of components, and some branches of manufacturing, such as the car industry, have developed large American markets. If we disengage ourselves from the United States, the export manufacturing industries will also have to shrink, and we shall have to develop domestic sources for the many raw materials and semi-fabricates that we now import. These changes would be painful not only for capitalists but for workers. Our government would have to develop a programme of import substitution and input reallocation. That is, Ottawa would have to arrange for the transfer of labour and equipment from the export industries into the import replacing industries. Unfortunately, some labour is not readily transferable, and a great deal of the specialized plant and equipment cannot be transferred at all. There is little that a nickel mine can do, except produce nickel. Hence we could not attain our goals simply by transferring inputs: we should have to build new plant and equipment on a really enormous scale, and we should have to retrain many workers and retire many more. If we are to judge by the experience of other countries that have tried to manage this sort of disengagement from the world market, the transition would be very painful indeed. Consumers, of course, would have to learn to abstain from a wide range of foreign goods and services. For many years, the whole economy would have to use more productive capacity for investment, and less for consumption. In the early years of the transition, this high investment would almost certainly create inflationary pressures, depress the external value of the currency, and reduce living standards substantially. Less essential goals, such as housing and urban improvement, would probably be sacrificed to make room for the import-replacing investment.

In the longer run, our standard of living could begin to rise again, but it would be rising from a lower level than would have been attained in the absence of the import-substitution and export-destruction programme. It is hard to believe that the economy could quickly work itself up to the level from which the programme would have displaced it. Indeed, many economists would argue that it *never* could: by sacrificing the gains from trade, a small economy such as Canada's is likely to remain permanently poorer.

To transform the economy so drastically, our government would have to direct the economy far more systematically and forcefully than it now does. It could not hope to achieve much by nudging the economy in the desired direction through tax incentives, selective subsidies, and exhortation. Once more, the observer can learn a good deal from the experience of Eastern Europe, where socialist regimes have opted for relative self-sufficiency. Ottawa would certainly have to plan, and to control the building of all new plant and equipment. New export plant would be proscribed; only import-replacing equipment would be allowed. Less essential building, such as housing, would probably be curtailed. The government probably would have to subsidize the new import-replacing installations, or to build them itself. It would certainly have to control both imports and exports through a system of licensing. If inflationary pressures became severe, it would probably control both prices and wages. Labour could hardly expect to be left free to bargain collectively; indeed, it might be necessary to introduce a system of labour-direction, such as we used in the Second World War. Paradoxically, the import-replacement programme could create a need for foreign currency: much of the import-replacing plant and equipment would have to be imported, and the high investment programme would indirectly create demand for new imports of consumer goods. Hence the government might have to control foreign exchange transactions, limiting the outlays that were not required for the programme of import-substitution. Foreign travel, in particular, might be sacrificed.

Perhaps we should undertake this restructuring of our economic organization. We should certainly recognize that if we want to move sharply toward self-sufficiency we should have to undertake it. Yet in economic reorganization nothing is easy. We should recall the adventures of Mr. Diefenbaker. Soon after taking office, he said that he would try to redirect 15 per- cent of our import trade from American to British suppliers. At the time, this seemed a not unreasonable idea. We were selling more to the British than we were buying from the British, while we bought more from the Americans than we sold to them. Why not try to balance our trade more neatly?

The answer came quickly enough. The British could not supply all the goods that Canadians were used to obtaining from the United States, and when they could supply their prices were often higher and their quality was often lower. Canadian firms could not readily turn to British suppliers for the semi-fabricated components that they incorporated into their American-designed products. Only by damaging *Canadian* manufacturers could Mr. Diefenbaker have done anything much for British exports. When the British proposed an Anglo-Canadian free trade area, our prime minister retreated in confusion. Canadians heard nothing more of the 15 percent diversion; British officials concluded that Mr. Diefenbaker was frivolous, confused, or both. It would be surprising if some Whitehall officials did not recall the behaviour of R. B. Bennett at the Ottawa Conference of 1932. In the 1950s, as in the early 1930s, it seemed, Canadian Conservatives mixed imperial sentiment with unreflecting industrial protectionism. Still, no Conservative government, and no Liberal government, would undertake the kind of thorough-going economic planning and control that would have been needed if we were to achieve any such major or fundamental change in our economic structure. In the present paper I have argued that we need not undertake any such reorientation, because our present trading arrangements give us large gains at small cost and with little risk. The matter of gains and costs cannot be disputed. As for the risks, different observers do reach different conclusions.[6]

Notes

1. On the misdoings of the bank of Canada and its Governor in the late fifties, see Scott Gordon, *The Economists versus the Bank of Canada* (Toronto: Ryerson Press, 1962) and the *Canadian Annual Review* for 1960, 1961, and 1962. Canadian economists generally argue that Mr. Coyne's version of economic nationalism made the Canadian recession significantly worse than it need have been.

2. This and subsequent American attempts to improve their balance of payments in ways that affected Canada are also discussed in chapter 5 of this volume.

3. Here as elsewhere in this paper, America's current-account balance is the balance on goods and services, not including unilateral transfers. If such transfers are included in the current account, the United States ran current-account deficits in 1968-69.

4. See below, chapters 4 and 5.
5. It is conceptually better to use gross domestic product, instead of gross national product, in these comparisons, but because few people understand the difference, and because the difference is tiny, we have used GNP instead.
6. This paper covers material on which the professional literature is not very extensive. What exists is diffuse and not very helpful to the student, because it is largely concerned with other matters. The writings on the foreign ownership question are not very relevant to the questions of commercial policy on which I have concentrated here. Canada's international trading posture, and our continuing troubles with the United States, are chronicled in the volumes of *Canada in World Affairs* (Toronto: Oxford University Press for the Canadian Institute of International Affairs), and of the *Canadian Annual Review* (Toronto: University of Toronto Press). The Canadian Institute of International Affairs' occasional publications are also helpful, as are the studies on free trade that emanated from the Canadian Trade Committee. On the American dollar, see Herbert G. Grubel, "The Rise and Fall of the U.S. Dollar 1945-1971", in John Chant and Keith Acheson, eds., *Canadian Perspectives in Economics* (Toronto: Collier Macmillan Canada, 1972). The negotiations that led to the erection of the international financial and commercial institutions can be traced in Keith Horsefield, *The International Monetary Fund* (Washington: International Monetary Fund, 1972), a volume which contains some Canadian documentation. Also helpful are R. F. Harrod, *The Life of John Maynard Keynes* (London: Macmillan, 1951), and Richard Gardner, *Sterling Dollar Diplomacy*, expanded edition (New York: McGraw Hill, 1969). On the behaviour of foreign-owned firms, the basic serious scholarly work is A. E. Safarian, *Foreign Ownership of Canadian Industry* (Toronto: McGraw-Hill, 1966). The international aspects of American economic diplomacy are explored in Andrew Shonfield, ed., *International Economic Relations of the Western World* (London: Oxford University Press, 1976), which was not available when this chapter was being prepared.

CHAPTER 2

"THE CANADIAN CONNECTION": CANADA AND EUROPE

Robert Bothwell

Back in the 1930s a Canadian diplomat remarked that one of the problems with the conduct of the nation's foreign relations was that the country was prone to indulge a champagne appetite on a beer budget. Put more concretely and less colourfully, there was a disproportion between ends and means in Canadian foreign relations. During the 1930s, this meant that the choices open to Canadian policy-makers were drastically limited: there developed a large gap between those professionally or altruistically interested in Canada's foreign policy and the substance of that policy. It is a recurring problem.

In the 1970s attention has been focused on the so-called "third option" of Canadian foreign policy, an option which calls for "a comprehensive long-term strategy to develop and strengthen the Canadian economy and other aspects of its national life and in the process to reduce the present Canadian vulnerability." The third option takes on meaning and force from two other options: the preservation of the status quo in Canadian foreign policy, or a closer integration between Canada and the United States.[1] These three policies are not by themselves the full tally of Canadian alternatives, since other, more fanciful, propositions have been frequently advanced. They are, rather, the ones which have some hope of commanding sufficient political support to be feasible.

The third option is most obviously proposed as a change from the status quo, since the option of closer integration with the United States would hardly evoke warm and fervent responses in the country's journalistic and intellectual communities. Under the status quo, Canada's international relations were anchored between two poles: the United States, the predominant western economic, political and military power, and Europe, including Britain, in whose economic survival and prosperity Canada has long taken a deep interest. For a decade after 1945 the United States offered the only certain refuge, economically and politically, if the rest of the world (meaning Europe) failed to recover from the devastation of war, or fell over the edge into Communism. In periods of pessimism, the Canadian government prepared schemes for the complete integration of the Canadian and American economies. Had the worst come, and Europe as a whole aligned itself with the Soviet bloc, there can be little doubt that Canada would have been forced into an economic union with the Americans.

Of course, the "worst case" never came about. Western Europe did recover from the aftermath of war. At the same time, most of western Europe became Canada's ally in NATO, while the GATT agreements helped to reduce tariff barriers. Canadian exports to Europe grew in value from $329,355,000 in 1948 to $2,842,018,000 in 1971. At the same time, trade with the United States increased steadily as a proportion of total trade, from 37.4 percent of exports and 76.8 percent of imports in 1947 to 67.8 percent of exports and 70.2 percent of imports in 1971.

Canadian efforts to diversify this country's economic relationships were persistent, but if diversification is measured by percentages, they were unsuccessful. Canadian trade expanded, to be sure, through the multilateral concessions of GATT. Canadian attempts to establish special relationships with Europe were not as rewarding. In 1949, at Canadian insistence, Article 2 of the NATO Treaty was inserted, to provide for non-military (economic, social, and intellectual) co-operation among the member states of the North Atlantic Alliance. "Atlanticism", a concept which is not peculiarly Canadian, but which offers manifest advantages to Canada, seemed to have found statutory embodiment. The Americans, as is well known, balked over Article 2, predicting that its sweeping general promises of good will and co-operation would never be fulfilled. What is perhaps not as well known was the genuine reluctance of the Europeans to go along with the "Canadian article". However, the inclusion of Article 2 depended on American, not European, good will. In the event, European and American gloominess proved well-founded: Canadian enthusiasm and American acquiescence had produced a dead letter.

The conduct of economic relations between Canada and Europe therefore remained within the structure of GATT, although trade among Commonwealth countries was still encouraged under the aging Commonwealth preferential system. The Commonwealth still basked in the fading glamour of the defunct British Empire and seemed to offer the possibility of political solidarity and a distinctive identity, as well as security for Canadian exports. Canadian trade with Britain, the most important market, was still a large proportion of total Canadian exports in the late 1940s (23.6 percent in 1949), but the proportion sank gradually through the 1950s. The dollar figure represented by British trade was still quite respectable, and its loss or diminution could not be regarded with equanimity.

The Commonwealth was a two-way illusion in the 1950s. For Canadians, it helped to bolster the Canadian identity; for the British it helped to mask the decline of British power and prestige, thereby maintaining the fiction that Britain was still a power with a future distinct from Europe's. When the European Common Market was formed in the mid-1950s, the British remained aloof. The Canadian government was acutely interested in, and perhaps even feared, the emergence of the Common Market. It was hoped that Europe's economic and political institutions would be strengthened, but the appearance of trade bloc naturally raised the possibility that Canada's trade with Europe would be reduced.

Canada's concern centred on the possibility, and then the probability, that Britain would seek membership in the Common Market. The highly publicized opposition of the Diefenbaker government to the proposed entry of the United Kingdom into the Common Market in 1961 pointed up Canada's worry that it would lose one special trading relationship without gaining another in compensation. Although the French veto of the British application postponed the issue for the balance of the 1960s, it could not do so for ever.

There remained the other pole of Canadian policy, the "special relationship" with the United States. Canadian and American societies were very similar; the two powers had common security interests; the predominance of American power simply extended English-speaking domination of the international political system. There was, then, a continuity rather than a break between the British Empire and the hegemony of the United States.

The identity of the Anglo-Saxon powers conferred prestige on Canada during the 1950s. The accretion of prestige also brought with it an accumulation of resentment, particularly in France. De Gaulle vetoed Britain's application to join the Common Market because he saw too great an identification between British and American interests. Although Canadians in general were perhaps rather slow to realize it, the same objection applied to Canada. In a period when Europe was weak and divided, that had little significance. If, however, the attractions of Europe to Canada were to increase, it would matter very much.

During the 1960s, Canadians decided that it did matter very much. The discovery that Europe saw Canada as part of an undifferentiated "America" — if they thought of it at all — was wounding to Canadian self-esteem, but only because the ingredients that went to make up that self-regard were changing. This distressing development overshadowed the foreign policy of the Pearson government. Within Canada, it helped to create and feed an impatience with the traditional policies of alliance and multilateral trade pursued by the government, and it strengthened as well a feeling of antagonism toward the United States. Outside Canada, there was impatience with the Canadians' insistence on separate treatment, and with the manner in which this was demanded.

Pearson's diplomacy, then, came under fire during a time of national crankiness at the end of the 1960s. The most vocally unhappy segment of Canadian opinion, largely composed of academics and journalists, pointed out the country's obvious reliance on and identification with American policies around the world. For some, any connection with the unseemly Americans was too much; others suggested that Canada should seek understanding elsewhere, in the Third World; still others argued for a change of emphasis in Canada's traditional policies. In the event that was what was done.

The Trudeau government underwent a laborious process of self-contemplation after taking office. It soon announced a reduction in Canada's NATO forces in Europe, thereby arousing the indignation of the Europeans as much as of the Americans. Simultaneously it sought ways of diversifying Canada's relations

27

abroad, with the object of lessening the close identification with the United States and American interests. Trudeau, of course, had to contend with what his countrymen would accept as a plausible policy for Canada, and with what Canada's allies would tolerate. It was inherently improbable that public opinion could swallow a facile identification between Canada and the Third World. Some commentators were obsessed with the similarity between dependent economies largely relying on the exploitation of natural resources. Such an identification was not made easier by the affluent style of life that Canadians enjoyed. A Canadian Third World Option might have flourished in the Theatre of the Absurd, but like other such policies it found its way from time to time into the public forum.[2]

So instead of the Third World Option there had to be the "Third Option". This implied a renewal of Canada's links with Europe, economically and politically. In the government's foreign policy statement of 1970, *Foreign Policy for Canadians,* the Trudeau government took note of the forthcoming expansion of the European Economic Community (Britain was applying again, along with several other countries), pointed out the economic strength and market potential of an enlarged Community, and promised that it would seek "appropriate consultative arrangements which will take account of mutual Canada-EEC interests".

There was some uncertainty as to what "appropriate consultative arrangements" might be, and even more doubt as to the substance of "mutual Canada-EEC interests". Canada already had political links to the present members and all but one of the proposed new members of the EEC through NATO. NATO served not only as a military alliance but as a centre for political consultation between its members. The European members of NATO are fond of stressing the symbolic importance to them of a Canadian military presence stationed in the possible battlefield of a European war. The benefits of a common defence aside, it is often asserted that Canada gains "invisible earnings" of good will and information through its mission to NATO headquarters in Brussels. Such sentimental assets are like the "invisible hand" in classical economics. If all goes well, then good will and sentiment may be presumed to be doing their work; if badly, things could always be even worse. Certainly association through NATO had done little to improve Canada's relations with a nominal ally like France. Would it prove an asset in connection with the Common Market?

Canada had first accredited an ambassador to the Common Market in 1961. However, he was also and primarily the Canadian Ambassador to Belgium. Now the tempo was stepped up. The ministers of external affairs and industry trade and commerce descended on the Community Headquarters in Brussels. Signor Malfatti, president of the EEC, visited Ottawa in September, 1971, just in time to meet a chastened Canadian government reeling under a new shock. Just a few days before, in August, President Nixon announced a series of unilateral American measures designed to get the Americans' international accounts in order. There would be trade restrictions and surtaxes, affecting not only a large segment of Canada's trade with the United States, but of the Canadian economy as a whole. As in the past, Canadian ministers trooped down to Washington to seek exemption from the surtaxes; but, this time, they failed.

August, 1971 marked a watershed in the tone and character of Canadian-American relations. These had been notably less close and cordial for some time. The Americans had disapproved of Canada's reduction of forces in Europe; military collaboration was less specific than it had been; and complaints about Canadian incursions into the American automobile market (a consequence of the Auto Pact of 1965) were being forcefully made on Capitol Hill. The unstated agreement on a common economic interest which had guided American trade policy toward Canada since the late 1940s was coming unstuck, and the acrimonious discussions that followed between Canadian ministers and U.S. Treasury Secretary Connally were the outward expression of a deteriorating situation.

Although bad personal relations could be remedied (in part through a change in the personalities involved), the underlying problem could not. The Canadian economy was vulnerable to external pressures, as economists had repeatedly pointed out; indeed this had been the common theme of Canadian political economists from the 1930s forward. The policy adopted by the United States could have meant, if it had been drastically implemented, a return to a Canada producing raw materials, facing low or no duties in the United States, while manufactured goods were excluded. The August crisis therefore sent a chill through Ottawa. Inevitably and naturally attention turned to the

29

possibilities afforded by Canada's other great trading partners, Europe and Japan. Of the two, Europe had pride of place, partly because the advantages of an arrangement with Europe were more evident than those of an agreement with Japan, and partly because Europe was still as it had always been, the Canadian alternative to a one-sided relationship with the United States.

With de Gaulle passed from the scene, the British application to join the EEC was faring better: British membership now seemed a virtual certainty. This meant, of course, that the British preferential tariff would be dismantled, as far as trade between Canada and the United Kingdom was concerned, and this would affect, Canadian officials estimated, between $600-million and $700 million of Canadian exports. Although there was some talk of special arrangements for Canadian exports to Great Britain, it was clear that any compensation to Canada for the loss of British markets would have to come through discussions under GATT. Eventually, this happened, with Canada doing rather better than both Canadian and European officials expected. The agreement respecting compensation was signed in March, 1975, covering about $600 million of exports.

In fact, however, the prospects presented to Canada by an enlarged Common Market were not all that favourable. British entry into the European Community was not likely to make the Community better disposed toward Canada; as Alastair Buchan has commented, British governments since 1945 had shown almost total indifference to Canada. Nor did a visit to London by Prime Minister Trudeau in December, 1972 seem to produce very many results.

Some — a very few — Europeans were willing. The most familiar to Canadians was Claude Julien, of *Le Monde*, who in 1965 had proclaimed Canada to be "Europe's last chance", an opinion he reiterated to a Canadian parliamentary committee in 1970. Julien told his audiences, after a recitation of Canada's mineral and agricultural wealth, that the possibilities were staggering. But of what and for whom? It was hardly in the Canadian interest to exchange the role of storehouse of minerals for the United States for that of Europe's mining provisioners.

Julien's argument was at least a start, an introduction for Canada to a continent where Canada and Canadians were unknown and ignored. How indifferent Europeans could be Canadians soon learned. But even indifference was to be preferred to the cold hostility of some sections of the French Government vis-a-vis Canada in the months and years after de Gaulle's disastrous visit to Quebec in 1967. Trudeau and the other Quebec ministers in the federal cabinet could not afford to compromise on the issue of the external recognition of Quebec, and Franco-Canadian relations entered their ice age. The resignation of de Gaulle, the death of Premier Daniel Johnson of Quebec, and the election of a Liberal government in Quebec more kindly disposed to federalism in one form or another, made the situation less acute.

There was still a long way to go. In 1973 the Nixon administration decided to mend its European fences, so long neglected during the Vietnam War. 1973 was to be the "Year of Europe" for the Americans, and presumably the Year of America for the Europeans. It looked as though no-one had as much as a day to spare for Canada. Soon plaintive noises began to come out of Ottawa, as External Affairs Minister Sharp rebuked the American proposal and the European response for leaving Canada out of account. According to Sharp, Canada was seeking a "meaningful long-term relationship" with the Common Market rather than a simple declaration of harmony and good intentions. Such a declaration was still desirable, of course, but it seemed clear enough that for all the time that might be spent it might end up as yet another meaningless document. The Canadian government, even so, discussed ways and means with the Europeans. In response to a European inquiry, the Canadian government set out a series of propositions in an aide-memoire for the Europeans to ponder. Canada once again stressed the seriousness of its intention to diversify its foreign relationships. Europe had a prominent role to play in this regard. The Canadian government hoped for an expansion of European-Canadian relations in as many areas as possible, from the cultural through the environment through trade.

It was one thing for Canada to propose, but it was not the European Community that disposed. The Community was in some important respects still a bureaucratic convenience, and rivalries between the Community and important or cantankerous member states were resolved in favour of the latter. For the Community to enter upon an international agreement on its own would be a quasi-sovereign act, and this was something that could not be tolerated by countries concerned for their sovereignty. Equally, the countries composing the Common Market were having problems of their own among themselves. The triumph of British entry and the expansion of the Six to the Nine was accompanied by the third Middle East war and the imposition of large oil price increases. It was a matter of interest and importance for Canada to know whether there would be a Community still in place with which to negotiate.

The Europeans reciprocated such feelings with interest. Canada's constitutional and racial troubles were not unknown in Europe and the increasing noise made by Canadian nationalists attracted attention. Some Canadian actions, such as the Foreign Investment Review Act, also distressed investors in Europe, as touring Canadian officials found. Measures intended to mitigate American ownership and control in the Canadian economy could be interpreted in a sense unfavourable to the Europeans as well — indeed, they had to be so interpreted.

The Canadian aide-memoire was handed to the Commission of the European Community and to the nine member governments in April, 1974. By late September there had been little in the way of positive response. In an official communication to the Political Coordination Committee of the Nine, the Canadian government reiterated its abiding interest in getting some kind of agreement down on paper. Canada wished to strengthen relations with Europe; equally it wished to be differentiated from the United States. Unfortunately, the Canadian government observed, there was still considerable reluctance in Europe to see a real difference between Canada and the United States. The best way of establishing a real link between Canada and Europe was a trade agreement, but in the meantime a statement of agreed principles was desirable.

Prime Minister Trudeau again visited Europe in October. There had been some hope that his visit to the Community Headquarters in Brussels would produce the desired formula, an agreed contractual link, but the hope was vain. Trudeau visited Paris, meeting President Giscard d'Estaing and Premier Chirac, and receiving verbal bouquets at the level of friendly banalities. This represented a considerable advance in public Franco-Canadian relations, but it stopped short of a passionate embrace. The addresses of welcome did suggest French interest in exploring what Canada had to offer, but remained cautiously noncommittal.

32

Trudeau presented his foreign policy options to the Europeans. His "third option" — co-operation with the United States but expansion of relations with Europe — represented "a determined effort . . . for the preservation of Canada's identity". But if things continued to drift as they were doing, Trudeau warned, "our economy will be more involved with the U.S. than with anyone else's." The problem was, of course, that this was already true. The discussions with the French demonstrated that an agreement might be obtained, but on the terms suggested by Julien long before — the European interest in Canada's natural resources. The Canadian delegation was not prepared to make such a serious commitment, and in the minds of some diplomats it was not necessarily in the national interest to do so.

The character of the discussions changed when Trudeau went on to Brussels. The problem there was not so much French specifics as Canadian vagueness. Back in the spring Canada had supplemented its aide-memoire with a draft trade agreement for discussion with the Europeans. Most of the clauses of the agreement were carefully phrased to avoid any possible violation of the GATT and consequently promised to do little that was new. There seemed little point in signing such an anodyne document, or so the Europeans believed. In Brussels, Trudeau admitted that the Europeans had found Canada's trade proposals "banal". He promised to do better next time.

The search for a contractual link with Europe continued. The Prime Minister gave it high priority and devoted sixteen days in March, 1975 to yet another European trip. This time Trudeau was more explicit. His discussions with European leaders covered present relationships and future possibilities, for example "package deals" for investments, made between countries rather than as the result of individual choice.[3] By the time Trudeau returned home, he had visited every Common Market capital but Copenhagen, and had received promises of support of varying warmth for his "contractual link" everywhere except Paris.

The Europeans took the opportunity to harp on two themes: foreign investment and the maintenance of Canadian troops in NATO. Trudeau stated in Bonn that the political character of NATO was "every bit" as important as its military character, but the Germans were reported to have indicated that in their opinion Canada had not taken its military commitments very seriously at all. Political leverage would have to be connected to military commitment.[4] Most of the Common Market countries approved the idea of a "Canadian connection", and deplored French reluctance. The French, in turn, confronted a dilemma. Relations with Canada had been improving steadily, and there were expectations of further improvement. While a Canadian relationship with Europe might present complications, it might be preferable to a closer Canadian integration with the United States. To some degree Canada could be useful in helping Europe to balance the United States. When the foreign ministers of the European Community met in Luxembourg in June, 1975, they quickly agreed to go ahead with negotiations for a contractual link. The Canadian ambassador to the Community expressed relief, "I have always felt the French would see their interests coinciding with ours in the long run."[5] Although warnings about NATO commitments continued to rumble out of Germany, the decision had been taken. The European interest, however was still in Canadian resources: "One can think in terms of your raw materials, your uranium," the vice-president of the Community's Commission remarked.

Problems persisted throughout the summer. The Europeans bickered among themselves over who should have the power to sign the agreement with Canada — the Commission or the representatives of the nine countries. With that question resolved, there was further dispute on what was going to go into the Europe-Canada accord. This was essentially the same issue that had been raised at the time of Trudeau's first trip to Europe in October, 1974. The link was to be just that — "Institutional link, perhaps", a Community official stated. "But there will be no contract, no promises to keep."[6]

The Canadian government had never intended very much in the way of promises. The Canadian draft trade agreement had carefully skirted the jurisdiction of GATT, leaving out the embarrassing issues of tariff preferences that could invite American concern or retaliation. Without trade concessions of a preferential nature, the agreement became a ratification of a change of form: the substitution of a connection with the Community for bilateral corrections with the individual member countries. As the Irish foreign minister put it during a visit to Ottawa, there was great good will toward Canada in Europe, and sympathy for the Canadian plight in relations with its overwhelming neighbour. "But", he added, "I don't think that anybody has come up with a way to harness that goodwill."

The agreement with the European community, when signed, as it seems it inevitably will be, will stand as a monument to Canada's skilful persistence in diplomacy. The participation of the Prime Minister undoubtedly played no small part in securing agreement where previously there was none. Canada will be, for the moment, prominent in the European consciousness. Canadians will be pleased to see that Europe does occasionally pay attention to them. Some Europeans will be dazzled at the thought of all those resources waiting for a buyer, and cheered at the thought that one supplier of raw materials does not regard them as played-out bandits whose hour has come. Unfortunately, by itself the contractual link need not mean very much. It is a link that must be carefully cultivated under a congenial time and a happy circumstance. Realistically, there is no reason to believe that time will be kind to the contractual link, or that other countries will refrain from demanding similar treatment for themselves. There is no evidence that Canada and Europe will be able to work out a sharing of resources and markets for manufactured goods, apart from such relative improvements that result from GATT negotiations.

The third option, so sensible, so necessary, so obvious, is an attempt to secure the triumph of politics over geography. The political advantages of a secure connection with Europe are as obvious now as they were in 1969. Internally, a relationship, presumably a close one, with Europe will offset the liaison with the United States. It will give Canadians the same psychological support, the same sense of differentiation, that they used to find in the great days of the British Empire. Canadians will find that they are both more and less than North Americans. Externally, there is considerable sense in the beleaguered democracies of western Europe and North America reinforcing their ties and affirming a common identity in the face of a general turning away from western political forms in the rest of the world. Any necessary sharing of resources, any growth in economic power, will have dividends.

Trudeau has attempted to anchor his third option in Canada's relationship with the United States, and indeed, has gone out of his way to explain it to them. This relationship will remain friendly; indeed, neither Canada nor Europe could accept a link that presumed more than a friendly rivalry with the Americans, and that in turn is the nub of the problem. The United States offers more, separately, to Europe than Canada can. Canada expects more from the United States than from Europe. The economic advantages of a link with the United States heavily outweigh those of a connection with Europe, and there is no denying the realities of geographical proximity or of economic power. Within strict limits, it is no doubt possible for shifts in trading patterns to take place, but there is no reason to anticipate such a shift from any possible separate agreement that Canada may conclude with Europe. A multilateral agreement among all important trading nations would be another matter.

Informed opinion would probably concur that a multilateral world would be the best of all possible worlds for Canada. But it is precisely because such a world is not in prospect that the Canadian government has pursued its "third option". The diagnosis of peril from isolation in the midst of powerful economic blocs is appropriate. The prescription, however, smacks more of placebo than of cure.

The options open to a small nation in its international relations are usually limited. Canadians, bombarded by descriptions of powerful statesmen bestriding the world, may expect too much of their own. An element of illusion in foreign policy is unavoidable, even desirable, but for Canada the effort to satisfy the public's demands for magic shadows may have gone too far with the ballyhoo surrounding the third option. The contractual link with Europe, when concluded, will turn out to be a modest achievement. It may open a small door in the common market wall. It is still unclear whether that door will lead to the servants' quarters or to the guest room.

Notes

1. M. Sharp, *Canada-U.S. Relations: Options for the Future,* a "special issue" of *International Perspectives,* Autumn, 1972.
2. See, for example, the interview with Ivan Head, foreign policy adviser to the prime minister, in *Le Monde,* September 1, 1974.
3. *Globe and Mail* (Toronto), March 7, 1975.
4. *Ottawa Journal,* July 8, 1975.
5. *Globe and Mail* (Toronto), June 28, 1975.
6. *The Gazette* (Montreal), September 20, 1975.

CHAPTER 3

CANADA
AND EUROPEAN
DETENTE

Donald Page

After three decades of uneasily watching the brinkmanship of Cold War confrontations in Europe, Canada is happily engaged in the first full-scale attempt at reducing tensions and increasing co-operation between the East and the West. In *Foreign Policy for Canadians,* the Canadian Government outlined what its involvement should be. "The Government", said the authors of the White Paper in 1970, "has no illusion about the limitations of its capacity to exert decisive or even weighty influence in consultations or negotiations involving the larger powers. But it is determined that Canada's ideas will be advanced, that Canada's voice will be heard, when questions vital to world peace and security are being discussed."[1] Through trial and error Canada has learned the benefit of active and informed participation in international conferences. At the Paris Peace Conference in 1919, she discovered the fate of the unprepared bystander, and this experience, *inter alia,* led her to play a more important role in peace-making after the Second World War. Her diplomats learned that agreements that emerge from international conferences are the products of intricate intra-allied and across-the-table bargains and trade-offs that no outside observer of Canada's stature can hope to change or re-open for further debate. Therefore, as long as peace and security are cardinal aims of her foreign policy, she must try to have a hand in establishing European détente, the absence of which has cost her so much in years past.

The climate for détente has been established by others through the Strategic Arms Limitation Talks (SALT), the Four Powers Agreement on Berlin and treaties between the Federal Republic of Germany and her Communist neighbours. Collectively, they provided the groundwork for the breakthrough represented by the multilateral Helsinki consultations on measures for European security and détente in which Canada participated at the end of 1972. Whereas détente at first meant merely the absence of tension or peaceful co-existence, it has now come to mean an active pursuit of co-operation, accommodation, and inter-relationship that Canada hopes will make its reversal more difficult.

The Helsinki consultations had their immediate origin in the 1966 Bucharest statement of the Warsaw Pact countries advocating a European conference on security, to which Canada and the United States would not be invited.[2] In the view of Soviet propaganda such a conference was to preside over the dissolution of the Warsaw Pact Organization and the North Atlantic Treaty Organization. On the NATO side, the Harmel Report on the future of the alliance opened up the possibility of negotiations on balanced force reductions, which was endorsed, except by France, as NATO policy at the Reykjavik ministerial meeting in the summer of 1968. But whatever immediate interest the Warsaw Pact Organization might have had in responding to NATO's overture was curtailed by the Czechoslovakian crisis. Out of this crisis came the Brezhnev doctrine of limited or shared sovereignty for the Soviet Union's socialist partners and with this confirmation of the Soviet Union's hegemony, both Eastern and Western European statesmen realized that détente could not be achieved through expanding bilateral contacts.

When the Warsaw Pact Organization renewed its call for a European security conference in March 1969, NATO demanded as its price of attendance some substantive evidence of Soviet willingness for the reduction of tension around Berlin. Within a short time, significant steps were being taken on the German front. The Soviet Union and the Federal Republic of Germany made surprisingly rapid progress in settling long-standing differences over boundaries and in concluding a non-aggression treaty.

This progress was acknowledged at the Rome ministerial meeting of May 1970 when NATO produced a detailed statement on the basis for exploratory talks on Mutual Balanced Force Reduction (MBFR). The statement called for verifiable, phased and balanced reductions of stationed and indigenous forces and their weapon systems without placing either side at a military disadvantage in relation to the other. With some justification, the Soviet Union at first saw MBFR as an American and British propaganda device to frustrate the convening of their more general European security conference; nevertheless, in June 1970 the Warsaw Pact states agreed that their proposed conference would also discuss the more specific NATO proposition for the reduction of foreign armed forces on the territory of European states. Brezhnev again advanced the possibility of such discussions at the 24th Party Congress and confirmed this in his meeting with Prime Minister Trudeau in May 1971 and later with other Western leaders.

Thus far both sides appeared to be talking at rather than to each other. To overcome the deadlock, Canada suggested at its June 1971 meeting that NATO send an emissary to the Soviet Union and other interested governments for exploratory talks over the groundwork needed before formal talks could begin. General NATO agreement was not forthcoming though former NATO Secretary-General Manlio Brosio was made the emissary of those members who agreed with the Canadian proposal. Brosio's mission, however, was ill-fated as was another Canadian suggestion for a group approach to multilateral preparatory talks, until the full German settlement was in force.

A four power agreement over Berlin in September 1971 broke the stalemate by guaranteeing unhindered civilian access to the city and the conduct of West Berlin's interests abroad by the Federal Republic of Germany. When inter-German negotiations seemed stalled, Brezhnev had personally intervened to convince the German Democratic Republic that West Berlin was a thorn to be lived with and not extracted. With the status quo recognized in a series of bilateral and multilateral agreements rather than by a peace treaty, remaining confrontations could be diverted to other avenues of expression without menacing super-power and bloc accommodation. Both sides were finally ready for preparatory consultations on a Conference on Security and Co-operation in Europe (CSCE).

In the final analysis, the negotiating stance for Canada and its NATO allies depended upon their perception of Soviet sincerity in pursuing détente. Soviet rapprochement with the West is not new; it was tried briefly in 1955, 1959 and off and on since 1963. What then makes the present Soviet posture appear to the West generally, and Canada specifically, as more than a tactical episode capable of an easy reverse?

Because of her location, Canada unlike some of her allies sitting next to the powder keg, has been able to afford the luxury of a more detached view of Soviet fulminations in Europe. Therefore when signs of a friendlier Soviet Union coalesced into overtures for détente in the late sixties, Canada took up the gauntlet. Her optimism rests upon her analysis of perceptible changes within the Soviet Union. Khrushchev's basic operating assumptions that the dissolution of Western colonial empires would open up possibilities for Soviet aggrandizement, that a world Communist movement would form under Soviet leadership, and that within a decade the Soviet Union would surpass the United States economically, have all been buried or muted by Brezhnev. Instead, Soviet dominance has been rejected by the liberated colonies and its leadership challenged. At the very same time when traditional indicators of economic power suggested that the West could be matched by the Soviet Union, Western technology widened the gap. Out of the 24th Party Congress in 1971 came a remarkably frank admission of Soviet economic failures — a declining growth rate, sluggish productivity, diminishing sources of labour, and failure to invent and apply scientific technology. For the first time, long-term foreign assistance was sought to close the gap and it is precisely this long-term prospect for economic co-operation that provides the human contact aspect of détente an opportunity to work. More than merely rescuing the Soviets from poor harvests and short-falls in five-year plans, it weans the Soviet economy away from its past self-sufficient isolation into a two-way form of economic integration with the West.

By turning to the West for assistance, it must never be forgotten that the Soviet Union is pursuing mutually incompatible ends, for détente threatens its ideological purity at home and its attractiveness abroad for the less developed countries. Western technology brings with it captivating ideologies for potential Soviet dissidents who are only held in check by increasing internal security services and extending further Communist ideology into the daily life of Soviet citizens. For the present, intellectual and religious dissidents will be destroyed or rendered impotent through exile or confinement after the usual character defamation. What will happen to them in the longer run, when a generation of leaders with more extended contacts with the West takes over, will largely depend upon the success or failure of the present leadership in controlling the ambitions of the more strident and aggressive nationalists within the hierarchy who see the maintenance of rigid ideological purity as the means to world dominance and leadership.

Peaceful co-existence does not mean ideological co-existence, Brezhnev has repeatedly warned. Soviet foreign policy remains a struggle to be pursued unremittingly in politics, economics and ideology. But victory now means the use of force in only certain circumstances while accommodation and on occasion even collaboration with the enemy are viewed as inevitable and sometimes desirable. Within this framework, there appears considerable room for jockeying among the competing trends in the present Soviet leadership represented by the Stalinists, the neo-Stalinists and the reformers.

Proponents of Stalinist Cold War policies have diminished rather than disappeared. Their influence is seen in occasional vitriolic propaganda attacks and in incidents such as the Czechoslovakian invasion. Many of their less violent ideas have been taken over by the neo-Stalinist group who actively seek world dominance by splitting any form of Western coalescence. Thus the Conference on European Security and Co-operation becomes, for the neo-Stalinists, a tool for splitting and beheading Western opposition in Europe by seeding discord among the members of the European Economic Community and encouraging distrust of United States leadership. Meanwhile, Soviet status in the world will be maintained only through military might, hard-nosed bargaining, and ideological purity protected from subversive contacts with the West. Economic deficiencies can be covered up by external successes if need be.

In opposition to these hard-line traditionalists are the reformers who have been on the upswing in the seventies. The more conservative among them believe in developing a better domestic economy through more disciplined work habits while projecting a peace-loving image abroad that will remove the West's excuse for building a nuclear deterrent in Europe. The more radical reformers believe in stretching the policy of peaceful co-existence into a détente based primarily on Soviet-American co-operation. Within this framework of a super-power stabilization of the international environment, efforts could then be made to develop more co-operative links with Western economic, technological and scientific communities.

From what little is known of the decision-making apparatus of the Soviet Union, it would appear that the present leadership of Brezhnev rests on a delicate balance of these three groups. One of the West's most difficult tasks is the assessment of what and when concessions can and cannot be pushed at the conference table without producing counterproductive results. Too much Western exuberance may bring Brezhnev to Khrushchev's fate. It remains to be seen whether his greater caution and skill can build the internal support required for changing and integrating domestic and international policies. Because Brezhnev has so closely identified himself and his new foreign secretariat with détente, he cannot afford to back down — but neither can the West afford to let him down. Whether we are witnessing a respite or a historic turning point in East-West relations depends as much on pace as substance.

Since the scenario of improved East-West relations rests upon varying assessments of Soviet intentions in SALT, in Cyprus, in the Middle East etc., different NATO perceptions of what is desirable, attainable and at what agreed cost are inevitable. The accommodation and testing of these perceptions will mean at best an uneven advance for détente. A fairly rapid pace for détente is unlikely because it assumes a succession of soluble problems in adjacent areas, a continuing Soviet predisposition for détente, an absence of harsh Soviet disciplinary measures against any of her satellites that would be offensive to Western co-operationists, a stalemate continuing in Sino-Soviet relations, a continuing cohesion among NATO members, and a rapid solution of the West's economic problems that makes continuing co-operation with the West attractive for the Soviet Union. Much more likely is a slower pace for détente in which tensions would remain with more concessions on such issues as Jewish emigration and external revolutionary movements. Instead of an immediate lessening of the risks of strategic military confrontations and improved opportunities for greater cross fertilizations in economic and technological developments, there would be few opportunities for intimate Western involvement in the development of Warsaw Pact countries, only slightly reduced military expenditures and the postponement of the next stage of SALT.

A more unlikely alternative scenario would be a piecemeal erosion of the détente process characterized by friendly Sino-United States or Sino-Soviet relations, harsh quelling of any dissidence in Eastern Europe, opportunities for strategic gains in outside areas, internal destruction of Western cohesion or by a triumph of neo-Stalinism in the Soviet leadership. What makes these possibilities unlikely is that neither side sees much to be gained in a return to Cold War tensions. Ultimately, such a course would entail increased costs and risks for the Soviet Union as the price of strengthening the Warsaw Pact, and reduced access to Western investment and technology. Moreover, anything that would likely unify the opposition would certainly not be in the Soviet interest unless absolutely required for the maintenance of her own dominance over her satellites.

These prognoses rest upon the further assumption that neither side will accidentally or deliberately initiate a nuclear war during the remainder of the seventies. The foreign policy of the U.S.S.R. for the next few years will likely be based on the realities of the world's present power alignments and will aim at consolidating its post-war gains in Europe, altering its aggressive image in the West, reducing the need for American economic and military influence in Europe and strengthening its economy to make it more internationally competitive as a means of dealing with Western European and non-European challenges to its power base. There is no indication that European détente *per se* will contribute to a lessening of super-power rivalry in other theatres, though it may prompt attempts at defining constellations for multi-polar diplomacy.

As this Canadian view of Soviet intentions and prospects for détente evolved during the last decade, Canada has cautiously measured each new Soviet action or lack of action against the U.S.S.R.'s professed sincerity in pursuing détente rather than a mere propaganda show. For this reason Canada supported the preparatory nature of the Helsinki consultations to ensure that sufficient common ground for discussion existed before embarking upon a formal round of negotiations. That is why Mitchell Sharp personally sought Soviet Foreign Minister Gromyko's assurances that they would really be discussing détente and not just a better means of peaceful co-existence. Thus it was Canada, who, in conjunction with her NATO allies and most of the neutral nations in Europe, appealed for a "step-by-step approach" to the items on the CSCE agenda, thereby allowing confidence to be built around the agreement on each individual item before proceeding to the next, as well as testing the Soviet's resolve to proceed.[3] Further, the various commissions of the preparatory conference would elaborate on each item on the agenda by drawing up guidelines for future talks. Canada's strategy involved the using of this building block approach in accelerating the pressure that deterrence had already put on Soviet behaviour.

Canadian statesmen have often stressed the need of finding "something better than the balance of mutual fear and deterrence on which the present uneasy structure of global security rests".[4] In Canada's view, Mutual Balanced Force Reduction of itself would not mean détente. It would have to be accompanied by parallel steps in the field of co-operation. Canada herself had moved in this direction in the early seventies through a series of bilateral exchange agreements and an unprecedented number of official visits to countries in the Warsaw Pact.[5] These interests would not be advanced by just a super-power accommodation on European arms. Therefore, one of Canada's major diplomatic achievements was in persuading the United States that MBFR should not precede the Helsinki consultations on security issues, economic co-operation and cultural co-operation. In short, MBFR and CSCE should be parallel but separate talks; armed force reductions, security and human contacts together would produce lasting détente.

Discussion at Helsinki focused around the declaration on the guiding principles governing relations between states. The Warsaw Pact states argued that this meant the renunciation of both the threat and use of force and a declaration of respect for and inviolability of existing European borders. NATO offered continuing *de facto,* but not *de jure* recognition of these boundaries. To do otherwise would have initiated a wave of protest among those Eastern Europeans who have fled to Western Europe, and among Canada's ethnic peoples, many of whom are in Canada as a protest against Soviet domination of their homelands. Nor would the West accept any doctrine that would legitimize Soviet hegemony or interference in the internal affairs of Eastern European states. Canada was most anxious that security be buttressed by a series of confidence building measures and moves toward co-operation. She was particularly responsible for two of these. She suggested the possibility of arrangements for the advance notification and observation of military movements and manoeuvres to accompany MBFR. In the field of co-operation, she particularly stressed the need for freer movement of people, as Mitchell Sharp stated: "If we don't achieve something in this direction — including the basic freedom of families to reunite — then the conference will have failed to achieve one of its more desirable goals."[6] A NATO communiqué echoed this concern and Moscow reluctantly accepted it as part of the agenda.

When Czechoslovakia proposed the establishment of a permanent body for continuing discussion on European security and co-operation, Canada wisely argued that a United Conference of Europe was premature. If such a body was in the offing, it would have been tempting to defer discussions of the more contentious items to it, thereby destroying Canada's systematic step-by-step approach. Moreover, Canada knew from past experience that institutional proliferation is useless unless confirmed by agreement on basic objectives and a united will to see them fulfilled. Canada was intent on building a lasting détente by not allowing the Soviet Union to play leapfrog over contentious issues.

The Helsinki consultations were important in charting the future of both Europe and Canada, for through her participation as a member of NATO, Canada gained European recognition of her right, which the Soviet Union had originally denied, to be involved in the settlement of European issues. After four intensive sessions spread over seven months, the consultations ended on June 8, 1973 with an acceptable set of mandates for future discussions. The Final Recommendations prescribed the organizational procedures for the next conference and four groups (baskets) of mandates: 1) questions relating to security in Europe, 2) co-operation in the fields of economics, of science and technology, and of the environment, 3) co-operation in humanitarian and other fields, and 4) follow-up to the conference. However, the Warsaw Pact states tended to view the Helsinki consultations as an end in themselves, whereas Canada and her NATO allies saw the recommendations as merely the first steps that must later produce actions.

Movement into the second stage of CSCE talks at Geneva was a horrendous task, for it called for the translation of principles into facts on the basis of consensus among all 35 participants on every item and procedure. Because consensus must be reached on each issue and votes are taken only at the very end, the trade-offs are multitudinous. Precisely what Canada's contribution is to this game of scrabble is difficult to discover. The Department of External Affairs has chosen not to publicize its adventures in CSCE in order not to generate unwarranted expectations in Canada for pushing the Soviet Union either farther or faster. With only *Le Devoir* and a handful of academics showing any interest in the subject, External Affairs will not have to defend or reveal its hand. Likewise the Opposition in Parliament has given the Government *carte blanche*.[7] Even in her specific objectives, it is difficult to ascertain exactly what Canada wants because many of her objectives are intended only for bargaining and trade-offs on behalf of her NATO allies. Moreover, she is faced with a constant struggle in keeping her viewpoints on the table since the nine members of the European Community are using CSCE as a proving ground for a new collective approach in foreign policy. Canada's main influence is in the fifteen member NATO caucus, where she along with Norway appears interested in making the NATO position something more than a U.S.-EEC accommodation.

Within the NATO caucus at CSCE, Canada has been given particular responsibility for advancing NATO's policy on the Human Contacts portion of Basket III. The Federal Republic of Germany would have been a more logical shepherd of family reunification, but other more important concerns allowed her to pass it on to Canada, who was found happily waiting in the wings since she was unable to contribute much in the security field. Quite properly, Canada took seriously the development of realistic means for promoting contacts between peoples. Only very recently have some of her diplomats recognized that human diplomacy is a valuable and sometimes essential servant of the more traditional forms of secret diplomacy. Although its possibilities have been hitherto largely unexplored, even totalitarian regimes have constituencies susceptible to the influence of human diplomacy. "Unless the Conference on Security and Co-operation in Europe tackles the question of human contacts seriously," warned the Canadian delegate at Helsinki, "we are not going to be able to achieve the improved conditions in Europe which this conference is supposed to create. It is perhaps not too much to say that the successful treatment of this item will be a touchstone for the success of the conference as a whole."[8] The United States and others would not see it that way, but they have a narrower view of what is required for détente. Traditionally, Canadian diplomats have argued that "whatever tends to separate men makes them suspicious, discontented and ill-disposed, and thus encourages the feelings of insecurity which we have experienced (in Europe)."[9] Her task in CSCE was to convince the Warsaw Pact states that relations between peoples of different countries should be widened from strictly state sponsored contacts to permit privately initiated individual contacts that would allow for the greatest possible degree of freedom of thought and movement of peoples.

In addition to their more general effect on peace in Europe, the enlargement of human contacts will satisfy certain Canadian constituencies who hitherto have received little comfort from Canada's bilateral agreements with Warsaw Pact countries or from debates at the United Nations. As illustrated in Table I, Canada has been the recipient of considerable numbers of Eastern European refugees, who naturally have a direct interest in matters of family reunification and freer movement of peoples and goods in both directions. Too often, we in Canada think merely of opening the Iron Curtain so that Western freedoms and development can be admired without realizing that exchanges will bring revelations for both sides. With the exception of the Czechs, the bulk of the eastern refugees and immigrants came before 1960, and most of them dwell too often on unfortunate experiences of the past without realizing that conditions and attitudes in their homelands have changed. Over the last three decades each side has developed its own over-simplified and emotionally charged stereotypes of the other that have obscured the real nature of the conflict. It is the challenge of people-to-people diplomacy to cultivate more realistic perceptions and appreciations.

Ethnic Canada is not the only interested supporter of freer access. Those with fraternal ties are equally concerned. For those Christians who believe that peace on earth is more than the absence of armed conflict, détente provides the prospect of closer ties with their co-religionists who eagerly reach out to those several hundred Canadian missionaries who bring them Bibles, tracts and fellowship. In conjunction with Jews,

TABLE I
IMMIGRATION FROM WARSAW PACT COUNTRIES TO CANADA, 1945-1973

	Bulgaria	Czechoslovakia	Hungary	Poland	Romania	U.S.S.R.	Totals
1945-49	160	3,577	3,202	30,071	1,054	9,572	47,636
1950-54	664	6,686	9,061	31,217	2,320	20,303	70,251
1955-59	189	1,209	38,344	13,980	726	3,382	57,830
1960-64	87	367	2,370	10,962	567	887	15,240
1965-69	78	2,989	2,519	7,074	271	1,014	13,945
1970-73	68	1,293	1,556	4,437	491	1,028	8,873
Totals	1,246	16,121	57,052	97,741	5,429	36,186	213,775

Source: *Canada Year Book, 1945-55; Annual Immigration Statistics, 1956-73.*

academics, and civil libertarians, they are anxious to uphold those who suffer persecution for their faith, beliefs or dissidence. There has also emerged, as a result of cultural exchanges at the state level in the past few years, an artistic community in Canada and Eastern Europe that desires longer term exchanges at the personal and institutional level. The freer movement of tourists also enables those who admire or reject Soviet applications of the Marxian system to observe more of the leviathan at first hand.

Rather than advocating the overthrow of the socialist system, these contacts are directed toward the mutual acceptance and accommodation of systems in an interdependent and changing world. This was the thrust of Secretary of State for External Affairs Allan MacEachen's speech to a group of academics on September 6, 1974:

> From the point of view of Canadians it will not be good enough if the answer is the mere replacement of opposing armed camps of steel with closed camps of the mind. While there may be a stability of sorts through mutual deterrence, there can be little prospect of peaceful change and development in a mutually-antagonistic political and intellectual life . . . But co-existence without an element of change — without the ability to adjust to our rapidly developing world and its new challenges — will bring a rigidity and even a brittleness that cannot help but endanger both sides.[10]

If Basket III emerges as a collection of pious generalities, then the Soviet Union will have gained Western trade, credits, technology, limited armament control and a degree of security without having satisfied Canadian interests. Unless some equivalence is accepted, détente will simply mean a unilateral disarmament of an already demobilized Western ideology.

The very fact that CSCE goes beyond an East-West accommodation, beyond the limited scientific, academic and cultural exchanges of the past into complex trans-national interactions makes it a threat to certain Soviet groups. That is why the Soviet press accompanied its report of the Helsinki consultations with renewed appeals for relentless struggles against alien bourgeois ideology. Canada is aware of the limitations to

Soviet change. Denunciations by Canada in November 1973 of the Kremlin's policies respecting national minorities and dissidents provoked Mr. Gromyko to remind Mr. Sharp of Canada's own difficulties with poverty, native peoples and unemployment. A joint communiqué expressed their wish for "extending co-operation and contacts between people in Europe", but a later *Pravda* release indicated that the Soviets interpreted this reference to "people" as meaning the exchange of only official delegations and not private individuals as Sharp had thought at the time.[11] Similar linguistic legerdemain was used by Gromyko to confuse immigrant with visitor status when presented with a list of individuals known to be seeking emigration to Canada for purposes of family reunification. In spite of this, the prospects are not entirely gloomy. Approximately half of the cases contained in lists presented in 1971 and 1973 have subsequently found release. As time goes on, aging relatives of Canadians now in the Soviet labour force will become more expendable and if suitable financial arrangements can be made they may have an opportunity to emigrate.[12]

It is in this context that Canada began the negotiations by submitting a list of five areas requiring discussion: liberalizing exit procedures; permission for family reunification and regular family contacts and marriages between nationals of different states; liberalizing of restrictions on the validity of passports; elimination of closed zones; and assurances of access to diplomatic, consular or other officially sponsored foreign establishments. NATO's bargaining strategy emphasized the freer movement of people and ideas as a prerequisite for Soviet security in Europe. This strategy reduced the possibility of trade-offs between economic (Basket II) and human contact (Basket III) issues, thereby favouring the Canadian presentation. But throughout Phase II (January-March 1974) of CSCE the Soviet Union rejected Western proposals for freer flows of information and people as a trade-off for its cherished desire of Western acceptance of the "inviolability" of European frontiers. Although Moscow has been willing to countenance some further human contacts, she has steadfastly rejected any freer flow of information.[13] Canada was prepared to spin out the negotiations until the autumn of 1975, but the Soviet Union pleaded for a rapid advancement to Phase III, the final summit meeting, early in the summer.

Before capitulating to Soviet insistence, further concessions were sought. Under this pressure the Pearsonian school of diplomats in the Department of External Affairs had an opportunity of demonstrating their finesse in hatching acceptable compromises. Exactly what laurels they deserve remains unclear but the Soviets on several occasions have credited the Canadian delegation with being the most realistic of the Western delegations. In a very real sense, they credit Canada with seeing both sides, an ability that leads to the discovery of solutions that NATO can accept and the Soviets can live with.

Instead of the harbinger of the millennium, we obtained only the minimum principles acceptable to all for the evolution of better solutions to long-standing problems in the final text signed by the government heads at the Helsinki Conference in July 1975. Predictably, the text fell short of Canadian demands for juridically defined rights. While no item on the original agenda was ignored, the vaguely worded agreements leave many loopholes. Sections on the reunification of families and cross-border marriages, for instance, say only that "participating states will examine favourably and on the basis of humanitarian considerations" such requests. Moreover, resort can always be made to a more clearly defined section which says that "participating states will refrain from any intervention . . . in the internal or external affairs falling within the jurisdiction of another participating state". While these uncertainties remain, the real breakthrough is not found in the text but in getting Communist leaders to discuss these sensitive issues at all. Their speeches at Helsinki at least contained passing references to the principles of human contacts while emphasizing the inviolability of frontiers. Negotiations on Canadian diplomatic exchanges with the German Democratic Republic that were stalled throughout 1974 over these very issues have now been completed. CSCE principles have now become the measuring stick for acceptable conduct abroad and Canada is interested in a follow-up to CSCE in 1977 where Communist governments can be held accountable to the letter and spirit of this declaration of intent, however vaguely defined. In the short run, the first fruits of détente for Canada may well be, as one reporter suggested, "herring and capelin", for Trudeau and Brezhnev took advantage of the occasion and the spirit of détente to begin talks leading toward the early settlement of that vexing bilateral prob-

51

lem of over-fishing in the North Atlantic.[14]

Peace, trade and prosperity have historically been the ingredients of Canada's policy in Europe. At the Paris Peace Conference in 1946, the Canadian delegate announced: "We believe that peace is not merely the absence of war, but the positive establishment of prosperity. Trade between nations, like the well-being of the people within each nation, is a main pillar on which to build the structure of a lasting peace."[15] While Canada's presence as a major trading nation at CSCE was not emphasized, she was no less concerned with the outcome of Basket II, dealing with commercial exchanges, industrial cooperation, science and technology, and environment. Because she is not a member of any trading bloc in an era of enlarging, closed, trading systems, she must remain at the forefront of expanding commercial relations with COMECON, the Eastern bloc's Council for Mutual Economic Assistance. Otherwise an aggressive EEC caucus will gain a monopolistic edge that already sees West German pipelines bringing Siberian gas to Western Europe and Fiats on Soviet shopping lists.

Statistics in Table II on Canadian trade with COMECON countries from 1970 to 1973 indicate a steady though largely inflation-induced growth in the dollar value of imports and a much larger but fluctuating export market. Hitherto, general trade has not been substantial because both sides produce similar products and resources for export and the socialist bureaucratic barriers to trade have been depressing. Moreover, an easy growth in Canadian exports to the United States in the sixties prevented the search for more aggressive and imaginative ways of penetrating Eastern European markets. Present Soviet interest in Western capital and technology and an anticipated interest in Western consumerism suggests a better future for Canadian trade with COMECON countries.[16] Thanks to the application of President Nixon's surcharge to Canada, Canadian trade diversification is becoming more of a reality, in line with the Third Option for lessening Canada's economic dependence on the United States. Since European markets seem better attuned to the global supermarket of the future, in which our secondary industry must compete, and more receptive to the more established Canadian exports of mining equipment, construction machinery and heavy electrical equipment, we should focus our attention there rather than on the longer range poten-

TABLE II
CANADIAN TRADE WITH COMECON COUNTRIES, 1970-73

	Imports		Exports	
	Four Year Average in Thousands	Percentage Change from 1970-71 to 1972-73	Four Year Average in Thousands	Percentage Change from 1970-71 to 1972-73
Bulgaria	1,428	+44	1,320	-74
Czechoslovakia	33,795	+32	6,782	+10
German D.R.	4,483	+30	3,423	+104
Hungary	10,326	+52	6,036	+11
Poland	19,602	+87	27,247	+128
Romania	10,187	+92	9,951	+82
U.S.S.R.	14,976	+76	199,960	+151
Total	94,797		254,719	

Source: *Trade Statistics*, a quarterly issued by Statistics Canada.

tial of Third World markets. Overcoming Canada's past reliance on laissez-faire manufacturing policies and opposition to diversification of markets will require substantial changes in her industrial strategy. Now that Eastern European economic planners have recognized the limitations within which the Soviet Union allows for their functioning, Canada must take advantage of this situation by developing a system of centralized marketing to overcome the traditional inhibitions of Canadian businessmen in dealing with unfamiliar markets and state trading corporations. This also requires federal government support for private trading houses and consortia, as well as the development of better financing and contractual arrangements for long-term, large export commitments. Both contractual and equity joint ventures must be developed if Canada wishes to protect her markets in an age of multinational enterprise. Naturally some rationalization of Canadian industry will flow from these contacts but it should not be at the expense of Canadian workers who fear unfair competition practices. The new industrial strategy must have the support of manufacturers, labourers, exporters and importers.

In developing these contacts, it must not be forgotten that détente is a two-way street. A Canadian business presence in Communist countries must be matched by a Soviet business presence in Canada. Only then will the commercial ties that make for irreversible détente be made secure. By insisting that visiting businessmen, engineers, managers and scientists not live in national ghettos when abroad, we can expect that new attitudes, aspirations, standards, and knowledge of other societies will develop eventually. In the border regions, these contacts may well raise the consciousness of the workers to discrepancies in living standards. But workers' revolts in Eastern Europe have not been numerous (German Democratic Republic 1953, Hungary 1956, Poland 1970-71) and are not likely to be tolerated as agents of change. Effects of commercial contacts on the political leadership will be minimal as long as it recruits on the basis of party orthodoxy and bypasses the managerial and technocratic classes. This is why détente must have a broader base than increased business co-operation and why Canada must not be satisfied with simply a dollar return from détente.

By resorting to vague generalities on the most contentious issues, the 35 participants in CSCE have found it much easier to reach agreement than the 19 nations involved in talks on Mutual Balanced Force Reductions. But, as Canada has said so often, détente will be illusory unless European security is buttressed by a reduction in the concentration of military power in the area. In the words of Mitchell Sharp, the task is how to combine "continued defence preparedness with pursuit of détente, alliance solidarity with willingness to seek accommodation with the other side, and firmness on basic principles with flexibility on means."[17] The spirit of accommodation initially produced by the balance of deterrence has been submerged in arguments over complexities while, almost oblivious to it all, the superpowers move onto another plateau of rivalry in long-range cruise missiles at the same time as they retire the obsolete in SALT. Meanwhile, in the European theatre the prospects for the deployment of mini-nuclear warheads alters the existing conventional and strategic balances.[18]

The two main issues dividing NATO and the Warsaw Pact at MBFR talks are the sequence and nature of force reductions. The Warsaw Pact countries want an immediate reduction of the forces of all direct participants while NATO desires an initial agreement for super-power force reduction and deferment of reductions in other forces to a second phase. NATO believes that the equilibrium should be achieved through phased reductions to a common ceiling on ground forces of approximately 700,000. The Warsaw Pact countries, arguing from a numerically superior position, reject any move toward conventional military balance in favour of proportional reductions across the board. Thus far, neither side has made any substantive changes in their positions though discussions have moved from balanced to asymmetrical reductions (MFR) and viewpoints have been clarified in negotiations over equivalence. The problem in resolving the debate over military equivalance is very simply illustrated in Table III. How accurate these facts and figures are has not been determined because the Warsaw Pact countries will neither accept NATO's figures nor present their own. The equation becomes more complex when types of divisions, their strengths, deployment, characteristics of equipment, availability of reinforcements, and so on, are added with the stipulation by both sides that reductions should not disadvantage any country.[19]

Canada is at the MFR talks because of her membership in

TABLE III
1974-75 MILITARY BALANCE BETWEEN NATO AND THE WARSAW PACT

NATO	Manpower in thousands	Tanks	Aircraft
United States	190	2,100	240
Britain	55	600	130
Canada	3	30	40
Belgium	65	375	140
Netherlands	77	500	160
West Germany	340	2,950	600
	730	6,555	1,310
France*	58	325	400
Total	788	6,880	1,710

Warsaw Pact	Manpower in thousands	Tanks	Aircraft
Soviet Union	460	7,850	1,250
Czechoslovakia	155	2,900	500
East Germany	100	1,650	330
Poland	220	3,100	730
Total	935	15,500	2,810

*France is taking no part in the discussions; therefore, her troops and any Soviet and NATO troops stationed outside of the area presently under discussion (Poland, Czechoslovakia, Federal Republic of Germany, German Democratic Republic, the Netherlands, Belgium and Luxembourg) are not being considered.

Source: *The Military Balance, 1974-1975* (London: The International Institute for Strategic Studies, 1974), p. 101. (Reproduced by permission of the publisher.)

NATO. While the military function of NATO has been somewhat downgraded by détente, there is no indication that the Government is considering withdrawal.[20] The articulate minority who pleaded in the late sixties for Canadian non-alignment and leadership of the Third World have lost much of their steam. Moreover non-alignment has become less meaningful in a multi-polar world and there is little indication at the present that the Third World's Group of 77 would accept the leadership of a fat cat whose economy is so closely integrated with the bastion of imperialism. When, in the early seventies, the politicians finally heeded the civil servants' plea for greater Canadian attention to Europe as an alternate source to the United States for capital and markets, her membership in NATO found even greater significance. In the first place, the NATO forum has largely replaced the embassies in obtaining information about major diplomatic initiatives and in ensuring Canadian influence in crisis management. While we are kept waiting in the capitals, we are briefed in Brussels. Of increasingly less value is the degree of low cost security provided by NATO though the advantages of technological spin-offs and contracts help balance the budget. A few thousand Canadian hostages in Europe soothe Europe's historical sensitivities while providing a means of gaining favour with members of the EEC. When combined with the support for the Federal Republic of Germany's position on frontiers in CSCE it led to a contractual link for Canada with the European Economic Community.

The main advantage for Canada in participating in MFR talks is the opportunity for establishing European security on a footing that will allow NATO to be transformed into the kind of alliance originally envisaged by Pearson: something beyond a defender of the West, something based on Article II of the North Atlantic Treaty, on consultative machinery and on co-operation in the non-military fields. Then the removal of Canadian land forces and obsolete equipment from Europe in favour of roles more in line with actual threats and Canadian defence interests will be practical.

This does not mean unilaterally throwing the sponge in on the defence of Europe. Any move toward unilateral demobilization in the present stage of MFR talks, either for her own selfish reasons or to add weight to similar viewpoints in the United States represented by Senator Mansfield, would weaken our capacity for negotiating with the Warsaw Pact which interprets such action as a sign of weakness worth exploiting. Withdrawal now would unnecessarily damage our relations with the European Community, who see behind the Canadian forces an enormous storehouse of supplies, and with the United States, without bringing us any closer to what we are striving for in détente. Moreover, at the present juncture, a withdrawal of conventional forces would compel European deployment of tactical and strategic nuclear weapons and the development of a Western European Defence System that would provoke the Soviet Union into another round of escalation.[21]

Given Canada's support of MFR in Europe, what can she reasonably expect to accomplish in the light of current negotiations and intra-NATO disagreements over means and ends? The easiest course, and the one most likely to bring success, would be support for a simple super-power reduction formula with other reductions left for a future phase. While this would undoubtedly win favour in United States circles, it would be counterproductive in terms of Canada's European objectives — since siding with the United States and removing one of Western Europe's bargaining assets would antagonize some EEC members of NATO whose favours in other areas Canada has so avidly sought.

A traditional Canadian role would be mediating a NATO-Warsaw Pact consensus, but such an objective is unrealistic since present negotiations illustrate more divergence than convergence. Such a course also assumes that the Soviet Union would accept a *quid pro quo* between CSCE and MFR with Western concessions already granted in the former, balanced by concessions in the latter. At the present there is no indication that such a balance could be constructed. Moreover, it is doubtful whether Canada has either the political or military influence required of a successful bridge builder, unless both sides confer this honour upon her.

The only realistic course for Canada to follow is in the resolution of intra-NATO differences that will allow for NATO participation in arms control in Central Europe without losing its overall military balance. When it is known how much détente the Soviet market can consume, and what further concessions the NATO allies are prepared to make, then machinery must be made available for advancing to a further stage of troop reductions and withdrawal of tactical nuclear weapons. Canada must facilitate this interchange and assist in the development of that machinery. She must also persuade both sides that CSCE-MFR is not a zero-sum game, where a gain for one side automatically amounts to a loss for the other. Only over a period of time and a whole range of relations can a workable and mutually acceptable balance be found. Stability does not automatically follow the reduction of armed forces, for they are not the cause of conflict. Conflict is rooted in man's depravity and the nature of his imperialism, and that is why human diplomacy is such an essential ingredient of détente.

A significant by-product of European détente will be changed Canadian-American relations. In spite of our different perceptions of the East-West confrontation and relations with Communist countries, Cold War bipolarity has made it more difficult for Canada to reduce her economic, political and military dependence on the United States. European détente will free Canada from some of these constraints because the United States will no longer feel so obliged to line up the troops behind her, and Canada will no longer have to use quiet diplomacy out of deference to the united Western front. The Soviet Union may never become a counterweight to the United States, as Prime Minister Trudeau precipitately suggested at the time of his visit to Moscow in 1971, but the Warsaw Pact countries will certainly become part of that inter-dependent world that collectively allows Canada greater options for diversification. By participating independently in the process of European détente, Canada has confirmed, for those who need reminding, that North America is not a monolith.

At the mid-point of the seventies, it has become imperative that old skeletons be buried so that we can meet unencumbered the new crises associated with inflation, famine and diminishing resources, disparities of wealth and technology. For Canada, the switch to international economic issues means both greater influence and greater solitude. Canada's major antagonists over the seabed, pollution and foreign investment are her old military allies. She must now search for new allies who will strengthen her hand in dealing with such problems. In this realignment, international organizations will take on greater significance and responsibility and she must help free them of Cold War antagonisms. Canada enters this new era of conference diplomacy with many natural assets, just as she did after the last European war. She must again rise to the challenge by producing another group of brilliant conference diplomats who make their points by the vigour of their intellectual arguments, and through a new Post (Cold) War Hostilities Planning Group, stimulate new ways of thinking about European issues. There is no realistic alternative if we are to get on with the future.

But however grand or promising, a diplomatically arranged détente is only a band-aid solution to a much deeper problem. The key to lasting détente will not be found in the diplomatic corridors, but in people's hearts as they are transformed by the renewing of their minds in obedience to the Spirit of God which alone can transcend all of man's political, economic and social barriers. Only then will nations and peoples learn to speak to each other and to bear one another's burdens in such a way that real peace may be found. If European détente is to be sustained, that is the ultimate challenge facing those who promote people-to-people diplomacy.

Notes

1. *Foreign Policy for Canadians*, (Ottawa: Queen's Printer, 1970), p. 38.

2. For a history of the steps leading to the Helsinki Consultations, see Karl E. Birnbaum, *Peace in Europe: East-West Relations 1966-1968 and the Prospects for a European Settlement*, (London: Oxford University Press, 1970) and Michael Palmer, *The Prospects for a European Security Conference*, (London: Chatham House, PEP, 1971). A different view of the origin is found in Walter C. Clemens Jr., "Shifts in Soviet Arms Control Posture", *Military Review*, LI (July 1971), pp. 28-36.

3. See the opening speech of the Canadian Ambassador to Finland, Department of External Affairs, *Statements and Speeches*, 73/3.

4. Statement by Secretary of State for External Affairs, M. Sharp to the United Nations General Assembly, September 29, 1969, *Statements and Speeches*, 69/14.

5. Peter C. Dobell, "Europe: Canada's Last Chance?" *International Journal*, XXVII (Winter 1971-72), pp. 126-128.

6. Statement by Secretary of State for External Affairs, M. Sharp, at a press briefing following a meeting of NATO, 1972, quoted in Murray Goldblatt, "Canada and European Security", *International Perspectives*, January-February 1973, p. 37.

7. Approval was given for Canadian participation by all parties in the House of Commons on June 5, 1972. However, the Standing Committee on External Affairs and National

Defence could muster only 22 MP's for three hearings on the subject, only two of whom attended all three sessions. In May 1975 a select group of academics fared better by being taken into the Department of External Affairs bosom on CSCE.

8. Statement of Canadian Ambassador, E.A. Côté, at the Helsinki Consultations, Department of External Affairs Communiqué No. 6, January 16, 1973.

9. *Ibid.*, No. 17, February 8, 1973. See also *Statements and Speeches*, 73/13.

10. Speech of Secretary of State for External Affairs, A. MacEachen, to the Banff '74 International Conference on Slavic Studies, September 6, 1974, *Statements and Speeches*, 74/10.

11. David Levy, "Making a Mark in Moscow. . . " *International Perspectives*, January-February 1974, p. 22.

12. Henry F. Heald, "Scanning the Broad Implications of Sharp's Trip to Soviet Union", *International Perspectives*, January-February 1974, p. 17.

13. For a more complete summary of Phase II of CSCE, see Jean Laux, "CSCE: Symbol of the Search for East-West Co-operation", *International Perspectives* September-October 1974, pp. 23-26.

14. See Ross Henderson, "Trudeau and Brezhnev meet in Helsinki, open way for talks on fishing dispute", *Globe and Mail*, August 1, 1975 and George Bain, "Spirit of Helsinki may outweigh lack of legal force", *Toronto Star*, August 2, 1975. The full text of the agreement will be published by the Department of External Affairs as "The Final Act of the Conference on European Security and Cooperation".

15. Statement of the Hon. Brooke Claxton to the Plenary Conference of the Paris Peace Conference, October 8, 1946.

16. For an explanation of the difficulties encountered by a capitalist nation dealing with a socialist market economy see J. Wilczynski, *The Economics and Politics of East-West Trade: A Study of Trade Between Developed Market Economies and Centrally Planned Economies in a Changing World*, (London: Macmillan, 1969) and S. Pisar, *Co-existence and Commerce: Guidelines for Transactions Between East and West*, (New York: McGraw-Hill, 1970). The official Canadian view on "Business in Eastern Europe" is found in *Canada Commerce*, LXXXIX (April

1975), pp. 1-27.

17. Canada, *House of Commons Debates,* June 5, 1972, p 28-30.

18. The long-range cruise missile now under development can be launched from a submerged submarine, a plane or a land vehicle. It will have a range of over 1300 nautical miles and a capacity to fly at altitudes between tree-top and over six miles. Its sophisticated electronic package will allow it to be retargetable while in flight and capable of producing its own counter-missile defences. See Kosta Tsipis, "The Long-Range Cruise Missile", *Bulletin of the Atomic Scientists,* XXXI (April 1975), pp. 15-22. On mini-nukes see Colin S. Gray, "Mini-nukes and Strategy", *International Journal,* XXIX (Spring 1974), pp. 216-41.

19. For a recent succinct discussion of the problems in arms reduction in Europe, see J.I. Coffey, *New Approaches to Arms Reduction in Europe*, Adelphi Paper No. 105, (London: International Institute for Strategic Studies, 1974). For brief insights into MBFR see Walter C. Clemens, Jr., "European Arms Control: How, What, and When?", *International Journal,* XXVII (Winter 1971-72), pp. 45-72 and A. Legault, "Stage One of the MBFR Talks", *International Perspectives*, September-October 1973, pp. 14-17.

20. See Mr. Sharp's remarks of April 17, 1973 to the Canadian Parliamentary Association on "NATO: How It Serves Canadian Interests", *Statements and Speeches,* 73/12. The NATO debate has produced much literature. The opposing views are examined in Harald von Riekhoff, "NATO: To Stay or Not To Stay", in S. Clarkson, ed., *An Independent Foreign Policy for Canada,* (Toronto: McClelland and Stewart, Carleton Contemporary, 1968), pp. 160-72, in the "Beyond NATO" issue of the *International Journal,* XXIX (Spring 1974), in Bruce Thordarson, *Trudeau and Foreign Policy: A Study in Decision-making*, (Toronto: Oxford University Press, 1972), in Lewis Hertzman *et. al., Alliances and Illusions*, (Edmonton: M. Hurtig, 1969), and Colin S. Gray, *Canadian Defence Priorities: A Question of Relevance*, (Toronto: Clarke Irwin, 1972).

21. For a discussion of the consequences of a unilateral United States withdrawal, see John Newhouse *et. al., U.S. Troops in Europe: Issues, Costs, and Choices* (Washington, D.C.: Brookings Institute, 1971).

CHAPTER 4

CANADA AND MULTINATIONAL ENTERPRISE

David Leyton-Brown

In recent years, increasing attention has been focused on aspects of world politics which previously were overshadowed by a traditional emphasis on relations between governments. This broader perspective is commonly referred to under the label of transnational relations — "contacts, coalitions, and interactions across state boundaries that are not controlled by the central foreign policy organs of governments."[1] By this definition, transnational relations is a residual category, encompassing everything excluded or underestimated by the conventional analysis of interstate relations. A major part of current investigation concerns the behaviour and effects of transnational organizations, identified as relatively large, hierarchically organized bureaucratic structures performing limited and specialized functions across international boundaries.[2] Prominent among these transnational organizations are businesses which operate internationally, and which are customarily known as multinational enterprises (MNEs).

It is a common misconception that all MNEs are alike in structure and behaviour. That is certainly not the case. There are qualitative differences among MNEs engaged in raw materials extraction, manufacturing and services. Some MNEs are structured so as to integrate all global operations under the command of a single decision-making centre, while others allow considerable autonomy to their foreign subsidiaries, even to the extent of international competition with the parent company. Some become "good corporate citizens" of the countries in which they operate, abiding by local legal requirements and accepted standards of conduct, while others appear insensitive to local policies and concerns. Despite the diversity of firms knowns as MNEs, it is possible to look for general patterns in the behaviour of MNEs and the concerns of governments, to determine the effects on government policy of these increasingly important actors.

Before doing so, however, it is necessary to clarify the object of our investigation. There is considerable disagreement among analysts as to the definition of the term multinational enterprise, with different writers pointing variously to criteria of ownership, size, geographical extent, importance of foreign operations, decision-making structure, and so on.[3] For the purposes of this political analysis, an MNE can be identified as a large business enterprise with significant operations in several countries, whose foreign subsidiaries are responsive to, if not totally controlled by, decisions of the parent.

It is particularly appropriate to study the interactions between MNEs and Canada, because of the unusual extent of foreign ownership in the Canadian economy. The Gray Report has stated that the degree of foreign ownership and control of economic activity is substantially higher in Canada than in any other industrialized country, with one-third of total business activity in Canada undertaken by foreign-controlled enterprises.[4] If foreign ownership is indeed increasing in other economies, and if the activities of MNEs are becoming more extensive, Canada might well be looked on as a foremost case of a spreading condition. Canada's experience as a host to foreign MNEs could be indicative of what lies ahead for other host countries, as foreign penetration of their economies increases. Furthermore, Canada is not merely the host to foreign MNEs. It is also the parent country of a number of Canadian multinationals.

In their pathbreaking work on transnational relations, Nye and Keohane suggested several possible effects of transnational interactions and organizations on interstate politics. Two of these are of particular relevance to Canada and the MNE. The first is "the emergence of autonomous actors with private foreign policies that may deliberately oppose or impinge on state policies". The second is "increases in the ability of certain governments to influence others".[5] These hypothesized effects will form the organizing base for this analysis. Firstly, the MNE will be studied as an autonomous actor, and resulting interactions and conflicts with the Canadian government will be examined. Secondly, we will assess the ways in which MNEs have been used as instruments of government policy in dealing with other countries, either by the parent or host governments.

Seen in this light, the problems raised for the Canadian government can be divided into seven different issue areas: 1) proposed takeovers of existing Canadian firms by foreign investors, 2) proposed investments by foreigners to create new enterprises in Canada, 3) internal operations of foreign-owned subsidiaries in Canada, especially concerning labour relations, 4) controls by the parent government over exports from Canadian subsidiaries, 5) extension of antitrust regulations of the parent government to activities of Canadian subsidiaries, 6) efforts by the parent government to improve its balance of payments position by influencing the investment, profit repatriation, and production location decisions of its MNEs and their Canadian subsidiaries, and 7) initiatives by the host Canadian government to exploit the unique characteristics of foreign-owned MNEs as an instrument of its own policy.[6]

Takeovers: The acquisition of Canadian businesses by foreign investors is the most visible and often the most contentious aspect of the foreign ownership question in Canada. The screening of foreign takeover bids was the original task assigned to the Foreign Investment Review Agency (FIRA), at the time of its creation in 1973. It would be wrong, however, to assume that prior to that time the Canadian government was powerless to prevent or affect takeover attempts. Though a great many takeovers took place without attracting noticeable government response (for example, 100 in 1968 and 130 in 1969)[7], in some significant cases the government was able to intervene to block or attach conditions to a takeover attempt, even though no organized machinery for that purpose existed.

The most prominent of these cases was the Mercantile Bank affair, in which the Bank Act was amended in 1967 to restrict foreign holdings in Canadian chartered banks. Since all other Canadian chartered banks were Canadian-owned, this legislation applied only to the Mercantile Bank, which had been purchased (from Dutch owners) in 1963 by the First National City Bank of New York (Citibank), despite warnings from Canadian officials and the Minister of Finance that the government would act retroactively to limit Mercantile's growth. Citibank charged retroactive and discriminatory treatment, and sought an exemption from the legislation, enlisting the support of the United States government in their struggle. The struggle became heated indeed, featuring an exchange of diplomatic protest notes between the governments, threats by Citibank to close down Mercantile, threatened retaliation against Canadian banking operations in the United States, and a highly publicized negotiating process. When the smoke cleared, the legislation had passed, Mercantile had been given a temporary five year exemption from the Canadian ownership provisions, and had begun issuing new shares to Canadian residents to bring the level of Canadian stock ownership in the bank up to 75 percent. The Canadian government had succeeded, in the face of powerful corporate and diplomatic pressures, in maintaining Canadian control of the banking sector.

Another vital sector, that of resource exploitation, was involved in two other recent cases. In 1970, a controlling interest in Denison Mines, Canada's largest uranium producer, was sought by an affiliate of the Continental Oil Company of the United States. Acting under the authority of the Canadian Atomic Energy Act, Prime Minister Trudeau forbade the sale. Despite threats to close the mine, and a lawsuit against the Prime Minister by the outraged Canadian owner, the government successfully prevented the takeover. New non-retroactive regulations were introduced to restrict further foreign ownership in Canada's uranium industry. A year later, in 1971, without any apparent legislative authority, the Canadian government disallowed the sale of Home Oil Ltd., Canada's largest independent oil producer, to Ashland Oil of the United States, and made money available to make Canadian offers equally attractive.

It is not always the federal government which acts to block undesirable foreign takeovers. On at least one occasion a provincial government has also done so. In 1971, the owner of McClelland and Stewart (publisher of this volume) suffered from a lack of working capital, and sought a buyer for the company. Only American publishers expressed interest, and finally the Ontario government provided a $1 million loan to keep the company under domestic ownership.[8]

Of the large number of takeovers which occurred each year, only a small number became politically salient. It appears that government intervention was prompted by the key sector occupied by the Canadian firm in question. Over a matter of decades, Canadian control or participation in certain key sectors has been guaranteed by a succession of measures including legislation to restrict foreign ownership in different industries, and the creation of publicly-owned enterprises. The historical key sectors in Canada are financial institutions, communications, transportation and more recently resource exploitation. Even in these key sectors, however, the will of the Canadian government does not always prevail. In 1969, one of Canada's largest investment dealers, Royal Securities Corporation, was acquired by Merrill, Lynch, Pierce, Fenner and Smith, the American brokerage house. Despite the sensitive sector involved, and despite the statement of official governmental disapproval, the sale was completed, because of the absence of prior legislative authority and competing provincial jurisdiction.

It is impossible to know with certainty whether the failure of the Canadian government to block any other takeovers reflects satisfaction or impotence. The ability of the Canadian government in the pre-FIRA period to act decisively when it wished has been demonstrated. Some indication of whether its wishes were mobilized frequently enough can be gained by an examination of the performance of FIRA since its inception. Applying its specified criteria of "significant benefit to Canada", FIRA reviewed 214 takeover applications from April 9, 1974, when the first phase of the act came into effect, until August 31, 1975. Of those, 43 were still pending, while 115 were accepted, 26 were refused, and 30 were withdrawn.[9] Of the 171 applications which were disposed of, 67 percent were accepted and 15 percent were refused. By far the majority of takeovers are still viewed favorably, though rather more have been refused or renegotiated than before FIRA came into being.

New Investment: Much less public controversy has been associated with investment by a foreign MNE to create a new enterprise in Canada. Nevertheless, some instances of policy problems in this area have occurred, and the second phase of the Foreign Investment Review Act, which came into effect on October 15, 1975, gives the government an established mechanism to screen prospective new investments as well as takeovers. Under the second phase, any foreign company seeking to enter the Canadian economy for the first time, and any foreign-controlled Canadian company seeking to make acquisitions or new investments in unrelated fields, must receive prior government approval. With this screening mechanism in place, it is likely that new investments will continue to be relatively removed from public attention, though the government now possesses a regularized means of screening out disadvantageous investments.

The blocking of undesired new investment has not been a concern of Canadian policy in the past. Dating back to the days of the National Policy, when tariff walls were built to encourage investment in Canadian plants by foreign producers, and continuing up to the present through regional development incentives offered by the Department of Regional Economic Expansion, the general thrust of Canadian policy has been to invite new investment, and not to discourage it. Some provincial governments have been so eager for the development and employment benefits associated with additional investment that they have competed with one another in offering attractive inducements to investors, or subsidized a new enterprise to an uneconomical extreme.[10] This eagerness for investment enables a prospective investor to play off competing provincial governments against each other, or even to threaten to locate new facilities in another country entirely, in order to obtain the most favorable assistance possible.

On two notable occasions, the Canadian government's encouragement of new investment has led to political difficulties. Awareness of the increasing possibility of energy shortages, and a public commitment to development of the Athabasca oil sands, made Canadian federal and provincial governments feel vulnerable to a threatened collapse of the Syncrude project in late 1974. Faced with rising costs and declining Canadian oil exports, Atlantic-Richfield, one of the four participating United States oil companies, withdrew its participation, and the remaining partners announced their inability to continue alone. After two months of frenzied federal-provincial-corporate negotiations, the project was salvaged, and equity participation by the Alberta, Ontario, and federal governments was achieved, but at the cost of $800 million in public funds from the three governments, and significant tax and pricing concessions to the oil MNEs.[11] The threat to discontinue the new investment appears to have produced more favorable investment conditions.

In the early 1970s, the Michelin Company of France proposed to build an automobile tire factory in the Maritimes to supply the entire North American market. The Canadian government willingly offered grants and other incentives under the regional economic expansion program. The United States government interpreted these regional development incentives as export subsidies, and imposed a countervailing tariff on Michelin tires exported to the United States. It is interesting to note that even where a foreign MNE is not American-owned, its activities in Canada can spark a Canadian-American dispute. This case contrasts with the present Domestic International Sales Corporation program of the United States government, by which American production for export can be subsidized, which can have the effect of discouraging production abroad by American MNES.

Labour Relations: The two previous issue areas have involved the entry of an MNE to the Canadian economy. This issue deals with the internal operations of an established branch of an MNE in Canada. The most visible and sensitive aspect of the internal operations of a firm in which government and corporate objectives can conflict is labour relations. The basic problem is the greater concern of an MNE for uninterrupted integrated production and global profit maximization than for customary industrial relations practices or particular governmental policy goals in a host country.

In the mid 1960s, while the Canadian government was urging voluntary limits on wage increases to stem inflation, the major automobile companies, at the urging of an international union, negotiated an inflationary wage settlement providing for progression to wage parity between Canadian automobile workers and those in the United States. Satisfying the demands of American union leaders, and preventing the disruption of production at larger American plants, appear to have been the primary motivations. On August 15, 1971, President Nixon of the United States announced a ninety day freeze on wages, prices and rents. Canada's Secretary of State for External Affairs announced that the Canadian government would not tolerate the importation of the freeze into Canada. Nevertheless, some American companies did extend the freeze to their subsidiaries in Canada. Chrysler of Canada deferred a scheduled 5 percent wage increase for its administrative and supervisory employees, and Douglas Aircraft Ltd. broke off contract negotiations with its Canadian employees, even though the existing contract expired before the end of the freeze.[12] In 1974, United Aircraft transferred production from its strikebound plant in Longueuil, Quebec, to a factory in Hartford, Connecticut, though some $73 million in federal grants and loans had been received to subsidize Canadian production. Only Prime Minister Trudeau's threat of nationalization brought about resumption of production in Longueuil. In all of these cases the Canadian government was unable through normal government policy to dissuade MNEs from undesired changes in their internal operations in the labour relations area.

It is not only foreign MNEs whose internal operations can conflict with Canadian government policy. On occasion, Canadian MNEs have behaved in a similar fashion. In 1968, when confronted with a strike by Canadian workers demanding wage parity with company employees in the United States, Massey-Ferguson threatened to withdraw its operations entirely to the United States. The strike was settled without wage parity. Massey-Ferguson used similar arguments in persuading the Canadian government to alter its proposed implementation of some recommendations of the Carter Commission on Tax Reform. A Canadian MNE, with the bulk of its assets and operations abroad, may have a stake in the Canadian economy functionally equivalent to that of a foreign MNE, and so be led by pursuit of corporate objectives into conflict with the Canadian government.

The relative ineffectuality of the Canadian government in attempting to affect the internal operations of foreign MNEs is not confined to labour relations. Even such major internal policy instruments as monetary policy have limited effect. Kari Levitt has pointed out that during the year following the devaluation of the Canadian dollar in 1962, the value of total imports into Canada rose by 6 percent, but the value of imports by United States subsidiaries from parent companies increased by 15 percent. Remembering that these inter-affiliate transfers constitute about one-third of total Canadian imports, it is clear that the purchasing policies of the subsidiaries inhibited the substitution of domestic for imported goods, when the latter rose in price as a result of the devaluation.[13]

Export Controls: Nothing is more likely to inflame the passions of Canadian economic nationalists than discussion of the United States Trading With the Enemy Act. Under the terms of this act, the United States government controls all commercial and financial transactions with specified proscribed Communist states, not merely of American residents, but of all American citizens. If some of those American citizens are fortunate enough to own a subsidiary in Canada, or happen to serve as directors of Canadian companies, then the attempt by the United States government to treat all of its citizens in an even-handed and nondiscriminatory fashion can understandably appear to Canadians as an extraterritorial imposition of American jurisdiction over the activities of Canadian companies, in opposition to Canadian trade policy. In fact, the number of specific cases is relatively small (though somewhat greater than the public is aware[14]), the total economic impact on Canada and the proscribed customers has been minimal, and the political gains by the United States have been negligible. The strains imposed on the Canadian-American relationship appear to have outweighed any positive benefit for the United States.

The impact of American export controls burst upon Canadian consciousness in the late 1950s, when directors of American companies were subject to legal penalties if their non-United States subsidiaries participated in transactions with China, North Korea and North Vietnam. In 1957, it was charged that the Ford Motor Company of Canada had refused to sell trucks to China because of these controls. The ensuing dispute became a heated issue in the 1958 Canadian election campaign, and led to a joint Canadian-American probe which resulted in the so-called Diefenbaker-Eisenhower agreement. Under the terms of this agreement, a consultation procedure was established whereby an American parent company could apply to the United States Treasury Department, with Canadian government support, for a special licence to exempt its directors from legal liability, thus allowing completion of a sale by a Canadian subsidiary. The agreement was intended to depoliticize future conflicts in this issue area and to lessen tensions, but not to guarantee freedom of export activity by Canadian subsidiaries. The principle of extraterritoriality was implicitly accepted, and exemptions were not guaranteed. It was, however, made clear that an exemption would be more likely to be forthcoming if refusal of the order would have significant detrimental effect on the Canadian economy, and if the order in question could be filled only by an American-owned subsidiary.[15]

This consultative procedure was used in several later cases involving proposed sales to China, and did succeed in limiting public outcry. Exemptions were received for the sale to China of pulp and paper by the Canadian subsidiary of Rayonnier, and for the reconditioning by the Canadian subsidiary of Fairbanks-Morse of locomotives owned by Canadian National Railways for sale to China. In both of these cases, though an exemption was obtained from United States export controls, the sale ultimately did not take place. It has been suggested that some Chinese orders might not have been genuine, but might have been merely ploys to embarrass American subsidiaries in Canada and to aggravate tensions.[16]

In 1963, the two year old American trade embargo of Cuba was brought under the Trading With the Enemy Act. In contrast to the previous practice, there was no explicit limitation on the ability of foreign companies owned or controlled by Americans (i.e. Canadian subsidiaries) to make sales to Cuba, but American directors or officers of those subsidiaries were to be held legally liable for violations of the controls. Only the form of the controls changed; the effect remained the same. Several cases were handled administratively through licensing and exemption consultations, but the first case which came to public attention concerned the refusal of American-owned flour mills in Canada to supply flour in connection with a wheat sale to the Soviet Union involving the shipment of flour to Cuba. Canadian-owned companies were found to fill the order. Because domestically-owned suppliers existed, and because no damage to Canadian economic interests had been demonstrated, no exemption would have likely been forthcoming. More recently, in 1974-75, when the Canadian government has been actively promoting Canadian trade with Cuba, a multi-million dollar sale of locomotives by a subsidiary of Studebaker-Worthington and a sale of office furniture by a subsidiary of Litton Industries were blocked. In both cases, word of the cases was leaked to the press, and Canadian cabinet ministers took firm public stands. In the former case, no exemption was received, but the sale went through when American directors were removed from the board of the subsidiary for the decision. The subsidiary has since been acquired by a Canadian-owned company. In the latter case, an exemption was granted.

Following Richard Nixon's rapprochement with China, that country was removed from the "enemies" list. The ban on sales to Cuba by foreign subsidiaries was lifted by the United States government in August 1975, following the lifting of the Organization of American States trade embargo against Cuba. Nonetheless, the issue has not disappeared from the Canadian-American agenda. Cambodia and South Vietnam have been added to the list of proscribed countries, and though at present there is little Canadian interest in trade with those countries, the potential for future tensions still exists. The Canadian government has introduced legislation, as a part of its new Competition Bill, to forbid any company operating in Canada from following a foreign law or directive in any manner injurious to Canadian trade.[17] This legislation, which is not yet law, may solve the problem for all time, as its supporters contend. On the other hand, it may confront corporate executives with two mutually exclusive legal liabilities, so that they are damned if they do and damned if they don't.

Antitrust: Another extraterritorial extension of American jurisdiction has occurred through antitrust policy intended to prevent restraint upon American business, whether that restraint occurs domestically or in a foreign country. American antitrust policy with respect to American MNEs in Canada has been used in four different ways.

The first application of American antitrust policy to the Canadian economy has been designed to effect a restructuring of Canadian industry, a matter surely considered within Canadian jurisdiction, by compelling American parent companies to divest themselves of their Canadian holdings. An American court found that the joint ownership of Canadian Industries Limited by DuPont and Imperial Chemical Industries was part of a global understanding between the two companies not to compete anywhere in the world. DuPont was ordered to sell its interests in CIL, without regard to costs and benefits for the Canadian economy. Similarly, the Aluminum Company of America was ordered to divest itself of its controlling interests in the Aluminum Company of Canada (Alcan). This intrusion of American courts into the structure of the Canadian economy aroused considerable resentment.

The second aspect of American antitrust policy which affects

Canada has been the attempt by United States courts to sub-poena documents from Canadian companies. The 1950 attempt by the United States Department of Justice to obtain discovery and inspection of records and documents from American-owned pulp and paper companies in Canada was successfully resisted by a diplomatic protest from the Canadian government, and the passage of the Business Records Protection Act by the government of Ontario. This act prohibits the removal of corporate records from Ontario in compliance with the requirement or subpoena of any authority outside Ontario. Similar legislation was later passed in the Quebec Business Records Concerns Act.

The third impact of American antitrust policy on Canada is somewhat paradoxical. American takeovers of Canadian firms have in some instances been overturned by American courts, rather than by the Canadian government. Such a refusal is most likely to occur when the acquiring company dominates a highly concentrated American industry, and when new competition in the industry is most likely to come from the acquired foreign company.[18] For this reason, the Joseph Schlitz Brewing Company was prevented by United States courts in 1966 from ac-quiring John Labatt Ltd., a Canadian brewer, because of Labatt's possible future expansion in the American beer market.

The fourth use of American antitrust policy has been to com-bat perceived illegal restraints on the possibility of exports from the United States to Canada. In the 1950's, the Canadian sub-sidiaries of General Electric, Westinghouse and Philips took part in a radio patents pool, in which all holders of Canadian radio and television patents cross-licensed each other, and agreed not to license anyone for import into Canada from abroad, but to license any outsider on a reasonable basis for manufacture in Canada. The patents pool had been investigated by Canadian anti-combines authorities, who suggested certain reforms for rationalization of the industry, but basically ap-proved. In 1959 a United States court found the patents pool to be an illegal restraint upon American exports, and ordered the American parent companies to break up the pool and license other American manufacturers for export to Canada. During the prosecution of this case, Canadian public sentiment was for-cibly expressed, but to no avail. This case, however, did give rise to another bilateral agreement to establish a consultation procedure and ameliorate tensions. The 1959 "Anti-Trust

Notification and Consultation Procedure'', popularly known as the Fulton-Rogers Agreement after the two Attorneys-General, provides for, but does not require, prior consultations in antitrust investigations. In practice, it has meant that the United States government informs Canada of its proceedings in cases involving Canadian-based companies.

The existence of countervailing Canadian legislation, such as the proposed Competition Bill, is often suggested as the cure for American extraterritoriality. Countervailing provincial legislation effectively prevented the removal of corporate records by United States courts, which would seem to confirm the contention. However, the investigation and approval of the radio patents pool by Canadian anti-combines authorities did not prevent its breakup by American courts. Countervailing legislation, to be effective, must be respected by American authorities.

Balance of Payments Policy: Increasing deficits in its balance of payments in the 1960's led the United States government to use American MNEs as instruments of its economic policy. In February 1965, the United States government initiated a program of voluntary guidelines, requesting 600 (later 900) participating corporations to decrease net capital outflow from the United States by expanding exports, limiting direct investment in developed countries, increasing the proportion of foreign investment financed through borrowing abroad, and increasing the return flow to the United States of foreign earnings and of short-term assets. Canada was exempted from the restriction on capital outflow, but not from the direct investment and earnings repatriation guidelines. Canada achieved its exemption by arguing that such a course of action was in the American interest — failure to maintain the flow of capital to Canada would impair Canada's ability to purchase American exports, thereby damaging further the American balance of payments. Canada also accepted a lowering of its exchange reserves ceiling by $100 million, to lessen pressure on the American dollar. As time went by, opposition in Canada grew to the idea that the United States government was dictating the reinvestment, purchasing, dividend and financial policies of Canadian companies. To indicate norms of behaviour for Canadian corporations in line with Canadian interests, the Minister of Industry, Trade and Commerce on March 31, 1966, issued "Some

Guiding Principles of Good Corporate Behaviour for Subsidiaries in Canada of Foreign Companies". These Canadian guidelines were not mandatory, however, and it was the American exemption, not the Canadian countervailing guidelines, which changed corporate behaviour in this instance, and in the following case.

In January 1968, the United States guidelines were made mandatory. Though the guidelines were directed mainly at Western Europe, and though Canadian government officials initially viewed the measure with equanimity, heavy corporate repatriation of funds put increasing pressure on the Canadian dollar. In March 1968, Canada was formally exempted from the guidelines in return for a commitment to institute controls to prevent Canada from being used as a "pass-through" to third countries for American funds (in effect to enforce the American guidelines), and to convert $1 billion of Canadian foreign exchange reserves into non-liquid United States Treasury Securities rather than dollars, again in order to lessen world pressure on the American dollar.

The Canadian argument of the interdependence of the two economies was persuasive.[19] The American exemptions and the Canadian concessions were looked upon by both governments as prices well worth paying. Nonetheless, economic nationalist critics have charged that these cases were highly unfavorable for Canada, because of the limitation of Canada's monetary independence.[20]

On August 15, 1971, the United States government instituted the next phase in its balance of payments policy — a 10 percent tariff surcharge on most categories of imports. The surcharge, which applied to most imports of manufactured or processed goods from Canada, but not to most imports of raw materials, threatened major dislocations in patterns of inter-affiliate trade by American-owned companies at a time when the Canadian government was trying to increase exports of manufactured goods. The following weeks saw the same emergency mission to Washington, the same argument about the interdependence of the two economies, and the same Canadian request for an exemption. This time the exemption was not forthcoming. Canadian legislation was passed to provide offsetting funds to Canadian companies hurt by the surcharge, but the damage was less than had been forecast at the outset. The surcharge was removed shortly, when the Smithsonian Agreements on world currency exchange rates were concluded.

These cases, more than those in any other issue area, have impaired the image of American MNEs as good corporate citizens of the other countries in which they operate. If an MNE's parent government can compel it to act counter to the economic interests of its host country, the fears of some critics may appear justified, and the good intentions and behaviour of many firms may be unable to counter the resulting suspicion. The cases in this issue area have all involved the United States government and its efforts to influence the foreign activities of American MNEs. Other parent governments, including even that of Canada, could attempt related policies.

Host Government Initiation: It is not only the parent government which can endeavour to use MNEs as instruments of its policy. A foreign-owned subsidiary is simultaneously an outpost and a hostage, and interdependence does not always work to the disadvantage of the smaller party. A host government may also try to make use of the unique characteristics of one or more foreign MNEs as instruments of its own policy. In the issue areas discussed above, American control of the Canadian activities of its MNEs have generally been in the context of maintaining a general, international policy program rather than for the achievement of some immediate policy goal vis-a-vis Canada. Canadian initiatives have tended to arise in pursuit of particular objectives, involving the prospect of considerable gain or loss, and frequently involving more intense conflict.

In 1963, the Canadian balance of payments deficit was aggravated by the great volume of imports of automobiles and automobile parts from the United States. To reduce this deficit, and to encourage additional automobile production in Canada, the government intended to reduce imports by raising duties on imported parts, and to increase exports by permitting a rebate of the duty on imported parts equal to the value of exports by the same company. After discussions with Canadian government officials, the American automobile companies planned substantial investments in new Canadian production facilities. The United States government disapproved of the impending shift of capital and employment to Canada, and wanted no increase in tariffs while the Kennedy Round of trade negotiations was in progress.[21] The two governments, and the four American automobile companies, entered into negotiations culminating in the Canada-United States Automotive Agreement of 1965. The pact was designed to provide economies of scale for Canadian automobile production and continental rationalization of the automobile industry, by allowing duty-free trade by manufacturers in new automobiles and automobile parts. Transitional safeguards, still in effect, were provided, *inter alia,* to protect the level of Canadian production under the agreement. The automobile companies not only took part in the negotiations, but also attached formal "letters of undertaking", in which they agreed to an annual increase of Canadian value added in relation to sales.[22] Though difficulties with the agreement have since been experienced by both governments, the signing of the pact was viewed as a triumph for Canadian economic policy. Though foreign control of the Canadian automobile sector was a major cause of the agreement, the involvement of the American automobile companies greatly facilitated the negotiations, and made the pact workable.

Significant political rather than economic gains were achieved when the Canadian government extracted recognition of its Arctic jurisdiction from an American MNE, against the wishes of the United States government. When the Canadian government enacted the Arctic Waters Pollution Prevention Act, proclaiming a 100 mile pollution-free zone in the Arctic, the United States government objected, claiming the Arctic to be international waters and hence beyond Canadian jurisdiction. The Humble Oil Company had already sent the tanker *Manhattan* on an exploratory voyage through the Northwest Passage, and intended a second voyage. Because of the experience of the *Manhattan's* first voyage, Humble Oil realized that the second voyage could not take place without Canadian icebreaker escorts, and was persuaded to recognize Canadian authority over the pollution-free zone, abide by Canadian regulations, and sign formal letters to that effect.[23] The fact that an American MNE had accepted Canadian jurisdiction created a useful precedent for the Canadian government position.

Some host government initiatives, though, are less than spectacular successes, and since these initiatives tend to involve higher stakes, the penalties of failure can be expecially costly. The dominant position of *Time* and *Reader's Digest* in the Canadian periodicals industry has long been of concern to the

Canadian government. It was recommended by the Royal Commission on Publications in 1960, and proposed in the 1965 Canadian budget that income tax deductions for the cost of advertising in a newspaper or periodical more than 25 percent owned by non-Canadians be removed, in order to stimulate the development of alternative Canadian publications. After diplomatic pressure from the United States government, threats to close both magazines, publicity campaigns organized by the magazines, and the conviction in the Canadian government that passage of the budget measures would result in defeat of the auto pact which was then pending, *Time* and *Reader's Digest* were both exempted from the provisions of the 1965 budget. Ironically, this left the two magazines in an even stronger position than before, because the incursion of other American competitors was prevented. The exemption was a bitter defeat for those who had sought to limit the dominance of these magazines and assert Canadian cultural sovereignty.[24] Since 1974, the Canadian government has been once again studying the removal of the special tax status of *Time* and *Reader's Digest*. Legislation to that effect has been introduced, but not yet passed. A similar corporate response has been evident (predictions of economic disadvantage for Canada, and attempts to raise public support), but there has been no apparent involvement of the United States government on this occasion. While the prospects seem favorable, only time (or *Time*) will tell if this initiative will succeed.

One other recent successful Canadian initiative is worthy of mention here. In 1973, the Canada Development Corporation, initially funded entirely by the Canadian government, purchased over 30 percent of the shares in Texasgulf Inc., at a cost of approximately $270 million, thus bringing the American-based MNE under Canadian control. Though a majority of Texasgulf's assets are located in Canada, it is noteworthy that the CDC sought control not of the Canadian subsidiary, but of the parent company. This purchase not only brought a dominant firm in Canada's resource sector under Canadian control, but it also gave the CDC access to the information flow and decision-making criteria of a world resource oligopoly.

Conclusions: The relative durability of these issue areas over time, and in different countries, suggests that future problems involving Canada and multinational enterprise are likely to fall

79

in the same areas. The Canadian government is not hostile to MNEs. It is aware of and desirous of the benefits such firms can offer the Canadian economy, such as regional development, employment, increased exports, access to technology and management skills, and so on. However, while anxious to maximize these benefits in its dealings with MNEs, the Canadian government is also conscious of the need to minimize possible costs. Therefore it is likely to continue to be the case that Canadian policy will be more reactive than initiatory, with most issues being placed on the agenda by the actions of MNEs or of other governments.

The Canadian government has been relatively unsuccessful in attempting to affect the internal operations of subsidiaries of foreign MNEs.[25] Government efforts to prevent undesired behaviour in the labour relations area have been ineffectual. Measures to change the position of *Time* and *Reader's Digest* in the Canadian periodicals industry are now approaching fruition, but only after a decade of failure. Indeed, the United States government seems to have been more able than the Canadian government to affect some aspects of the behaviour of Canadian subsidiaries of American MNEs, through its balance of payments guidelines, its export controls, and its break up of the radio patents pool. On the other hand, Canadian government policy has been much more effective when applied at the border, to prevent or attach conditions to the entry of an MNE. Various takeovers were blocked, even before FIRA was established to screen all takeovers and new investment in light of government criteria. The success of Canadian government initiatives in the auto pact and Arctic jurisdiction cases was due in large part to Canada's border policy actions — proposed unilateral changes in the Canadian tariff structure, and threats to deny the *Manhattan* right of passage.

While Canadian policy seems most effective when applied at the moment of entry of an MNE, it is at that same moment that Canada is most vulnerable to the international mobility of the MNE. It all depends on which party most wants that entry to occur, and which has least to lose or most to gain if it does not take place. The Syncrude case is the best example of the bargaining strength and freedom of action of MNEs before their Canadian enterprise is established. This vulnerability is compounded by the interplay of federal and provincial jurisdictions and objectives. Some provinces have acted to restrain the expansion of MNEs or to rebuff parent government extraterritoriality, as Ontario did with its loan to McClelland and Stewart, and its Business Records Protection Act. Other provinces are so eager for foreign investment that they pressure Ottawa to relax its screening criteria.

Elsewhere I have argued that Canadian government satisfaction with the outcome of cases of this sort varies with the intensity of the conflict involved. In an examination of twenty-seven publicly identifiable cases of conflict generated by the activities in Canada of American MNEs from 1945 to 1971, it was found that the proportion of outcomes favorable to the Canadian government generally rose as the level of intensity of conflict rose.[26] A related observation is that tactical politicization, or the deliberate attempt to rally public support behind the Canadian government's position as a bargaining tactic, contributed to the achievement of Canadian objectives in several cases, such as the Mercantile Bank affair, and improved the balance of favourable over unfavourable outcomes. Of course, where tactical politicization occurred but the Canadian objective was not reached, as in the 1965 *Time* and *Reader's Digest* case or the 1971 surcharge dispute, the political costs of defeat were magnified. The statistical argument for the utility of tactical politicization must be set against the fact that the Canadian government voluntarily relinquished this tactic by concluding international agreements to depoliticize future disputes in two different issue areas — export controls and antitrust.

Only twice was an alliance observed between an MNE and a foreign government against the government of Canada. Pressures from the United States government in support of the American magazines compelled the Canadian government to exempt *Time* and *Reader's Digest* from the 1965 budgetary measures aimed specifically at them. American government pressures failed to overcome the resolve of the Canadian government in the Mercantile Bank affair. On other occasions, MNEs have relied on their own arguments and resources in dealing with the Canadian government, and have not sought the support of the parent government. In cases where the United States government initiated action, MNEs seemed to be more or less obedient servants rather than eager collaborators.

It is clear that the MNE can be both an autonomous threat to

81

the fulfillment of government policy and a potential instrument of government policy. MNEs have been used as policy instruments a greater number of times, and in a greater variety of ways, by the parent United States government than by the host Canadian government. Still, Canadian initiatives, though less numerous, have not been less important. All American efforts to exercise control over the activities of American-owned subsidiaries in Canada were merely instances in a broader policy program, and the net effects have been minimal. A handful of sales to Communist countries have been prevented, with little apparent damage to the economies of those countries. Antitrust actions in Canada had little visible impact on economic competition in the United States. The American balance of payments received only temporary relief from each of the succession of measures. On the other hand, the Canadian government, in a far smaller number of cases, has been able to use American MNEs to achieve impressive economic and political goals, in both the short and long term.

It is as an autonomous challenge to government power that the position of the MNE is less clear. Some governmental inability to understand or influence internal corporate decision-making has been demonstrated, while on the other hand, the government's control over initial access has at times been masterfully used. Those MNEs with internationally-integrated production, marketing and management structures are apt to be less responsive to national policies and concerns, and such structures appear to be the wave of the future.[27] If Canada continues to be a foremost case of what lies ahead for other countries, it is to be hoped that Canada will be an example of an increasing ability to pursue national objectives effectively, and to comprehend and influence the decisions of an actor of growing importance in world affairs.

Notes

1. Joseph S. Nye Jr. and Robert O. Keohane, "Transnational Relations and World Politics: An Introduction", in Robert O. Keohane and Joseph S. Nye Jr., eds., *Transnational Relations and World Politics* (Cambridge: Harvard University Press, 1972), p. xi.

2. Samuel P. Huntington, "Transnational Organizations in World Politics", *World Politics,* Vol. xxv, No. 3, (April 1973), p. 333.

3. Yair Aharoni, "On the Definition of a Multinational Corporation", in A. Kapoor and P. D. Grub, eds., *The Multinational Enterprise in Transition* (Princeton N.J.: Darwin Press, 1972).

4. Government of Canada, *Foreign Direct Investment in Canada,* (Gray Report) (Ottawa: Information Canada, 1972), p. 5.

5. Nye and Keohane, op. cit., p. xvii.

6. Elsewhere I have argued that these same seven issue areas characterize the experience of comparable countries such as France and the United Kingdom. See my "Problems of Host Governments", *International Perspectives,* Sept.-Oct. 1975.

7. Gray Report, *op. cit.,* p. 478.

8. Malcolm Levin and Christine Sylvester, *Foreign Ownership* (Don Mills: General Publishing Co., Paperjacks, 1972), pp. 22-24.

9. *Toronto Star*, Sept. 27, 1975, p. D7.

10. The tragi-comic story of Bricklin Motors in New Brunswick is a case in point.

11. Ottawa *Citizen*, Feb. 5, 1975, p. 9.

12. Levin and Sylvester, *op. cit.,* pp. 76-77.

13. Kari Levitt, *Silent Surrender* (Toronto: Macmillan of Canada, 1970), p. 125.

14. Charles Stedman, "Conflict in Transnational Relations: The Case of the U.S. Cuban Assets Control Regulations", unpublished manuscript.

15. Kingman Brewster Jr., *Law and United States Business in Canada* (Canada: Canadian-American Committee, 1960), p. 26.

16. I. A. Litvak, C. J. Maule, and R. D. Robinson, *Dual Loyalty* (Toronto: McGraw-Hill of Canada, 1971), p. 71.

17. Legislation of this sort has been called for by economic nationalists since it was proposed in the Watkins Report. *Foreign Ownership and the Structure of Canadian Industry* (Ottawa: Queen's Printer, 1967), pp. 355-62.

18. Jerrold G. Van Cise, "Antitrust Guides to Foreign Acquisitions", *Harvard Business Review*, Nov.-Dec. 1972, p. 83.

19. Gerald Wright, "Persuasive Influence: the Case of the Interest Equalization Tax", in A. Axline *et. al.* eds., *Continental Community?* (Toronto: McClelland and Stewart, 1974).
20. Levitt, *op. cit.,* p. 13.
21. Jack N. Behrman, *U.S. International Business and Governments* (New York: McGraw Hill, 1971), p. 176.
22. See Litvak *et. al.*, Appendix B1 for the relevant documents.
23. Gilbert R. Winham, "Choice and Strategy in Continental Relations", in Axline *et. al., op. cit.,* pp. 236-37.
24. Walter L. Gordon, *A Choice for Canada* (Toronto: McClelland and Stewart, 1966) p. 97.
25. In this connection, regulatory policy has been somewhat more effective than allocative or redistributive policy. These three policy types have been discussed in the writings of Theodore Lowi.
26. David Leyton-Brown, "The Multinational Enterprise and Conflict in Canadian-American Relations," *International Organization*, Autumn 1974.
27. Howard Perlmutter, "The Tortuous Evolution of the Multinational Corporation", in Kapoor and Grub, *op. cit.*

CHAPTER 5

CANADA
AND THE WORLD
PETROLEUM MARKET

John N. McDougall

The problem of supplying Canadian energy requirements has received a great deal of attention lately from politicians, journalists and academics alike. This chapter will not deal directly with many of the important issues which have been fully discussed elsewhere, such as the advisability of a subsidized Canadian price for petroleum, or the proper distribution of the revenues from oil production between different levels of government and between governments and industry. Rather, the purpose is to focus upon the international aspects of the matter of Canadian energy supply, to place oil and natural gas in Canada in a continental and international perspective, and to give an account of Canada's past and present foreign relations in this area.[1] The argument presented is that successive Canadian governments have taken decisions which have increased the country's dependence upon foreign supplies of petroleum, even though these policies at the same time promoted the expansion of the Canadian petroleum industry. This increasing foreign dependence is reflected in the growing number and diversity of the government's international involvements.

The first part of this article, then, is devoted to an analysis of the Canadian petroleum market, particularly its global and continental facets. The second part is a discussion of three areas of oil and gas policy which involve some degree of international action on the part of the Canadian government: Canadian participation in the International Energy Agency (IEA); the negotiation of a Canadian-United States treaty on pipelines; and the Mackenzie Valley pipeline proposals. The third part contains a critical assessment of present Canadian policies in these areas and an argument for considering some possible alternatives.

The Canadian petroleum market

Canada's imports and exports of oil are rather insignificant when measured against the world's trade in oil.[2] Moreover, our exports have gone exclusively to one country, the United States, while our imports have tended to come predominantly from one country, Venezuela.[3] In the light of these facts, it might be expected that Canada would be only minimally concerned with the world oil market and the international politics of oil; and when compared with the extent to which some other countries must be concerned with that market (consider Saudi Arabia, Kuwait, the United Kingdom, Japan, and India), it is perhaps fair to say that Canada's economic fortune is minimally affected by it. Nevertheless, the policies adopted by the federal government toward the transportation and marketing of oil and natural gas have always had a very substantial international aspect, which has consisted primarily of relations with the United States. The reason for this is, of course, that while they may be small in comparison with world trade, Canadian imports and exports have represented a very substantial portion of Canadian consumption and production of oil. Since 1961 and the declaration in that year of the National Oil Policy (NOP) Canada has imported roughly half of its petroleum requirements, has supplied the other half with domestically produced petroleum, and has exported a substantial share of domestic production.[4]

This decision to bifurcate the Canadian oil market along the famous Ottawa Valley line — imported oil for the east and domestic oil for the west — has had two consequences which should be noted in connection with this discussion: first, half of Canadian consumers of oil are totally dependent on the world oil market and are exposed to the effects of changes in the conditions of that market. Second, the producers of oil in Canada are heavily dependent upon exports to the United States for the full and efficient utilization of their productive capacity. At the time the NOP was declared, Canadian oil production was well below the full capacity of the industry; and it was increased exports to the United States, rather than a very much increased share of the Canadian market, which were to allow the increase in the rate of Canadian production which the industry and the Province of Alberta had insisted was necessary.[5]

The international political implications of the NOP, therefore, first appeared in the form of regular consultations and occasional disagreements between Canadian and American governments over the amount of Canadian oil imported into the United States. The United States has a long history of restrictions on the importation of petroleum, partly as a result of the political power of independent American oil companies aimed at preserving their share of the United States market, and partly as a result of the government's desire to minimize the degree to which the United States is dependent on "insecure" foreign supplies.[6] These factors were largly responsible for the mandatory import controls which the United States government imposed in 1959. Canada was granted an exemption to these controls on the basis that continental supplies, which reached American markets "overland" rather than "overseas", were as secure as the United States' own supplies.[7] However, the actual amount of oil imported from Canada on an annual basis was usually less than satisfactory from the Canadian viewpoint, owing to the continuing pressure from the independent oil companies on the U.S. government. Throughout the sixties, "implementation of Canada's national oil policy featured persistent overtures to Washington for more U.S. imports of Canadian oil and for a larger share of the oil market in the mid-continent."[8] Thus, Canadian crude oil was "not formally, but effectively" under United States import controls, and

> overall levels of imports of Canadian oil were the subject of regular consultation between United States and Canadian officials by which annual target levels were established. The National Energy Board allocated quantities that in aggregate would not exceed target levels. This system, dependent on the co-operation of the industry and government agencies, worked fairly well for over a decade. However, by 1970 Canadian oil became more than marginally attractive in comparison with other feedstocks and some United States refiners, for economic reasons, found it impossible to adhere to the voluntary levels. In order to restrain imports from Canada, the United States government placed them under formal control in March, 1970.[9]

There followed a period of almost continuous discussions between Canadian and American officials concerning a possible alleviation or elimination of these controls.[10] Concurrent with this series of negotiations was a wide-ranging public debate on Canadian energy policy, in which Canadian nationalists and conservationists insisted that the quotas against Canadian oil exports were being used by the United States as a lever with which to detach Canadians from their electrical power, water, and natural gas in a mammoth, continental energy package.[11] However, both the negotiations and the debate were soon to be superseded by events, which saw, among the most significant developments, the increased price of overseas supplies (a result of the concerted action of members of the Organization of Petroleum Exporting Countries — OPEC); the decline of oil-producing capacity in the United States; the escalation of exploration and development costs throughout the United States (excepting Alaska); the delays in gaining access to the huge reserves of Alaskan oil; and the successful environmentalist campaign in the United States against nuclear and coal-powered generation plants and petroleum refineries.[12] As a result, restrictions against Canadian oil were gradually relaxed, and by the end of 1972 Canada was producing at capacity and exporting to the United States at a record rate of 1.2 million barrels a day. Then, in a complete reversal of positions, Canada imposed export controls early in March 1973, shortly before the Nixon administration abandoned restrictions on imports to the United States from any source, in April of that year.[13] The Canadian government's position at present is that, owing to the declining producibility of established Canadian oil fields, the rate of exports to the United States should fall to 650,000 b/d in 1975, plus whatever portion of an additional 250,000 b/d, set aside for Eastern Canadian markets, is not actually consumed there.[14]

Before 1973, then, the international politics of the NOP consisted largely of negotiations with the United States government which were aimed to maintain the rate of production in the Canadian industry at something approximating capacity, through higher rates of exports. Since 1973, the issue has been, conversely, how far Canadian exports ought to be reduced by the Canadian government. Here the dependence of half the Canadian market on overseas supplies, the other side of the NOP coin, is of great importance; for, somewhat paradoxically, Canada cannot afford to cut its exports below a certain level without eroding its capacity to supply the eastern market, that is, to finance its imports.

While for some time Canada has been "self-sufficient" in oil in the theoretical sense that productive capacity has roughly equalled the size of the Canadian market, Canada has never been "self-sufficient" in the practical sense of not having to rely on foreign sources of oil. This was demonstrated during the oil embargo of 1973, when the federal government attempted to meet short-falls in the supply of foreign oil to Eastern Canadian consumers by making some Canadian oil available to them. The government faced two obstacles. In the first place, transportation facilities did not exist to allow this to be done readily; and some Canadian petroleum had to be carried by an existing pipeline to Vancouver and thence shipped to Eastern Canada by tanker, via the Panama Canal.[15] In the second place, beyond a certain point, Canadian oil allocated to Eastern Canada had to be diverted from American markets at a time when Americans were also concerned about shortages in supply, thus placing our actions on this front in the arena of Canadian-American relations.[16]

A further consequence of Canada's semi-independence of the international oil market has revealed itself since 1973 and the end of the oil embargo, namely, the difficulty Canada has faced, and continues to face, in maintaining a price for crude oil in Canada which is below the world price. While it is not within the scope of this paper to explore all of the ramifications of this issue — especially those involving federal-provincial relations — the essential points may be summarized as follows: First, Canada pays the world price for its imports of crude oil. Second, Canada has also adopted a policy to equalize (save for transportation costs) the price of crude oil across the country. Finally, Canada has determined that the price at which crude oil is sold across the country shall be held below the world price. At the time of writing (August, 1975) the differential between the Canadian well-head price of $8.00 per barrel and the world price is about three dollars per barrel.[17]

At present, the cost of maintaining this subsidized price for oil is roughly $1 billion per year.[18] This sum would have to be raised through general taxation were it not for the fact that Canada's exports total an amount of oil almost equal to the volume of its imports, and the fact that Canada charges the full world price for those exports. Thus, the rough equivalence of Canadian imports and exports of oil, combined with the fact that the

Americans are paying Canada international prices for their imports of Canadian oil, has meant both that Canada's balance of payments situation has not been as adversely affected by increases in world oil prices as that of most other major importers of oil, and that no general taxes have had to be raised to maintain a price across Canada which is below the world price.

This situation is contingent, then, upon the continuation of two conditions: the willingness of Americans to pay full international prices for their imports of Canadian oil, and Canada's capacity to maintain a rate of oil exports which does not fall below that of its oil imports. The first of these conditions seems fairly reliable. While some protests were raised in the United States to Canada's charging world prices for its oil exports, the administration in that country has expressed a somewhat grudging understanding of the Canadian position and, at any rate, has so far paid the prices sought by Canada.[19] The second of these conditions appears less reliable. There are indications that Canada's capacity to produce at current rates, and thus to export at current rates, will begin to decline by about 1980.[20] If exports are curtailed for this reason, and if world prices do not fall substantially, Canadians will then face a choice between, on the one hand, eliminating the differential between Canadian and world prices and, on the other hand, having to find other sources of federal revenue with which to maintain its import subsidy. In either case, there will be an immediate, adverse effect on Canada's balance of payments.

Thus, there are three main considerations which must be kept in mind with respect to the availability of petroleum to the Canadian market: the life-index of proven reserves of Canadian crude, that is, the ratio of total reserves to current annual production (which is declining); Canadian exports to the United States; and the maintenance of a price for oil in Canada below world levels. The three are inter-related. As long as some differential between the Canadian and the world price is maintained, exports to the United States must be continued to finance the subsidy, unless the subsidy is to come out of general federal revenues (the Canadian taxpayer's pocket). A way out of this which is sometimes suggested — namely that exports be halted and the production thus saved be substituted for imported oil, to reduce the import bill — solves only one part of the dilemma even in principle, quite apart from its practical difficulties; for the drain on Canada's available reserves would be just as rapid regardless of whether present production serves the United States market or an equally larger share of the Canadian market. The basic difficulties Canada will face in the future arise not out of the marketing of available production, but out of the imminent failure of the volume of production to equal the volume of Canadian consumption.[21] When this day arrives, the continuation of the subsidized price for Canadian oil would appear to be totally unjustified, if it isn't already.[22]

It is for these reasons that the eastward extension of the inter-provincial oil pipeline, and thereby the supply of the Montreal market with Canadian crude oil, is a change of little significance to the broad picture. Whether at its planned average throughput of 250,000 b/d, or its maximum throughput of about a million b/d, the truth remains that, at present levels of production, consumption, and proven reserves, any reduction in imports permitted by the line will of necessity be met by a corresponding reduction in exports — producing no net effect on our balance of payments; and our established reserves will continue to diminish at the same rate — doing nothing to put off the day when total Canadian consumption will exceed total Canadian production.[23] That is the day of the crunch, and the amount of oil from Alberta that is laid down in Montreal has nothing to do with it.

Another feature of the Canadian oil market should be noted. Canada's two largest markets for crude oil, those centring on Montreal and on Southwestern Ontario, are served by means of pipelines which traverse United States territory,[24] a situation with the potential for international problems. The United States could use their jurisdiction over these pipelines to gain bargaining power against the Canadian government and to press the Canadian government into positions more favourable to the United States on, for example, the price or the volume of Canadian oil and/or natural gas exports to that country. The threat of "shutting off" these pipelines has been raised from time to time by various senators and governors in the United States, though there is little public evidence to suggest the threat has been raised by the United States government. Nevertheless, the reaction in some quarters to some of the actions taken by the Canadian government since 1973 reveals, if nothing else, that Canada cannot be absolutely certain of tolerant understanding, especially among those Americans who stand to suffer materially from Canadian policies.

In one instance, the Governor of Maine raised the spectre of shutting off the Portland-Montreal pipeline when it appeared Canada was going to interfere with the supply of petroleum products to industries in his state, owing to Canadian shortages of the same products during the winter of 1973-74.[25] Also, twenty-nine United States senators, mostly from midwestern states supplied with Canadian crude oil, suggested the throughput of the Interprovincial Pipeline should be taxed as a means of their states' recouping the Canadian export tax on oil.[26] And the American ambassador to Canada has reminded Canadians that Ontario is as reliant on the United States for coal as some areas of the United States are reliant on Canadian natural gas, which is to say, almost totally in the short run.[27] Meanwhile, although it occasionally expresses "disappointment" or "surprise" at some measure taken by Canada, the American administration has tended consistently to reveal an appreciation of some of the constraints upon Canadian policy-makers, noted above.[28] The administration, however, seems to stop short of accepting any policy which would mean the sudden stopping of deliveries of either oil or gas to those communities and refineries in the United States which have become totally dependent on them, practically speaking. They have also complained that the reference-price employed by Canadian officials in calculating the export tax on Canadian petroleum is higher than the actual world price; and have further suggested quite clearly that American comsumers as a whole are not to be be placed, as American consumers of British Columbia's natural gas were placed in the winter of 1974-75, in the position of assuming the entire burden of Canadian gas shortages.[29]

Another problem with the Portland-Montreal pipeline as a means to supply Montreal, one that seems to have materialized in the course of the Saudi Arabian embargo of 1973, is that of Canada being automatically involved in politically inspired actions by oil producers against the United States. Since some oil destined for Montreal (and in winter all such oil) is unloaded at Portland, Maine, countries aiming to curtail supplies to the United States may not be able (or willing) to exempt oil delivered in this way to Canada, or, even if they are both willing and able to do so, the United States may not be prepared to allow the transhipment of foreign oil for Canada when it is facing a suspension of such deliveries itself. Some confusion surrounds the question of whether or not this potential problem did in fact materialize during the 1973 Arab embargo, but it nevertheless needs to be recognized as a possible limit upon the freedom of action enjoyed by Canadian authorities in similar circumstances.[30] (In all likelihood, however, the International Energy Agreement contains an answer to this problem, at least implicitly.)[31]

Finally, it is important to bear in mind that by far the largest share of the production and marketing of crude oil and of oil produced in Canada is carried out by companies based outside this country, several of which operate on a global basis and number among the largest corporations in the world.[32] It is difficult to identify precisely any international-political consequences of this. It is true, however, that Canada does not have a domestically-owned (and/or government-owned) petroleum company operating on a major scale in the international market, unlike the United States, Britain, and many of the countries of Western Europe. The extent to which international oil companies can and do serve to promote the interests of their home-countries internationally is a disputed point, but it is clear that there is no potential for any to do such service to the Canadian national interest. In this connection, it is interesting that Canada's major supplier of oil, Venezuela, proposed during the 1973 troubles that direct negotiations, by-passing the international companies, should take place between Canada and Venezuela on the matter of trade in oil between the two countries. Canada failed to act on this suggestion, apparently because the Canadian government had no corporate instrument available to negotiate and carry out such a sale.[33] At any rate, one important role for a publicly-owned petroleum company in Canada, according to Canadian Energy Minister Donald Macdonald, and others who advocate the creation of such a company, was to promote Canada's interests in dealing with foreign oil-producing countries, since the international oil companies could not be relied upon to do so.[34]

While the major concern of this paper is with oil, even a brief description of the Canadian oil market would be incomplete without some mention of natural gas. Natural gas is a competitive fuel in all Canadian petroleum markets except those east of Quebec, where natural gas service is non-existent. In the rest of Canada, natural gas may be used for residential, commercial, and industrial space heating; industrial processing; boiler fuel; and thermal generation of electrical power. Indeed, the only major portion of the market for petroleum which cannot also be served with natural gas is that of transportation.[35] Almost none of Canada's natural gas is imported, but about half of domestic production is exported, again, exclusively to the United States.[36] Also as with oil, the United States is involved to some extent even in our domestic consumption of natural gas, for one very important pipeline linking Alberta gas fields and Ontario consumers runs through the United States. About forty per cent of the natural gas used in Eastern Canada is transported by this line through the United States.[37]

A few important ways in which natural gas has become or may yet become associated with oil in matters of international politics will be mentioned here and discussed more fully below: First, as already noted, some Canadian critics have claimed that, in the days when the United States was demanding less oil than Canadian producers involved wanted to export, that country bargained with Canada using oil as a lever to exact high volumes of natural gas from Canada. Second, several United States markets have become very heavily, if not totally, dependent on Canadian natural gas as their source of fuel, making the issue of the availability and price of Canadian natural gas exports an overriding issue in some areas of the United States. Third, the possible (in fact, highly probable) construction of a Mackenzie Valley pipeline for natural gas from Alaska and the Canadian Arctic may pave the way for a second system for the transportation of Alaskan and Mackenzie Delta oil to United States and Canadian markets.[38]

Present international policies

Since about 1973, Canada's relationship to the international petroleum market has changed drastically from that of the previous two decades. Canadian crude oil has traditionally been at a slight price disadvantage in all markets east of the prairies.[39] While Alberta oil production had occasionally been a useful source of American supply during various disruptions in overseas supplies, very often Alberta producers could maintain markets for only about half of their capacity.[40] It required special action by the government, the National Oil Policy, to ensure adequate markets for Canadian crude oil. Also, as reported above, fairly constant surveillance by Canadian officials and occasional diplomatic exchanges with the American government were required through the 1960s to maintain Canadian production at levels satisfactory to Canada. Today, however, even greater government involvement, and perhaps a new national policy, may be required to obtain adequate domestic supplies for markets traditionally served with Canadian crude oil. Moreover, the marginal price disadvantage of Canadian crude oil appears to be a thing of the past, although a collapse of world prices is a possibility which few economists would dismiss lightly.[41] Short of that, present world prices provide a sort of umbrella, under which new domestic sources of energy may be developed that are comparatively economic under such circumstances.

In brief, the main direction of Canadian external relations in the matter of crude oil has done a 180-degree turn from one of expanding or maintaining markets for Canadian production to one of ensuring adequate future supply for Canadian markets. This new direction of policy has given rise to three major international involvements for Canadian decision makers, to be discussed presently: the International Energy Agency, the pipeline treaty with the United States, and the Mackenzie Valley pipeline system.

It may be noted, first of all, that the new developments appear generally to have given rise to a great increase simply in the number of our international involvements, as well as a corresponding increase in the number and variety of government offices engaged in them. At one time, an office of the National Energy Board (NEB) administered the National Oil Policy in conjunction with American officials and the Canadian industry, while other members of the Board or its staff represented Canada in all but the most sensitive of our international relations concerning oil. Today, much of Canada's involvement in oil discussions with the United States, the Organization for Economic Cooperation and Development (OECD) or the IEA, is conducted by officials within the departments of Energy, Mines and Resources and External Affairs, while External Affairs carries the ultimate responsibility for the negotiation of a pipeline treaty with the United States. Although the NEB is party to many of these activities at the Canadian end, through formal or informal interdepartmental consultations, the representation of Canada in international negotiations and discussions, while never a responsibility exclusive to the Board, is probably one in which it no longer even predominates.[42]

The IEA

Unquestionably the most important multilateral involvement for Canada in the energy field is its membership and participation in the International Energy Agency and its assenting to the Agreement on an International Energy Program. Canada has for some time participated in the proceedings of the energy committee of the OECD, and the OECD continues to provide the organizational context for various multilateral conferences and consultations, such as meetings involving oil consuming and oil producing countries. However, the International Energy Agency, as a sort of energy department of the OECD, is an extraordinarily powerful international agency which may well control conditions in the future under which Canada imports its foreign supplies of crude oil. In this connection, it is important to remember that in the near future Canada may well become not only a net importer of oil (owing to a decline in exports), but also dependent on imports to serve a larger share of the domestic market than at present. These possibilities remain contingent on decisions regarding the construction of pipelines and other means of enlarging available domestic supply, such as investment in oil sands and heavy-oils production. Be that as it may, Canada's dependence on international sources of crude oil is certain to remain, will probably increase, and may increase dramatically if the capital required for domestic developments is not forthcoming. Thus, an international agency which can, in the most urgent circumstances, allocate available supplies of oil to importing countries and can rule on the permissible rate of consumption in the member countries, is of considerable importance to Canada.

As party to the Agreement on an International Energy Program (which was struck in September, 1974), Canada has joined with fifteen oil-consuming nations (Austria, Belgium, Denmark, Germany, Ireland, Italy, Japan, Luxembourg, Netherlands, Spain, Sweden, Switzerland, Turkey, United Kingdom and United States).[43] The aim of the agreement and of the IEA, which it creates, is to formulate and manage an oil-sharing plan among consuming nations in the event of any supply disruptions, and to seek co-operation with oil-producing nations.[44] The program essentially requires member nations to institute demand restraint measures in the event of shortages, maintain emergency stocks equivalent to sixty days of imports, and to share equally the available supply. The sharing program comes into effect when a country or a group of countries is hit by shortages which affect seven percent of consumption. (A special clause in the agreement permits Canada and the United States to call for help if the shortage affects seven percent of *imports,* not total consumption.) If there is a disruption of supplies which affects the group as a whole, the program does not come into effect until the overall shortage reaches seven percent of group consumption. Then, when a disruption of between seven and twelve per cent occurs, available supplies are shared in proportion to net imports and, if the shortage exceeds twelve percent, all countries will have to reduce demand by ten percent. The sixty day emergency reserve that each country must maintain may be as oil, alternative energy sources, or in the case of Canada, shut-in production in western Canada. (Since at the moment Canada is a net exporter by the agreement's definition based on the previous year, it would not have to share the shortage beyond the requirement to cut consumption by seven percent. Moreover, given that it has a surplus of energy reserves, in the form of shut-in production, which exceeds sixty days consumption—the emergency reserve requirement—it could use the additional reserves beyond this level to avoid even the implementation of demand restraints.)

The agreement, therefore, has fairly favourable implications for Canada, primarily in that it assures against any extraordinarily large shortages of oil during an international crisis. Also significant to Canada, the agreement provides for research and development and technological exchanges regarding alternative sources of energy and means of energy conservation.[45] The, IEA, moreover, has endorsed the idea of a floor price for oil, that is, has resolved neither to force nor even to allow the international price of oil to fall below a certain minimum, a minimum which will be set so as to achieve a significant increase in investment in energy sources indigenous to the membership and to protect that investment. Finally, the IEA promises to become the instrument with which countries conduct relations with the international petroleum companies dominating the world market, creating the opportunity for a country like Canada, which is not the home of any of these giants, to deal with the companies on a multilateral rather than a bilateral basis.[46]

Given the powers of this international body, it is important to note that its decisions are binding on member states, even though it makes some substantial decisions on a majority or qualified-majority basis, rather than by unanimity. The actual number of votes assigned to each member may change as the size of the organization's membership changes, so they will not be discussed here. However, the principles of vote allocation are evident in the original agreement, and they are interesting: Each member begins with three "general voting rights". In addition to these, each member is assigned "oil consumption voting rights," which are distributed among members in proportion to their oil consumption. Thus, all countries obtain a number of what are called "combined voting weights," and these vary quite widely among the member countries. For example, the United States — which incidentally possesses fifty percent of the votes assigned on the basis of oil consumption — possesses just under forty percent of the total "combined voting weights" of the entire membership.[47] Likewise, the Common Market participants add up to a share just under forty percent. The corresponding figure for Japan is about thirteen percent and for Canada is about six percent. On the basis of this system, a "majority vote" consists of half the general voting weights and sixty percent of the combined voting weights. All measures already agreed to by the members can be implemented by such a majority vote, so it is in effect the case that members are legally bound in advance to undertake the measures outlined if a majority determines they are necessary. Two other interesting points emerge from this distribution of voting rights: The concurrence of half the membership, by number, is sufficient to pass a motion, provided the United States is included among their numbers. Conversely, the United States can defeat a proposal if it is joined by only one other state, regardless of that state's voting power. By this system, decisions affecting Canada's access to foreign oil, and even its use of its own oil in any future emergency or in the long-term future, will be taken and be binding on Canada, conceivably without Canadian concurrence. This situation, while somewhat disquieting, probably merely reflects, rather than contributes to the constraints upon Canada's freedom of action with respect to the world petroleum market and the other members of the Agency.[48]

The pipeline treaty and the Mackenzie Valley Pipeline
Canada's other major international involvements with respect to oil and natural gas are bilateral and, like the multilateral ones, are primarily concerned with access to future supplies, although in this case most of the fuel resources involved are Canada's own. The two bilateral issues are between Canada and the United States: the pipeline treaty and the Mackenzie Valley pipeline. The two issues are inter-related. The government of Canada appears to favour a Mackenzie Valley pipeline as the most effective way to gain access to a second generation of natural gas supplies in the face of an impending shortage of supply from the currently producing regions of Alberta and British Columbia.[49] In keeping with the tradition of federal policies on the construction of natural gas pipelines, the pipeline proposal most likely to win federal approval (Canadian Arctic Gas Pipeline — CAGPL) would provide for service to both United States and Canadian markets, from reserves in both Alaska and the Mackenzie Delta.[50]

The Mackenzie Valley project, however, has a rival in the United States, one which proposes to establish a transportation system for natural gas which would parallel the one for oil already under construction across Alaska.[51] This alternative proposal, sponsored by El Paso Natural Gas, may suffer a slight cost disadvantage compared with the Canadian route and the further possible disadvantage of serving most immediately the West Coast of the United States rather than the Midwest, which has fewer alternative sources of supply. However, while it cannot be certain at this point which of the two ventures the United States Federal Power Commission is most likely to approve as a means of delivering Alaskan gas, it seems certain that one of the two will be approved before very long. The urgency regarding a transport system for Alaskan gas is not merely its attractiveness as a new source of supply; it has also to do with the production of oil in Alaska, which will proceed rapidly once the Trans-Alaska oil pipeline is operating, since large volumes of natural gas are expected to be produced *in conjunction* with the production of oil. Given the value of the gas, and the cost of storing it, the producers in Alaska can be expected to push very hard to have some means of moving the gas to market in place or under construction at about the time when Alaskan oil is produced on a large scale.[52]

The pipeline treaty being discussed at the present time between the Canadian Department of External Affairs and the American Department of State is tied up with the Mackenzie Valley proposal for the simple and direct reason that the Americans will not accept the Mackenzie route in the absence of such a treaty.[53] It seems a little ironic to the author that, for at least a decade, over half the oil consumed in Canada, as well as a large part of the natural gas, has been transported via pipelines running through the United States without any apparent desire on the part of the Canadian government to obtain a treaty guaranteeing the terms under which such international pipeline systems operate. It is only now that a pipeline has been proposed for the primary purpose of transporting Alaskan gas to American markets that a treaty to cover such systems is deemed to be in the national interest of Canada.

Be that as it may, the terms of the treaty will apparently be strictly reciprocal, that is, guaranteeing to both parties the same treatment of pipelines across the other's territory. The most important provision is likely to be a proscription against discriminatory tariffs or taxes imposed by either country on the gas transported through its territory. This means that, in each country, no tariffs or taxes will apply to the other's gas which are not also applied to strictly domestic users of the same pipeline, or to comparable domestic pipelines. As the Prime Minister said at an early stage in the pipeline treaty discussions,

> I can see no reason why Canada should not give suitable undertakings as to the movement, without discriminatory impediment, of Alaskan gas through a pipeline across Canada to United States markets, provided all public interest and regulatory conditions are met in the building and operation of the pipeline. An undertaking of this kind would, of course, be reciprocal, with the same assurance being given to Canada regarding our oil and gas shipments through the United States.[54]

The recent negotiations on this matter reportedly do not involve the specific and substantial terms of any particular pipeline proposal, that is, for example, they do not involve the requirements which the Canadian government might impose upon the construction of the Mackenzie Valley pipeline.[55] For example, environmental protection would remain a matter for independent legislation and regulation. Thus, in reply to questions in the House of Commons regarding environmental protection and the implications of the proposed treaty with respect to the Mackenzie Valley pipeline, the Minister of Energy, Mines and Resources said that, if there is to be such a line, "it would be governed, but there would be no specific reference in a treaty of general application." Moreover, he added,

> each country which is to be host to a pipeline would, of course, have to determine its own environmental standards for that particular pipeline. In that sense the treaty would not cover this. This is handled by domestic law. There is recognition, however, that the standards which might be imposed, whether by way of local taxation or other requirements, should on the whole be mutual on either side. There should not be any exceptional charge disguised in any way for passage across the territory.[56]

Canada and the world petroleum market: An evaluation

Canada appears to be nearing the day when the amount of oil produced from conventional sources — the oil fields of Alberta and Saskatchewan — will no longer equal the volume of Canadian consumption. This prospect, even as it is anticipated today, let alone when it actually arrives, confronts Canadians with a choice between, on the one hand, committing large amounts of our total economic resources for the development of a "second generation" of domestic sources of petroleum — probably the oil sands and frontier deposits — and, on the other hand, becoming highly vulnerable to vagaries in the price and availability of oil in the world market. Even if Canadian production does, after enormous investments, keep abreast of Canadian consumption, thus maintaining the theoretical self-sufficiency we now enjoy, it is almost certain that Canada will never enjoy full self-sufficiency in the sense in which the term is normally used, that is, the meeting of total national requirements by means of domestic supply. The policies and actions of the present government would appear to reflect these circumstances, for Canada is engaged in a combination of domestic, continental, and multilateral programs, described

101

above, aimed at assuring the future availability of both foreign and domestic oil on the best possible terms. The question this raises is: are policies of the present government the best ones, under the circumstances?

It should first be clearly stated that it is impossible to say categorically what the best policies are, since a policy which appears conducive to efficiency today may become comparatively very costly a year from now, depending on the movement of world prices. A drop of 50 percent in the (constant dollar) world price of crude oil, a prospect which few observers would rule out, would make many of the present efforts to develop alternative sources, such as Alberta's tar sands, very expensive indeed by comparison.[57] (On the other hand, it is possible to take the position that self-sufficiency is a goal which is worth outlays for petroleum that are higher-cost than necessary.) In spite of these uncertainties, some assessment of the present situation and the responses of the Canadian government is made below.

It appears to this observer that there is one most prominent, most enduring, and most significant feature in the background to Canada's moves with respect to oil and natural gas during the 1970s. This feature is the actual and potential reserves of oil and gas in Alaska and their importance within America's strategy to reach *its* goal of self-sufficiency. Alaska's proven reserves of approximately ten billion barrels of oil represent roughly twenty-five percent of total United States reserves of oil. Alaska's reserves of thirty-two trillion cubic feet of natural gas represent about sixteen percent of total United States reserves of natural gas. More significant than these figures, however, are those indicating that Alaskan reserves are the equivalent of five years of oil imports at the current rate and the equivalent of around thirty years of natural gas imports at the current rate. However, most impressive of all are the figures comparing the success of exploration in Alaska as compared with the rest of North America, which suggest that Alaska's proven reserves of oil and natural gas will continue to grow, and grow for some considerable period of time, so long as adequate means are devised to provide them access to markets.[58] The figures on the rate of discovering reserves are staggering. Over the period 1965-1974, the reserves found per exploratory foot drilled in the lower forty-eight states of the United States were 78.0 barrels of oil and 346 million cubic feet (mcf) of natural gas. The comparable figures for Alberta were 126.1 barrels and 606 mcf. The comparable figures for Alaska were 5,367.3 barrels and 15,526 mcf. The reserves found per exploratory well drilled are equally incredible: 423,400 barrels and 1,858 mcf for the lower forty-eight states; 434,500 barrels and 2,191 mcf for Canada; and 49,229, 850 barrels and 142,409 mcf in Alaska.[59]

It would seem reasonable to assume that, in view of these figures, oil companies would prefer to search for new oil and natural gas supplies in Alaska than anywhere else in North America, other things being equal; but, of course, other things are not equal, for the additional reserves in Canada and the United States are more readily marketed than those in Alaska. However, at present prices in North America, the value of the proven and potential Alaskan reserves justifies huge outlays by the industry for the transportation systems necessary to bring them to market. Thus, it is not so much in the shape of the figures given above, but rather in the shape of a Mackenzie Valley pipeline corridor linking Alaskan reserves to American markets for oil and gas, that Alaska stands so prominently behind all other immediate considerations of Canadian energy policy, such as the evident decline in the supply potential of Alberta, British Columbia and Saskatchewan and the corresponding promise of reduced exports and/or increased imports of oil and natural gas. Canadians, having been told they can no longer look to the west for their fuel supplies, have been told to look north, to the Mackenzie Delta and a great joint Canadian-United States pipeline venture to bring natural gas and energy salvation. The loudest and most persistent voices carrying these recommendations have been the owners and would-be producers of adjacent Alaskan oil and gas — the same voices who counselled Canadians to export vast quantities of the gas from western Canada in 1969 and 1970 [60] If there is, in fact, any alternative to this scheme, one would be unwise to expect to hear of it from these voices or to find any evidence of its feasibility in the so-called facts and expertise they bring to the problem of future supply. Unfortunately, these doubts are not enough to demonstrate that a feasible alternative does exist. Neither are they enough to demonstrate that the Mackenzie Valley proposal is undesirable. An exploration of each of these two propositions will conclude this article.

It may be helpful to begin with an examination of what the

alternatives to the Mackenzie Valley pipeline might be, even in principle. A non-exhaustive list of such alternatives follows: a natural gas pipeline from the high (eastern) Arctic to Eastern Canadian markets; the substitution of manufactured gas for natural gas, using Albertan coal and the Trans-Canada pipeline system; intensified exploration and development in currently producing regions; accelerated development of the oil sands and Albertan heavy oils and the substitution of oil for natural gas in present markets, as required; off-shore exploration and development in the Atlantic provinces; increased importation of oil and substitution of oil for gas in its present markets, as required; substitution of imported and domestic coal for oil and natural gas in their present markets, as required; development of non-hydrocarbon energy resources.

No attempt will be made here to comment on the comparative feasibility and efficiency of these alternatives. This is well beyond the capabilities and probably even the comprehension of the author. The list is provided, rather, to highlight two aspects of Canada's present situation. First, half of these alternatives, failing massive public investments, would depend upon the co-operation of the petroleum industry for their success, even in principle; and, as argued above, the industry has already committed itself to the Mackenzie project, so is unlikely to co-operate in ventures which might make it appear to be less of a necessity than the industry would have us believe. If all the industry has at stake in Mackenzie is the prospect of bringing frontier gas to serve the needs of Canada, it is surprising they haven't, for example, shown more public enthusiasm for the eastern Arctic alternative, which at least promises enough Canadian gas at the far end of the pipe to fill it.[61] Some attention has been given to the idea of a pipeline down from the high Arctic in addition to (and following) the construction of Mackenzie, but little thought appears to have been given by either the industry or the government to the high Arctic as a substitute for Mackenzie.[62] Similarly, without imputing motives, it is interesting to note that the precipitous decline in the confidence we were all encouraged to hold in the oil sands and heavy oil of Alberta as future energy sources also has the effect of making Mackenzie appear more necessary. This confidence declined in direct proportion to the spiralling cost projections for tar sands development which, again, were released and widely publicized by the industry.[63] Indeed, if the energy prospects in the rest of the country are really as bleak as we are led to believe at the moment, it would be reasonable to say that the construction of pipelines down the Mackenzie Valley has the advantage (assuming it is an advantage) of facilitating future Canadian imports of Alaskan gas and oil to supplement Canada's declining production.

Again, the purpose here is not to compare the economic rationality and feasibility of the Mackenzie project with those of any other alternative. It is intended here, rather, to point out four things: First, alternatives to Mackenzie exist, at least in principle. Second, no serious consideration has been given by the government to these alternatives as potential substitutes for that project. At least, to my knowledge, no analysis comparing Mackenzie's costs and benefits with other schemes for future supplies has ever been published or even undertaken. Third, the industry's contention that Mackenzie is absolutely necessary for the availability of future oil and gas supplies is, speaking analytically, self-fulfilling, if at the same time the industry refrains from developing economic alternatives to it. Fourth, several of the leading firms in the Canadian industry are also very heavily committed in Alaska, and they (along with others in the industry, as well as the United States government) stand to gain enormously when Alaskan oil and gas are brought to market in the lower forty-eight states.[64] People in the industry would have to be more than human if they did not allow their judgment as to what is best for Canada (or their publicly stated stance regarding what is best for Canada) to be influenced by what is most beneficial to themselves. The facts and evaluations which they contribute publicly and through government agencies ought to be considered with this in mind.

However, nothing said so far establishes the case that the Mackenzie Valley project is, indeed, not a good thing. The present author submits that the construction of a Mackenzie Valley gas pipelines linking Alaskan supplies to American markets is not in the national interest of Canada. This argument is based on three political considerations, which I distinguish from the economic, environmental, and social objections which others have argued over the past few years. The first political consideration has to do with what some officials within the Department of External Affairs have privately termed "the canal-zone implications" of the line. This phrase alludes to an important set of implications arising out of an Alaska-to-Chicago pipeline across Canadian territory. The line, and hence the state of public affairs at all times in Canada, would be without question a major security interest of the United States. In the event of any political developments in Canada, even those of purely domestic character from a Canadian viewpoint, which to American eyes constituted a threat to the security of fuel supplies for one of that country's major centres of energy consumption, American intervention in the Canadian political process would seem highly probable. This seems to constitute an unnecessary and undesirable step in the direction of "Banana Republic" status for this country.

Some of the parties submitting positions to the Federal Power Commission in the United States have stressed that the Mackenzie Valley route involves very serious security implications for the United States, and that these ought to be weighed against any economic arguments in favour of that particular method of carrying Alaskan gas to American markets.[65] The Canadian debate on the issue seems much more largely concerned, if not exclusively concerned, with economic, environmental and social issues. It deserves to be emphasized that, if the Americans do opt for the Canadian route, this is not likely to be the result of a conclusion that American security is not involved at all but, rather, of a conclusion that the probability of any political developments in Canada which would pose such a threat is very low. Canadians, on the other hand, ought to calculate the risk of what the American government might be prepared to do to make sure of this.

The second political consideration arises out of the very probable necessity of continuous consultation between the Canadian and American governments, perhaps even to the point of joint administration, regarding the North American, and for that matter even just the Canadian, natural gas market. It seems inconceivable that the joint Canadian-American system could operate without a series of joint decisions regarding what Canadian and Alaskan gas will be allocated to what Canadian and United States markets and at what prices. This problem is complicated by the highly probable eventuality that deliveries from the Arctic and deliveries from the Canadian producing provinces will overlap in some markets, involving the latter in these decisions regarding markets and prices. The possibility strongly emerges, in other words, that the Mackenzie project will result in a situation in which even the conditions under which Canadian markets are supplied with Canadian gas will be determined in co-ordination with the American government.[66] Such decisions may or may not turn out to be rational from the Canadian standpoint. It might be argued that under these circumstances the entire North American gas market will turn out to operate more efficiently than it does now, but it cannot be argued that such a system does not greatly lessen Canada's capacity to decide in its own terms wherein the greatest efficiency lies, or to decide, independently, whether and to what extent efficiency ought to be compromised for the sake of other Canadian goals and interests.

The third political consideration is really an elaboration of the issue of independence versus integration just stated. This consideration involves not only the Mackenzie Valley pipeline, but also the pipeline treaty, the IEA, and Canadian-American relations in general, so that the present discussion can also serve to conclude this article. Leonard Waverman has stated that a nation may be justified in paying the additional costs (if any) for national self-sufficiency in energy to the extent that the nation values the capacity to set its own foreign policy.[67] America seems prepared to pay a high price for energy self-sufficiency, presumably (in part) because it does not wish greater dependence on Arab oil to set constraints on its policies toward the Middle East. For Canada the situation is only superficially similar. The policies which Canada seems destined to adopt in order to maximize Canadian independence of overseas oil may tend to place this country in a position of increased continental interdependence and lead to the integration of the North American oil and gas economy. Again, this may make sense, economically; and there is evidence in Waverman's own work to suggest that it would eliminate some diseconomies of the present situation.[68] However, if some trade off is to be admitted between economic rationality and political independence, Canadians should at least consider whether continental integration in energy matters does not place unacceptable constraints on Canadian freedom of action in other areas. Some degree of Arab leverage over Canada's policies in the Middle East may be a more tolerable burden for Canada than American leverage over some of our domestic policies, such as those regarding foreign

107

investment or resource taxation. This seems especially plausible if it is considered that Canada's policies toward the Middle East, or toward just about any international situation, are simply less significant to overseas oil producers than is the foreign policy of the United States. Canada is less exposed economically because it is less powerful politically.

Therefore, one of the options in the list provided above, namely an increased reliance on overseas imports of oil to replace declining supplies of domestic oil and gas, should not be dismissed without a thought. There is the problem of price, but it is quite conceivable that in the near future world oil will be available at prices equal to or even less than those of North American oil. A national Canadian oil company, backed by a bargaining package from the government, might be able to obtain oil from the government of Indonesia at a smaller cost to our economic resources than that for oil from Shell Canada or Texaco Incorporated. There is the problem of balance of payments, but if investment in the Mackenzie Valley corridor is sufficiently large to pre-empt an adequate level of investment in other new sources of Canadian energy, we may face that problem anyway.[69] The volumes of Mackenzie Delta oil and gas which are supposed to obtain a cheap ride on the back of pipelines from Alaska to the American Midwest may not be worth the price of neglecting developments which might have occurred elsewhere in Canada, such as heavy oils, for example. The proven reserves and discovery rate in the Delta are anything but world-shaking. There may be no rosy Arctic sunset on Canada's energy problem.

Most of these concluding remarks are speculative and based on highly contingent assumptions about the future. However, their burden has not been to establish the case that an economic alternative to the government's present policies — general encouragement of the Mackenzie Valley corridor, the quest for the Pipeline Treaty necessary for the United States acceptance of that project, and participation in multilateral arrangements to assure reliable access to overseas supplies (the IEA) — does in fact exist. Their burden has been rather that these policies are not being seriously measured against a possible substitute or substitutes. Every other feasible oil and gas development is presented by the government as the sequel to Mackenzie, or as a supplement to Mackenzie, but not, to my knowledge, as an alternative to Mackenzie. The one possible exception to this would be the "all-Canadian" pipeline down the Mackenzie Valley — the Maple Leaf project. The difficulty, politically, with promoting this scheme is, if one is prepared to allow any Mackenzie pipeline to prevail over the objections of environmentalists, native rights advocates, and economic critics, it might as well be CAGPL, for the sake of scale economies. (In this light, it is interesting that the government is structuring present pipeline debate to be on the question, not whether Mackenzie? but which Mackenzie?) Surely some of the theoretical substitutes to this development are worthy of analysis and study, if only to the point of permitting their comparison with it with respect to the total cost to Canada's economic resources versus delivered energy to Canadian markets. Prime candidates for such comparison might be a high Arctic pipeline, heavy oils, coal gasification, and further exploration and development in B.C., Alberta and Saskatchewan (or some combination of these).

Apart from all these considerations, there is a simple but an important thought which seems to get lost in the present energy debate in this country. It is that continental self-sufficiency does not mean Canadian independence. It does mean North American independence of the world (in energy matters), with which American decision-makers are legitimately concerned. By itself, it does not mean Canadian independence of America, with which this author believes Canadian decision-makers are obliged to be concerned. Indeed it seems to mean an even higher level of economic interdependence and political integration of the two countries than we know already.

Notes

1. I make no attempt to deal with issues other than the transportation and international trade of the oil produced and/or consumed in Canada. I do not, for instance, discuss the quite intense diplomatic activity between Canada and the U.S. on the environmental issues of Alaskan oil tankers off the British Columbia coast and the passage of the ice-breaking tanker, the *Manhattan*, through Canadian Arctic waters.

2. Canadian production of crude oil was approximately 630 million barrels in 1974, which represents roughly 3.8 per-

cent of the combined production of non-Communist countries in 1974. Our *total consumption* of approximately 651 million barrels in the same year represents a slightly larger percentage of total non-Communist consumption, and represents about 3.1 percent of the oil consumed everywhere in the world in 1974. Canadian *imports* of roughly 305 million barrels represent approximately 2.4 percent of total 1974 production outside North America and the Communist countries and constitutes about the same percentage of total "Free World" trade in oil. Roughly the same would be true of our exports of almost 320 million barrels.

However, Canadian exports were a relatively significant 24 percent of U.S. imports in 1974, a decline from 29.5 percent in the previous year. In both these years, Canada was the largest single foreign supplier to the U.S., a position which it seems destined to lose in 1975 owing to a sharp decline in the volumes of Canadian oil approved for export. It must be remembered, however, that until 1975 the U.S. was the world's largest oil producer and in 1974 imported less than 40 percent of its total requirements for that year, so that Canadian oil constituted slightly less than 5 percent of total U.S. supply in 1974. See *World Oil*, (February 15, 1975), pp. 70 and 123. (Figures have been rounded and percentages calculated by the author.)

3. In 1970 for example, Canada imported a total of 207,633,062 barrels of petroleum, of which about 130 million barrels (62 percent) came from Venezuela. The next largest suppliers were Iran and Nigeria, each with about nine percent, and Saudi Arabia with about 7 percent. This pattern, however, had shifted fairly sharply by the end of 1974, with Venezuela's predominance as a Canadian supplier diminishing and the share of countries in the Middle East increasing. Thus, of total Canadian imports for 1974 (291,155,897 barrels), Venezuela's share was down to 44 percent. The next largest suppliers were Iran (25 percent) and Saudi Arabia (11 percent). Over the same period, Canadian dependence on Arab suppliers has increased from about 15 percent to about 25 percent of our total imports, and our dependence on supplies from the Middle East as a whole has increased from 25 percent to 53 percent of our

annual import requirements. See Statistics Canada, *Imports by Commodities*, 31, 12 (December, 1974), (Ottawa: Information Canada, 1975), p. 61; *ibid*, 27, 12 (December, 1970). Percentages are based on calculations by the author.

4. Foreign sources provided 46 percent of Canadian refinery receipts in 1961, or 366,000 barrels per day (b/d) out of a total Canadian consumption of 793,000 b/d. This was the same percentage as in 1960, the year before the NOP was announced. By 1965, total Canadian consumption was 967,000 b/d of crude oil, with foreign sources accounting for 41 percent. In the years 1971 and 1974, imports were 52 percent and 53 percent of Canadian consumption, respectively.

Regarding exports as a percentage of total Canadian production, the pattern is less consistent. In 1960, the year before the announcement of the NOP, about 21 percent of net Canadian production was exported. This figure climbed to roughly 35 percent in 1962, the year following the announcement of the NOP. By 1965, exports as a proportion of total Canadian production had risen slightly, to about 37 percent; by 1971, to about 57 percent; and by 1974, it had dropped again to just under 50 percent. Exports as a percentage of production reached a peak of 59 percent in 1973. Sources are the Canadian Petroleum Association, *1971 Statistical Yearbook; Canada Yearbook*, 1961, 1962, 1966; and *Oilweek,* February 17, 1975, p. 33. Percentages were calculated by the author.

5. The NOP, however, did have the effect of preserving a share of the Ontario market against further encroachments from foreign suppliers. See the announcement of the policy by the Minister of Trade and Commerce: Canada, Parliament, House of Commons, *Official Report of Debates,* Fourth Session, Twenty-fourth Parliament, Vol. II, February 1, 1961, p. 1941. (Hereinafter, debates in the House of Commons will be cited as *Commons Debates*.) On the shut-in capacity of the industry, see below, n. 40.

6. M. A. Adelman has concluded, "there is ample evidence that imports into the United States have always been limited. The widely held belief that they were only restricted in 1959 is wrong by at least ten years." *The World Petroleum Market* (Baltimore: Published for Resources for

the Future, Inc. by the Johns Hopkins University Press, 1972) p. 159. Adelman argues this case in pages 150-59. He seems to attribute the controls to government protection of the domestic industry, and complains that talk of "security" is generally vague and deceptive. On the other hand, he declares at one point, "this is not to deny that the United States has a security problem, or to assume that it should import freely. We need only the proposition that the U.S. government considers restricted imports and high world prices to be in its own national interest." p. 242, n. 164. See also pp. 245-6.

7. There is the implication here that Canadian productive capacity was regarded as an important reserve capacity for the U.S. in the event of an international emergency. See J. G. Debanne, "Oil and Canadian Policy," *The Energy Question: An International Failure of Policy, Volume II, North America,* E. W. Erickson and Leonard Waverman, eds. (Toronto: University of Toronto Press, 1974), pp. 131-2. Adelman gives an account of the attractiveness of Canadian imports in *The World Petroleum Market,* p. 154.

8. Debanne, *Oil and Canadian Policy,* p. 134.

9. D. M. Fraser, "Energy Resource Development in Canada: Interdependence or Autarky," Address for The Chicago Council on Foreign Relations Conference on The Nature of The Canadian-United States Relationship at The Johnson Foundation, Racine, Wisconsin, April 18-19, 1975, (Ottawa, National Energy Board, Mimeo), pp. 18-19.

10. J. J. Greene, Canada's Minister of Energy, Mines and Resources, met with the United States Secretary of the Interior on the matter of Canadian access to the U.S. market as early as December 5, 1969. Between this meeting and June 23, 1970, when the U.S. quotas against Canada began to ease slightly, the matter of the quota's being used as a lever to extract other energy resources from Canada was raised repeatedly in the House of Commons, especially by T. C. Douglas of the NDP. See indexed references to Canadian oil exports to the U.S., in *Commons Debates,* Second Session, Twenty-Eighth Parliament, Vols. II-VIII.

11. Perhaps the peak of this debate was reached in June, 1970, when T. C. Douglas read to the House a letter written by a Presidential aide, which said in part,

the national security of the United States requires the conclusion of a comprehensive agreement with Canada with respect to all energy matters and the imposition of some quantitative limitations on the entry of Canadian petroleum pending the conclusion of such a pact.

Ibid., Vol. III, p. 8275. See also James Laxer, *Canada's Energy Crisis* (Toronto: James Lewis and Samuel, 1974), pp. 74-5.

12. Debanne, *Oil and Canadian Policy*, p. 135.

13. *Ibid.* See also Laxer, *Canada's Energy Crisis,* pp. 38-9.

14. See National Energy Board, *Report to the Honourable Minister of Energy, Mines and Resources, in the matter of the Exportation of oil,* October, 1974, (Ottawa: Information Canada, 1974) pp. 4, 11-12.

15. "During the Arab oil embargo, Canada developed two emergency transportation systems to move western oil to eastern refineries. Approximately 115 thousand b/d can be moved throughout the year from Vancouver to eastern refiners via the Panama Canal. An additional 100 thousand b/d can be moved down the St. Lawrence while shipping lanes are open", *Ibid.,* pp. 2-16.

16. Generally in 1974, as compared with 1973, deliveries of Canadian-produced crude oil to Canadian users rose by 125,000 b/d, while total production in Canada dropped by 117,000 b/d. This appears to have been done at the expense of exports to the U.S., which declined by 238,000 b/d, which is roughly equal to the sum of the additional Canadian demand on Canadian production plus the decline in Canadian production (125 plus 117 equals 242 thousand b/d). See *Oilweek,* February 17, 1975, p. 33.

17. The actual differential varies over time and among various grades of crude oils and petroleum products. Three dollars per barrel is very likely accurate within plus-or-minus ten percent, assuming that Ottawa pays out the subsidy on the basis of the same reference-price as it uses to set its export charge on oil to the U.S. See National Energy Board, "Increased Export Charge on Crude Oil," *Press Release,* Ottawa, August 5, 1975.

18. On the same assumption as that in the preceding note, and on the further assumption that total imports in 1975 are the same as those in 1974 (approximately 307 million barrels),

the subsidy would amount to over $900 million. The cost of the import subsidy under the old Canadian domestic price of $6.50 a barrel and at 1973 levels of imports has been given as $1.6 billion in W. D. Gainer and T. L. Powrie, "Public Revenue from Canadian Crude Petroleum Production," *Canadian Public Policy*, Vol. I, No. 1 (Winter, 1975). p. 5.

19. The U.S. reaction to recent Canadian decisions is elaborated upon below.

20. The NEB has forecast that the "potential producibility" of established areas (Alberta and Saskatchewan) will begin to decline almost immediately from its present rate of approximately 2 million b/d to less than 1.6 million b/d in 1980 and less than 1 million b/d a decade from now. Indeed this decline appears to have begun (see "Crude Output in the West may fall 1.2 percent," *The Globe and Mail,* Toronto, August 14, 1975, p. B1). The NEB also has forecast that the requirements for indigenous crude oil or equivalent for use as feedstocks in Canada, at present about 1.2 million b/d, will increase to about 1.4 million b/d by 1985. Forecast Canadian supply, therefore will become insufficient to meet forecast demand in the Canadian markets it has traditionally served before 1985, in fact, around 1982. This leaves no room for exports and even threatens an increase in the proportion of the Canadian market served with imported oil, thus expanding Canadian reliance on overseas crude oil beyond the rate which will result simply from the growth in total Canadian consumption. See NEB, *Report*, Appendices 2-IV, 4-I. There are mutterings from the industry that Canada's supply picture may prove to be even bleaker than this report would indicate.

21. When that day comes, of course, the difficulty Canada must face is not merely the loss of the export tax as a means to finance the subsidy but also the foreign earnings with which to meet the total import bill, with a predictably severe strain on our balance of payments.

22. I have yet to encounter a convincing argument that the maintenance of a Canadian price below world levels is economically sound, or even equitable. As Leonard Waverman points out, too many supporters of the subsidy fail to mention that, while a higher price would in fact benefit

foreign-controlled producers, the subsidized price also benefits disproportionately many foreign-controlled users in Canada (for example, foreign-controlled firms in energy intensive industries such as pulp and paper). A higher price would have the further advantage of forcing Canada to become more energy-efficient, as other industrialized nations are learning to do to their long-term benefit. See "The Two Price System in Energy: Subsidies Forgotten," *Public Policy, op. cit.,* pp. 76-88. Another excellent analysis of the domestic price-ceiling, which also argues against it, except as "an interim means of easing transition" to world prices, is that of Gainer and Powrie, "Public Revenue from Canadian Crude," p. 6.

23. Data on the throughput and capacity of the Sarnia-Montreal pipeline were taken from National Energy Board, *Report to the Governor in Council In the Matter of the Application under the National Energy Board Act of Interprovincial Pipeline Limited,* May 1975, pp. 13 and 16.

24. The Montreal market, especially during the winter months, is almost totally dependent on deliveries via the pipeline to that city which transmits overseas crude oil unloaded at Portland, Maine. The Ontario market is served by Interprovincial Pipeline, which runs from the prairie provinces to Sarnia, Ontario, via a route which runs south of Lakes Superior, Michigan and Huron.

25. "May Have Right to cut flow to Montreal, Maine Leader says," *Globe and Mail,* December 18, 1973, p. 3.

26. Ross H. Munro, "Congressmen protest Canadian oil tax and phaseout," *Globe and Mail,* November 28, 1974, p. B1.

27. See, for example, a speech by U.S. Ambassador William J. Porter to a dinner sponsored by the Canadian Institute of International Affairs in Winnipeg, Manitoba, September 25, 1974, *News Release* (Ottawa: United States Information Service), pp. 6-7. See also John Bird, "Keeping lines with Washington open," *Financial Post,* February 1, 1975, p. C4.

28. See Ross H. Munro, "Washington Shows no surprise," *Globe and Mail,* September 6, 1973, p. B1; "U.S. angry with Ottawa for increase in oil price," *ibid.,* September 15, 1973, p. 1; "U.S. not surprised by higher tax", *ibid.,* November 3, 1973, p. B3; "Canada's plan to phase out ex-

ports causes concern, disappointment in U.S.," *ibid.*, November 25, 1975, p. 1; "Trudeau, Ford, hold 'great' round of discussions but make no commitments on oil, beef, defence," *ibid.*, December 5, 1975, p. 1. As early as March, 1973, the U.S. Secretary of the Treasury was able to say, "The United States would understand an oil supply policy which might cut back exports to the United States if necessary to cover Canadian needs." Quoted by T. C. Douglas, *Commons Debates*, First Session, Twenty-Ninth Parliament, Vol. IV, (May 28, 1973), p. 4163.

29. A good, concise summary of recent exchanges between the Canadian and American governments, which touches most of the preceding points on the U.S. reaction, is available in Hyman Solomon, "Energy Squeeze will bring anguished cries from U.S.," *Financial Post,* Toronto, April 26, 1975, p. D1. See also his, "All this posturing tells us nothing", *Financial Post*, November 9, 1975, p. 7. For an academic review of relations between the two countries in the energy area, see Ted Greenwood, "Canadian-American Trade in Energy Resources," *International Organization,* 28, 4 (Fall 1974), pp. 689-710.

30. I will leave conclusions on this matter to the reader's judgment. See references to the Saudi Arabian position in the index to *Commons Debates,* First Session, Twenty-Ninth Parliament, especially Vols, VII-VIII. One of the clearest statements by the Minister on the issue was given on November 22, 1973, in reply to a question from the Right Honourable J. G. Diefenbaker concerning Canada's status under the Arab oil embargo. The Minister said (*ibid.*, Vol. VII, p. 8034):

the position taken by the Arab countries with regard to Canada is different from that taken with regard to Holland and the United States. The position taken with regard to the Portland pipeline is due, of course, to the fact that it is a destination in the United States and the Arab embargo applies to any shipments to that country, whether for consumption there or in transit. The basic position with regard to Canada is that we are not in the same category. Shipments will be made to Canadian ports such as Halifax, Saint John or Montreal, but there will be an overall reduction in production and we will share in that.

The controversy was over the last statement of the Minister, that is, over whether Canada was included in the total embargo applied to the United States and Holland for their pro-Israeli policies or merely suffered the effects of the general reduction in production. My own assessment is that it is impossible to say for certain from the public record whether Canada was totally embargoed or not; and to draw inferences from data on actual oil deliveries to eastern refineries is complicated by the fact that, apart from Arab actions, the international companies may have had their own reasons for diverting some of the Arab oil that was available away from Canada toward other markets.

31. This Agreement is discussed in detail below.

32. The ten largest oil producers in Canada produced two-thirds of total Canadian petroleum production in 1974. Only one of these ten companies (and the smallest) was controlled in Canada. The real giants in Canadian crude oil production are Imperial Oil, Texaco, Gulf Oil, Mobil Oil and Chevron Standard, whose combined share of total production is a whopping 55 per cent. Three firms (Imperial, Gulf and Shell) moreover, account for over half of Canada's refining capacity. All of the firms named above are subsidiaries of international companies large enough to rank among the ten largest corporations in the United States. (Shell, of course, is a European company but has sales large enough to place it in the same league.)

Within Canada these companies are very large, as well. Imperial, Shell Canada, Gulf Canada, and Texaco Canada are all among Canada's twenty largest manufacturing, resource and utility companies ranked on the basis of 1974 sales. See *Fortune*, August 1974, p. 176; *ibid*., May, 1975, p. 210; *Oilweek*, May 12, 1975, p. 13; and *ibid*., August 4, 1975, p. 14.

33. See indexed references to discussions between the Canadian and Venezuelan governments in *Commons Debates*, First Session, Twenty-Ninth Parliament, Vols. VIII and IX, especially December 3, 1974, p. 8342. See also Terence Belford, "Ottawa turns down buying Gulf, Shell," *Globe and Mail*, November 3, 1974, p. 1. Belford reports that the

Minister of EMR brought this idea of nationalizing some such company back from discussions in Venezuela, where he had learned that the Venezuelan government wanted to deal with the Canadian government, not some international oil company. The cabinet was reported to be split on the issue for some time before the idea was discarded.

34. During the debate on Bill C-8, to create PetroCanada (a government-owned, Canadian oil company) Macdonald explained that it was "distinctly contemplated by the government" to use the company to enter into the international market to buy for Canada, "particularly when it is indicated to us that supplies would be available through the Canadian national corporation for the Canadian market where they might not be available through the international majors." *Commons Debates,* First Session, Thirtieth Parliament, Vol. I, (November 4, 1974), p. 1005.

35. For a discussion of inter-fuel competition in Canada, see The Minister of EMR, *An Energy Policy for Canada, Phase 1,* Vol. 1 (Ottawa: Information Canada, 1973), pp. 109-115. A dated, but superior theoretical discussion is available in John Davis, *Canadian Energy Prospects,* Study prepared for the Royal Commission on Canada's Economic Prospects (Ottawa: Queen's Printer, 1957), Ch. 12.

36. In 1974, for example, total Canadian production of natural gas was estimated to have been 2,445 billion cubic feet (bcf.) of which exports constituted 959 bcf., or nearly forty percent. This represents a small decline in the proportion of total production devoted to the export market, which was 44 percent in 1972 and 43 percent in 1970. Back in 1964, the comparable figure was also 44 percent. National Energy Board, *Annual Report, 1974* (Ottawa: Information Canada, 1975), p. 18; *Canada Yearbook,* 1965 (Ottawa: Queen's Printer, 1966), p. 568. Percentages were calculated by the author.

37. For details of this system, called "Great Lakes," and for a brief account of the debate over its construction — one of the most contentious decisions ever taken by the NEB — see my "Regulation versus Politics; The National Energy Board and the Mackenzie Valley Pipeline," *Continental Community: Independence or Integration in North America.* Andrew Axline, *et al.* (Toronto: McClelland and

Stewart, Carleton Contemporary Series, 1974), pp. 257-8. See also, William Kilbourn, *Pipeline: Trans-Canada and the Great Debate, A History of Business and Politics* (Toronto: Clark Irwin & Co., 1970), Ch. 12.

38. See Hyman Solomon, "U.S. wants to keep finger in our energy," *Financial Post*, January 12, 1974, p. 5.

39. Leonard Waverman, "The Reluctant Bride: Canadian and American Energy Relations," *The Energy Question, op. cit.,* pp. 219-20. Debanne also writes that the western provinces and the independent oil producers in western Canada, "had to face a calculated price differential of about 25 to 35 cents a barrel in favor of Venezuelan crude" in the Quebec market throughout the sixties. "Oil and Canadian Policy," p. 130.

40. See, for example, "Trends in the Canadian economy, oil industry and Imperial Oil Limited," booklet based on remarks delivered by W. O. Twaits, President, Imperial Oil Limited, to the New York Security Analysts, Inc., (undated), p. 14. See also, Royal Commission on Energy, *Second Report,* Table IX.

41. See Waverman, "Reluctant Bride," p. 235. Also, the upshot of Adelman's painstaking analysis of world prices would seem to be that, depending on the actions of the *consuming* governments, the OPEC cartel is either doomed or saved. His prediction of surplus capacity in the world market has already taken place (*Fortune,* May 1975, p. 191); and his anticipation that consuming governments would act to provide price protection for investment in alternative energy sources is borne out by the floor-price proposals before the IEA and the American tax on imported oil. Thus, while Adelman's analysis supports the view that there are enormous pressures building up to break the cartel and bring down prices, as producer-governments shave prices to increase their share of the market, a consumer-producer pact could keep them high — at least as high as the consuming countries want them. "Since most of the consuming countries . . . do want high oil prices for one reason or another, the prospects of an oil commodity agreement being made do seem at least fairly good: whether good enough one cannot say." *The World Petroleum Market,* p. 249; *passim.*

42. These impressions are based on the author's interviews with several officials in each of the agencies mentioned, conducted in Ottawa, April 1975.

43. I regretfully admit that the ensuing analysis of the IEA is based on information which is somewhat out of date. For example, the membership of the organization now stands at eighteen, but the new members are unknown to me, as is the present numerical distribution of voting rights among members which is discussed below. However, I very much doubt that the expansion of the membership has changed the proportional distribution of voting strength, as reported in my text, or the conclusions drawn from the analysis in my text; but the interested and meticulous reader may wish to test this conviction against the facts. I have also failed to get hold of the text of the Agreement as finally ratified, and the citations of the Agreement are from the draft text signed in September. Again, I have seen no indications of major subsequent changes in the agreement.

44. *Oilweek,* December 9, 1974, p. 8. This is the source of analysis provided in the remainder of the paragraph. See also the Minister, *Commons Debates,* First Session, Thirtieth Parliament, Vol. III, (November 14, 1975), p. 1325.

45. Chairman, Governing Board, IEA. Text of notes used for press conference, March 20, 1975.

46. One of the four "Standing Groups" of the IEA, on which each member country has at least one representative, is called the "Standing Group on the Oil Market," through which one or more participating countries may "consult with and request information from individual oil companies on all important aspects of the oil industry". *Petroleum Intelligence Weekly,* Special Supplement, (the full text of the Agreement on an International Energy Program), October 14, 1974, Article 37, p. 6.

47. *Ibid.,* Article 62, p. 8.

48. Before leaving the IEA, it may be worth noting that it appears to have been a formalization and institutionalization of earlier arrangements among the OECD membership to co-ordinate energy supply during emergencies, arrangements that go back at least to before the fall of 1973. When an MP asked, on October 18, 1973, whether any Canadian-Venezuelan agreement or offshore agreement

would be "over-ridden by the OECD which would be forced to initiate world-wide rationing," the Minister replied: "Any arrangement we may have directly with Venezuela would be subject to those other arrangements." *Commons Debates,* First Session, Twenty-Ninth Parl., Vol. VII, p. 6991.

49. This assertion seems scarcely to require documentation, but one of the many such expressions of the Government's attitude may be found in a major speech on energy policy by the Prime Minister, *ibid.,* Vol. VIII, December 6, 1973, p. 8482.

50. A rival, "all Canadian" scheme has been submitted to the NEB by Foothills Pipelines Ltd., to build a line connecting strictly Canadian Arctic gas reserves with existing gas transmission systems in southern Canada. For a comparison of the features of the two schemes, see W. L. Dack, "Which pipeline for Arctic Gas?," *Financial Post,* April 26, 1975, p. D5; "Do we share an Arctic line with U.S. or go it alone," *ibid.,* October 5, 1974, p. C-8.

51. See Hyman Solomon, "El Paso won't give up without a fight," *ibid.,* April 26, 1975, p. D5.

52. It has been estimated that there would be "a saving of several hundred million dollars in gas reinjection investment if oil and gas were produced jointly on the North Slope." C. J. Cicchetti, *Alaskan Oil: Alternative Routes and Markets* (Baltimore: Resources for the Future, Inc. through the Johns Hopkins University Press, 1972), p. 95.

53. See Hyman Soloman, "Assured passage, but no other guarantee on oil," *Financial Post,* May 4, 1974, p. 14; "Energy squeeze will bring anguished cries from U.S.," *ibid.,* April 26, 1975, p. D1.

54. *Commons Debates,* First Session, Twenty-Ninth Parliament, Vol. VIII, December 6, 1973, p. 8482.

55. Nevertheless, some Canadian officials have expressed the fear that American negotiators will seek to tie the treaty to some conditions regarding the price and volume of Canadian exports currently under contract to U.S. importers. Hyman Soloman, "U.S. wants to keep . . ."

56. *Commons Debates,* First Session, Thirtieth Parliament, Vol. 119, No. 100, March 20, 1975, pp. 4318-19.

57. There is a strong expectation among many observers that producing countries with comparatively very large total reserves of oil (e.g. Saudi Arabia) will eventually lower prices to a level just below the cost of alternative sources of energy (which, depending upon the location, is in the order of a constant dollar, oil-price equivalent of $6-8 per barrel) so as to maintain the largest possible world market for oil. The "floor price" proposals of the IEA would seem to be based on the assumption and the fear that this will or is very likely to happen, thus undercutting planned investments in alternative energy sources. However, far be it from me to rush in where Adelman fears to tread. He has said: "By 1985 the world energy outlook will have changed in ways we cannot foresee, and the current problems may be moot — or more urgent than ever. In the meantime, world oil looks to be more and more a politically dangerous struggle among companies and governments over markets, and between companies and governments over profits. The more they invest and make oil cheap, the more they will hold it dear . . . Somehow the oil will continue to be produced at ever-expanding rates. It will be an interesting story. No mere economist can hope to do it justice, but some will try." *World Petroleum Market,* p. 262.

58. See M. A. Adelman, "The Alaskan North Slope Discoveries and World Petroleum Supplies and Costs," *Change in Alaska; People, Petroleum, and Politics,* G. W. Rogers, ed. (University of Alaska Press, 1970), pp. 35-36, and *passim.*

59. *Oilweek,* April 28, 1975, p. 13.

60. A graphic description of the dependence of Canadian decision-makers upon information from industry sources is provided in Eric Kierans, "The Day the Cabinet was Misled", *Canadian Forum,* March, 1974, 4-8. I have described and criticized in more general terms the manner in which private interests are able to influence public choices in the guise of providing "technical" information and advice, in "Regulation vs. Politics" and "Oil and Gas in Canadian Energy Policy," *Issues in Canadian Public Policy,* G. B. Doern and V. S. Wilson, eds. (Toronto: Macmillan of Canada, 1974) pp. 122-29. A very good overview of the lobbying activities of the Canadian oil industry in a time of

crisis is presented in G. R. Berry, "The oil lobby and the energy crisis," *Canadian Public Administration,* Vol. XVII, No. 4 (Winter, 1974), pp. 600-635.

61. I exaggerate, but there is increasing evidence that neither the gas nor the oil reserves in the Mackenzie Delta are very large or very promising. A recent report published by the U.S. Interior Department has predicted that, over the next seven years, only 1.1 trillion cubic feet of gas will be added to the currently proved reserves there of 3.8 trillion cubic feet. Interestingly, the report states that these reserves are not sufficient to justify an all-Canadian project and that a joint U.S.-Canadian project is the only economic means of Canada gaining access to its Mackenzie reserves. See John Picton, "Pessimistic forecast of gas finds contained in U.S. agency report," *Globe and Mail,* August 16, 1975, p. B2. Some have argued that there is no need to go into the Arctic at all, and that southern regions have all the gas Canada needs in this century. See Joseph Yanchula, "The Politics of Petroleum: An inside look at Alberta Oil," *Canadian Forum,* November-December 1974, p. 5.

62. Thus, the EMR study, *An Energy Policy for Canada,* sets out five alternative "cases" of energy development and purports to do an economic analysis of the alternatives. The problem is that each case is predicated on the development of a Mackenzie Valley gas pipeline at some stage and the cases which include other types of development *also* include such a line, so that it is impossible to read from the results of the analysis how Mackenzie stacks up against these alternatives, none of which is examined independently of Mackenzie. See pp. 210-216.

63. The Appendices to *An Energy Policy for Canada* (i.e., Vol. II) give a clear indication of this optimism of only three years ago. While admitting that no separate economic analysis of the Alberta oil sands and Alberta heavy oils was undertaken, itself an interesting admission in view of the elaborate treatment afforded frontier deposits, the authors nevertheless offered the guess with respect to the Alberta oil sands that, "about 35 billion barrels can probably be recovered for a price of about $6 per barrel . . ." This volume of oil represents over fifty years of current Canadian production. During the last year, the industry has

been saying that nothing much will be forthcoming at prices of less than $10 per barrel. *Cf* Joseph Hanchula on the costs of oil sands projects in "The Politics of Petroleum," pp. 6-8.

64. As of 1969, the companies in strongest acreage position on the Alaskan North Slope were Atlantic Richfield, British Petroleum, Humble (Exxon), Mobil, Standard of California, Union of California, and Phillips. Wallace F. Lovejoy, "The Oil Industry: Its Structure and Regulation in Alaska and Other States," *Change in Alaska,* p. 51. The Canadian subsidiaries of these firms accounted for just under forty-five percent of Canadian oil production and just under forty percent of Canadian gas production, according to figures in *Oilweek,* May 12, 1975, p. 13.

65. See "U.S. gas group has harsh words for Canadian," *The Toronto Star,* Toronto, April 8, 1975; Hyman Solomon, "El Paso won't give up . . .,"

66. The problem is one of negotiating the best possible deal with the U.S. on the Alaska-Canada project, say with respect to the relationship between the share of initial financing borne by each country and the share of the line's throughput acquired by each country, without involving such matters as the price and volume of exports to the U.S. under current contract or other important economic interests. And then there is the problem of setting export prices and volumes independently of the rate and cost for domestic consumption. Of course, something close to joint administration of Canadian export policies is already in effect, practically speaking. See Hyman Solomon's account of current negotiations between Canadian and U.S. officials regarding the mutual sharing of Canada's impending gas shortages, where it appears the marketing of Canadian gas is not a matter of domestic policy. "U.S. officials take proposed gas cutbacks in stride," *Financial Post,* July 26, 1975, p. 3.

67. "The Reluctant Bride," p. 235.

68. His views on this point with respect to oil are argued in *ibid.* With respect to natural gas, see his *Natural Gas and National Policy* (Toronto, 1973).

69. Panic over the potential balance of payments deficit which may be occasioned by future deficiencies in Canada's oil productivity appears to be the next feature of the campaign

to stampede the country in the direction of Mackenzie. Again, a cautious and critical acceptance of this argument on the part of the government would seem warranted. Facing an oil supply deficit, there would appear to be two directions in which to proceed: Massive investment in Canadian energy supplies, or massive investment in other industries which could earn the foreign exchange with which to purchase supplies elsewhere (cf. Japan). Whether one strategy makes more or less economic sense than the other depends on Canada's comparative advantage (or disadvantage) in oil and petrochemicals as opposed to other industries, say forest products. (Perhaps Canada has less oil than the Arabs. It is fairly clear that it has more trees than the Arabs). Again, there is no proof here that such an alternative is possible. It is simply noteworthy that some superficially reasonable alternatives to present policies have not been given very careful (public) examination.

CHAPTER 6

SOVEREIGNTY, RESOURCES AND THE LAW OF THE SEA

L. C. Green

The failure of the recent United Nations Law of the Sea Conference, which held its first session in Caracas in 1974 and its second in Geneva in 1975, means that any attempt to analyze the problems relating to sovereignty and resources in so far as the law of the sea is concerned, whether from the specific standpoint of Canada or from that of the international community at large, must, in the absence of definitive conventions or treaties on these matters, be tentative at best. This is not to say, however, that there is no law in this field. As with any problem of international law, the legal regime is to be found in both customary and treaty law.

The difficulty with customary law is that, as with the similar type of law in the national legal system, it is unwritten and, despite the existence of the International Court of Justice, judicial settlement of international disputes is still comparatively rare. One must, therefore, seek the evidence of custom outside of the law reports, making use rather of what states have habitually done or regarded as legally binding upon themselves. It is not enough merely to assert that some states have normally pursued a particular line of conduct with regard to international maritime matters, for their behaviour may have been occasioned by convenience or some measure of comity or good-neighbourliness. Since international law may be defined as that system of laws and regulations which those who operate on the international scene recognize as being necessary for their orderly conduct, and which they recognize as being binding upon themselves in order to achieve that orderly conduct,[1] compliance by states with an alleged course of conduct or acceptance of a so-called rule or principle must be the result of a belief in an obligation to behave in this particular fashion.[2] The evidence of this customary law is to be found in official state papers, state practice consistently over a lengthy period, acceptance by other states, and judicial decisions by national courts, particularly those of such maritime states as Great Britain and the United States. It is also found in the writings of jurists to the extent that those writings have been accepted by states or by their courts, for it is not the writer who makes the law but the acceptance of his view by those who are alleged to be bound by the so-called rule. Perhaps the best example of this is to be found in the concept of the freedom of the seas as expounded by Grotius in his *De Mare Liberum*,[3] rather than the contrary view put forward by Selden in his *De Mare Clausum*.[4] One might likewise refer to the acceptance of one marine league or three miles as the outer limit of the territorial sea (that is to say the extent of the sea off the eoast, usually measured from the low-water mark) which a littoral or coastal state might claim as its own. In 1805 Lord Stowell, one of the greatest admiralty lawyers of all time, had to decide whether the *Anna,* captured by a British privateer at the mouth of the Mississippi, had in fact been lying in American waters at the time of its seizure. In his *De Domonio Maris*[5] the Dutch writer Bynkershoek had written that states conceded a right of ownership over a maritime belt no "farther out than it can be ruled from the land". He went on to say that "the control of the land (over the sea) extends as far as cannon will carry; for that is as far as we seem to have both command and possession."[6] Adopting this view, in the course of his judgment Stowell said[7] "We all know that the rule of law on this subject is *'terrae dominium finitur, ubi finitur armorum vis'*,[8] and since the introduction of fire arms, that distance has usually been recognized to be about three miles from the shore."

Over the centuries it became accepted that the territorial sea did in fact extend three miles seaward from the coast, although during the twentieth century various states, frequently to assert exclusive rights over coastal fisheries, sought to claim a wider territorial belt. A codification conference called under the auspices of the League of Nations failed to regularize the situation. Even in 1958 when a conference did succeed in drawing up four Conventions on different aspects of the international law of the sea, all that could be agreed was that "the sovereignty of a State extends, beyond its land territory and its internal waters, to a belt of sea adjacent to its coast, described as the territorial sea", and that for certain purposes a state might exercise its jurisdiction over the sea continguous to the territorial belt provided that "the contiguous zone may not extend beyond twelve miles fom the baseline from which the breadth of the territorial sea is measured."[9] Moreover, a subsequent Conference held in Geneva in 1960, primarily concerned with settling this question of the extent of the territorial sea, was equally unsuccessful since the proposed twelve-mile belt failed by one vote to secure the necessary two-thirds majority.

Since the 1960 Conference made it clear that most countries favored a twelve-mile territorial belt, it was perhaps not surprising that many states made unilateral declarations extending their territorial zone from three to twelve miles. In 1970 Canada joined their number. This was at the time of the passage of the *Manhattan* through Canada's Arctic waters and the decision of the Government of Canada to extend Canada's territorial limits to twelve miles and to introduce anti-pollution legislation. Moreover, realizing that other countries, and particularly the United States, which still asserted that international law would only concede a three-mile limit, might contest the legality of this legislation and attempt to secure a condemnatory judgment from the International Court of Justice, Canada considered it necessary to preclude any possibility of such recourse to the World Court. In accordance with the Court's Statute,[10] countries may make declarations accepting the jurisdiction of the Court in advance, agreeing to submit to that jurisdiction should a dispute with another country arise in the future. When making such declarations, countries are able to exclude particular types of dispute. Canada first accepted the jurisdiction in 1930, with some reservations, but in 1970 felt it necessary to amend the Canadian declaration[11] so as to preclude any "disputes arising out of or concerning jurisdiction or rights claimed or exercised by Canada in respect of the conservation, management or exploitation of the living resources of the sea, or in respect of the prevention or control of pollution or contamination of the marine environment in marine areas adjacent to the coast of Canada."

It is interesting to note the statement made by Prime Minister

Trudeau explaining the reason for Canada's actions:[12]

> The way international law exists now, it is definitely biased in favour of shipping in the high seas and in various parts of the globe. And in the past this has probably been to the benefit of the states of the world because there has been, because of this bias in international law, a great deal of the development of commerce in all parts of the globe . . . . International law has been developed in the past in order to have the concept of high seas which is favourable to navigation and to commerce everywhere. And this was fine in the past, but now with the advance of technology and the importance which is coming forth to us in all parts of the world — of not only thinking of commerce, but also of quality of life. We're saying international law has not developed in this direction. It's beginning, that's why . . . (Canada is willing) to participate in every aspect of the development of international regimes which would prevent pollution of coastal states. But until this international regime has developed we are stuck with the law as it has developed in the past centuries,[13] and the centuries before when in the era of steamships and sailing ships, there was no danger of pollution, and it was important for commercial and other reasons that the nations of the world could communicate on the high seas. . . .
>
> . . . . In one case, (the territorial zone), if there is a problem we will be taken to the courts,[14] and we'll fight it there and . . . . we have the trend of international law in our direction — the twelve miles. In the other case (the 100-mile anti-pollution zone), there is no law so we can't be taken to the courts.

It must not be thought that it is only Canada which has thus bluntly expressed its disapproval of what might be described as the traditional law of the sea. In the General Assembly's Committee on the Peaceful Uses of the Seabed, the Indonesian spokesman asserted that "the three-mile limit . . . had never been a rule of international law since a general international convention providing for it had never been accepted by all States and since it had never been practised by all States."[15] This statement merely reflects the view of many new states created since 1945 with regard to the rules of international law as they were described at the time of their birth, and by which they were alleged to be bound in the view of the states already existing and which had given them birth.[16] A view somewhat more in keeping with that of the Canadian Prime Minister was expressed by the Singapore delegate to the above-mentioned General Assembly Committee. In his view,[17] the new law of the sea "should be development oriented and aimed at improving the economics of the developing countries."

Statements of this kind show discontent not merely with the customary rules of international law in respect of the sea, but also with the established treaty law too. Perhaps one of the best expressions of this view is to be found in the Separate Opinion of Judge Ammoun of Lebanon in the *Barcelona Traction* case:[18]

> What the Third World wishes to substitute for certain legal norms now in force are other norms profoundly involved with the sense of natural justice, morality and humane ideals. It is, in short, a matter of a change of course towards natural law as at present understood, which is nothing other than the natural sense of justice; a change of course towards a high ideal which sometimes is not clearly to be understood in positive law, peculiarly preoccupied as it is with stability: the stability of treaties and the stability of vested rights.

The principal law of the sea treaties with which dissatisfaction has been expressed or which are no longer considered relevant since they have been outdated by advances in technology, as well as the Third World's ideas of natural justice, are those which were adopted at the 1958 Geneva Conference. These dealt with, in addition to the territorial sea and contiguous zone, the high seas, the continental shelf, and fishing and conservation of the living resources of the high seas. Of these, only that on the continental shelf has been ratified by Canada. It must be remembered that only seventy-two states, including the Holy See, San Marino, and the Federal Republic of Germany, none of which was a member of the United Nations, participated in the 1958 Conference, whereas now there are more than 130 members of that organization entitled to take part in any further Conference. Moreover, it is now well established that the Convention definition of the continental shelf, "the seabed and subsoil of the submarine areas adjacent to the coast but outside the area of the territorial sea, to a depth of 200 metres or, beyond that limit, to where the depth of the superjacent waters admits of the exploitation of the natural resources of the said area,''[19] is completely out of date. In addition, technological, ecological and conservation considerations have made many of the provisions of the Conventions appear to relate to some antediluvian era. The change of majority in the United Nations from an industrialized, developed group of states to a developing group has altered many of the basic principles of traditional international law. This, in turn, has led to an emphasis on sharing of resources and capabilities, together with a recognition of a concept of good-neighbourliness, whereby the developing states claim a legal right to share in the natural resources of the world, even though exploitation of those resources depends on the "know-how" of the older developed states.[20] Reference has already been made to one comment by Judge Ammoun which reflects this view, but in the same case he made a comment that was far more sweeping and expressive of this attitude:[21]

Policy does of course crop up under the veil of resolutions or declarations in the United Nations Assembly. . . . Policy, the policy of the great powers and the colonialist powers, dominated classic traditional law: it cannot be dissociated from law today any more than yesterday; but it is a new policy, one which does not escape the influence of the great principles which are destined to govern the relationships of modern nations. The 1969 Vienna Convention (on treaties, for example), took this consideration fully into account when it adopted numerous solutions to meet the suggestions included in individual opinions and propositions by new members of the international community . . . (Thus), the diplomatic protection of shareholders injured by a third state does not constitute an international custom that is unequivocally and unambiguously demonstrated by the web of precedents which form the material element, and definitively established by the conjunction of that element with the psychological element of *opinio juris.*[22] This conclusion is reinforced by the opinion . . . held by a multitude of States — new States and other, very numerous, developing States — with regard to the application of diplomatic protection, the rules of which are acceptable by them to the extent that they take account of their state of under-development, economic subordination and cultural stagnation, in which the colonial powers left them and in which they are in danger of remaining for a long time, in the face of Powers strong in industry, knowledge and culture.

We have noted that, in so far as the law of the sea itself is concerned, a somewhat similar view as to the future was adopted by the Singapore delegate during the discussions of the General Assembly's Seabed Committee.[23] He suggested that if the developed states were to establish exclusive zones off their coasts in which they alone would have the right to exploit the natural resources (a principle which finds favour with a variety of Canadian economic and fishing interests), these states should contribute a percentage of the revenue so derived to an international authority for the benefit of the disadvantaged states.

With such clearly conflicting ideological approaches to international law in general and the law of the sea in particular, it is perhaps not surprising that the Caracas Conference of 1974 proved little more than a manoeuvring exercise, with the various participants making statements of policy and seeking to sound out the views of others in the hope of securing some support for their own positions. It was hoped that the session of the Law of the Sea Conference held in Geneva in 1975 would prove more fruitful. Unfortunately, however, this was not to be the case and at one time it even appeared likely that the session would break up in complete disarray with nothing whatever achieved. Virtually at the last moment, however, the three Committees of the Conference were each able to produce "informal single negotiating texts . . . to serve as a procedural device and provide a basis for negotiations"[24] at the next session which is scheduled to be held in 1976. While these texts "must not in any way be regarded as affecting either proposals already made by delegations or the right of delegations to submit amendments or new proposals", it must nevertheless be borne in mind that they will constitute the working texts for 1976 and may well indicate the lines along which agreement will be ultimately achieved, even upon such controversial issues as sovereignty and resources which have so frequently constituted stumbling blocks in the past. Although these documents carry no official status of their own, they do provide actual written texts in the form of drafts which could easily constitute separate treaties, or form parts of one comprehensive convention on the law of the sea. They must, therefore, possess a cachet that will inevitably be denied to any proposals put forward by individual delegations. For this reason, any commentary on the law of the sea must pay full attention to the three hundred or more draft articles prepared by the Committees. The Report presented by Committee I was in the form of a draft Convention on the Sea-bed and the Ocean Floor and the Sub-soil thereof Beyond the Limits of National Jurisdiction; while the proposals put forward by Committee II covered the Territorial Sea and Contiguous Zone, Straits used for International Navigation, the Exclusive Economic Zone, the Continental Shelf, the High Seas including management and conservation of living resources, Land-locked States, Archipelagic States, Islands, Enclosed and Semi-enclosed Seas, Territories under Foreign Occupation or Colonial Domination, and the Settlement of Disputes — in other words, a group comprising some of the most controversial and contradictory national interests now existing. Committee III was concerned with somewhat more technical matters, and its Report related to Protection and Preservation of the Marine Environment, Marine Scientific Research and Development and Transfer of Technology.

In so far as sovereignty over the littoral sea adjacent to coastal states is concerned, the proposal put forward by Committee II is a marriage of customary principles and modern practice. Clearly reflecting the basic principles of traditional law relating to maritime sovereignty, it is acknowledged that

> The sovereignty of a coastal State extends beyond its land territory and internal waters, and in the case of an archipelagic State,[25] its archipelagic waters, over an adjacent belt of sea described as the territorial sea.
> This territory extends to the air space over the territorial sea as well as its bed and subsoil.
> The sovereignty over the territorial sea is exercised subject to the provisions of these articles and other rules of international law.

While the proposals accept that the normal baseline from which the territorial sea should be measured is that of low tide, the method for drawing baselines around archipelagic states is spelled

133

out in painful detail and is so complex as to be well nigh in-comprehensible to the layman. If applied, for example, to the Indonesian archipelago it would produce strange and perhaps even unfortunate consequences for both the Philippines and Singapore.

Reflecting the development in state practice since 1958 and lending support to Prime Minister Trudeau's stance of 1970, there is, for the first time, a clear abandonment of the tradi-tional three-mile limit for the territorial sea. To date, the only major maritime power that seems firmly determined not to ac-cept this change is the United States, which still clings to the three-mile limit, shown by its reaction to the seizure in May 1975 of the *Mayaguez* some eight miles from an island claimed by both Cambodia and the Provisional Government of the Repub-lic of Vietnam, as well as by the Republic of South Vietnam when that state was an ally of the United States. In accordance with the negotiating text prepared in the name of Committee I, "every State shall have the right to establish the breadth of its territorial sea up to a limit not exceeding twelve nautical miles" measured from baselines normally constituted by the low-water line along the coast "as marked on large-scale charts officially recognized by the coastal State". Concomitant with this exten-sion of the territorial limit is the provision that the ultimate limit of the contiguous zone will be twenty-four miles, whereas under the existing 1958 Convention the contiguous zone plus the ter-ritorial sea is not to exceed twelve miles from the baseline.

While the proposal is that the baseline shall normally be the low-water mark, the draft makes provision for the baseline to be drawn in a different fashion when geographic considerations so demand. This may be of importance when Canada finally decides where its baselines are to be drawn, and may in fact be the means for resolving some of the controversies that still exist between Canada and the United States concerning the exact location of disputed maritime boundaries on both the Atlantic and the Pacific coasts. Moreover, "where the coasts of two States are opposite or adjacent to each other, neither of the two States is entitled, failing agreement between them to the con-trary, to extend its territorial sea beyond the median line every point of which is equidistant from the nearest points on the baselines from which the breadth of the territorial seas of each of the two States is measured", although deviations are permitted where these are rendered necessary by historic title or special circumstances. The United States contends that such special circumstances are present in the Georgia Strait.

The acknowledged extension of the territorial sea to a permitted twelve miles immediately throws into question the issue of the right of innocent passage for non-littoral shipping, and this is a right which the United States Navy Department regards as essential to the security of the United States. Even prior to the 1975 session of the Conference, the right was already being questioned by a number of coastal states because of the increase in the size of oil tankers, liquid natural gas and bulk chemical carriers, the development of nuclear-powered ships and the increasing risk of coastal pollution. Coastal states have become increasingly concerned about their right to exclude or control the passage of such shipping as is evident from such legislative measures as the Canadian legislation of 1970 regarding Arctic waters pollution prevention, extending territorial limits and amending the Canadian Shipping Act,[26] which were met by bitter condemnation by the United States authorities.[27]

In 1949 in the *Corfu Channel* judgment[28] the World Court proclaimed that in so far as international straits are concerned, that is to say straits which join two parts of the high seas and are used for normal international navigation, innocent passage through such waters is to be enjoyed even by warships, despite the fact that the strait lies within a state's territorial sea:

> It is . . . generally recognized and in accordance with international custom that States in time of peace have a right to send their warships through straits used for international navigation between two parts of the high seas without the previous authorization of a coastal State, provided that the passage is *innocent*. Unless otherwise prescribed in an international convention, there is no right for a coastal State to prohibit such passage through straits in time of peace.

The Court construed innocence as depending upon the manner of the passage as well as its purpose. The attitude of the coastal state was not regarded as being a deciding factor. While there may be some doubt whether warships have any absolute right of passage through parts of the territorial sea not constituting an international strait, there is no doubt that such a right has traditionally been regarded as belonging to merchant ships. In fact, in the course of his Separate concurring Opinion in the *Corfu* case Judge Alvarez of Chile, who as early as thirty years ago was concerned about what he described as the "New International Law," stated the following:

> It may be accepted that, today, the passage through the territorial sea of a State, or through straits situated therein, and also through straits of an international character, is not a simple tolerance but is a *right* possessed by merchant ships belonging to other States . . . . Although (warships) may effect an innocent passage through straits forming an international highway between two free seas, in other cases the coastal States are entitled to regulate the passage, especially with a view to the protection of their own security or interests, but they are not entitled to forbid it. Warships only enjoy an unrestricted right of passage when they are engaged in an international mission assigned to them by the United Nations.[29]

The participants at the 1958 Conference were fully cognizant of these views and the Convention on the Territorial Sea reflects them, providing the following:

> ships of all States, whether coastal or not, shall enjoy the right of innocent passage through the territorial sea. . . . Passage is innocent so long as it is not prejudicial to the peace, good order or security of the coastal State. . . . Submarines are required to navigate on the surface and to show their flag. . . . The coastal State must not hamper innocent passage through the territorial sea. . . . The coastal State may take the necessary steps in its territorial sea to prevent passage which is not innocent. . . . Foreign ships exercising the right of innocent passage shall comply with the laws and regulations enacted by the coastal State . . . and, in particular, with such laws and regulations relating to transport and navigation. . . . If any warship does not comply with the regulations of the coastal State concerning passage through the territorial sea and disregards any request for compliance which is made to it, the coastal State may require the warship to leave the territorial sea.

The new states at the 1974 and 1975 sessions of the Law of the Sea Conference did not consider these provisions sufficiently detailed and were particularly concerned to achieve greater specification as to what was "prejudicial to the peace, good order or security of the coastal State" and, as such, sufficient to deny the "innocence" of the passage in question. The 1975 Committee Report provides, therefore, that "prejudice" arises from

> any threat or use of force against the territorial integrity or political independence of the coastal State or in any other manner in violation of the Charter of the United Nations;
> any exercise or practice with weapons of any kind;
> any act aimed at collecting information to the prejudice of the defence or security of the coastal State;
> any act or propaganda aimed at affecting the defence or security of the coastal State;
> the launching, landing, or taking on board of any aircraft;
> the launching, landing, or taking on board of any military device;
> the embarking or disembarking of any commodity, currency or person contrary to the customs, fiscal or sanitary regulations of the coastal State;
> any act of wilful pollution, contrary to the present Convention;
> the carrying on of research or survey activities of any kind;
> any act aimed at interfering with any systems of communication of the coastal or any other state;
> any other activity not having a direct bearing on passage [which is described as equivalent to "navigation"].

In so far as fishing vessels are concerned, as in the 1958 Convention, their "passage" is not considered innocent if they fail to observe coastal regulations aimed at forbidding foreign fishing within the territorial sea. The extension of the width of the territorial sea from three to twelve miles enlarges the importance of this provision.

The proposed draft also indicates the type of regulation that the coastal state may enact without denying the right of innocent passage. Thus, the coastal state may prescribe for the safety of navigation and the regulation of marine traffic, including the designation of sealanes, and tankers and vessels carrying nuclear or other inherently dangerous or noxious materials may be confined to such lanes. To some extent this is in accord with Canadian anti-pollution legislation, but the draft goes on to forbid the coastal state from laying down regulations as to the design, construction, manning or equipment of foreign ships unless expressly authorized so to do by international rules. This provision runs counter to the Canadian Arctic Waters Pollution Act in so far as concerns the 100-mile belt specified in that Act. It would appear, therefore, that the majority of the members of the international community are unwilling to accept the Canadian view that a coastal state may demand standards higher than those postulated by international law to be effective equally for both foreign and national shipping operating off its coasts. The other matters on which the coastal state may regulate foreign vessels exercising the right of innocent passage relate to the protection of navigational aids and facilities and installations, including those for the exploration and exploitation of the marine resources of the territorial sea and seabed and subsoil thereof; to the protection of cables and pipelines; to the conservation of the living resources of the sea and the prevention of infringement of fisheries legislation; to the prevention of the infringement of customs, fiscal, immigration, quarantine, sanitary or phytosanitary regulations as well as to "research of the marine environment and hydrographic surveys." Further, reflecting the new trends in international concern, particularly consequent upon the Declaration of the United Nations Conference on the Human Environment[30] held at Stockholm in 1972, coastal states may regulate for the purposes of "the preservation of the environment of the coastal State and the prevention of pollution thereto", but apparently not if such regulations relate to the construction, design or equipment of foreign vessels.

It sometimes happens that a coastal state might, for a variety of reasons,wish to exclude foreign shipping from passing through its territorial sea or a part thereof. Occasionally, the littoral state might want to exclude the shipping of only a particular state or group of states, while, for example, participating in naval manoeuvres with some of its own allies. The draft, repeating the provisions of the Geneva Convention of 1958, recognizes that for security reasons a coastal state may find it necessary to suspend the right of innocent passage through all or part of its territorial sea. However, as with 1958, the closure must be "without discrimination amongst foreign ships". This would seem to mean that if a NATO or similar naval exercise were taking place off the Canadian coast and the ships were lined up within the Canadian territorial sea, it would be impossible for restrictions to be placed upon, for example, Soviet merchant ships or for that matter warships exercising the right of innocent passage — assuming that a Soviet destroyer could ever claim to have legitimate right of navigation within twelve miles of the Canadian coast — unless similar restrictions were placed upon all foreign merchant ships or warships as the case may be. It would appear, therefore, that if an attempt were made to exclude Soviet fishing vessels, which had not in any way infringed Canadian fishing regulations, from approaching Halifax while the fleet was lined up in, perhaps, the vicinity of Sydney, Nova Scotia, similar restrictions would have to be imposed upon any United States vessel seeking to enter the Gulf of St. Lawrence in order to approach Cleveland or Detroit.

Among other issues considered at Geneva, which were of major concern to Canada as well as a variety of other states, was that of international straits and the right of passage through them, particularly in so far as the passage of supertankers might be involved.[31] Canada is of course particularly concerned in view of the issues that have arisen during the last five years or so resulting from the *Manhattan's* voyage through the Northwest Passage.[32] As to the latter, however, it might be contended that anything provided in the draft is irrelevant. As has been indicated, in the *Corfu Channel* case the World Court ruled that for a strait to be considered international it must be used as a navigational route for passing from one part of the high seas to another. If it be maintained that shipping, other than Canadian, has navigated the Northwest Passage, then all that is needed to deny its international status is evidence that such passage is neither regular nor frequent. In fact, it would seem that since Amundsen's first sailing in 1906 there have only been four Canadian and three non-Canadian crossings[33], hardly enough to describe the Passage as a navigational route of convenience or necessity. Moreover, it should be borne in mind that Canada considers the waters of the Northwest Passage to be internal and to have been so for a sufficiently lengthy period to enjoy such status by reason of an historic title or exclusive exercise of jurisdiction.[34] There is, therefore, no need to demarcate them by any baseline and they cannot be considered as constituting an international strait.

While the draft prepared at Geneva in 1975 contains no specific definition of a strait, it would seem that this document understands an international strait to be one used "for international navigation between one area of the high seas or an exclusive economic zone and another area of the high seas or an exclusive economic zone", with sovereignty over the strait, its bed, subsoil and airspace remaining with the coastal state. Moreover, the proposed regulations do not affect any internal waters within the strait, unless such waters constituted part of the high seas or the territorial sea prior to the drawing of straight baselines in accordance with the proposals in the draft. Normally, a right of transit will exist through or over all such straits, except when the strait is formed by an island of the strait state. No such transit zone will be enjoyed if a high sea route or a route in an exclusive economic zone of similar convenience exists seaward of the island. Transit passage is somewhat different from the concept of innocent passage, for it is defined as

> the exercise . . . of the freedom of navigation and overflight solely for the purpose of continuous passage and expeditious transit of the strait between one area of the high seas or an exclusive economic zone and another area of the high seas or an exclusive economic zone.

To enjoy the right of transit passage, ships and aircraft shall

> proceed without delay through the strait;
> refrain from any threat or use of force against the territorial integrity or political independence of a strait State or in any other manner in violation of the Charter of the United Nations;
> refrain from any activities other than those incidental to their normal modes of continuous and expeditious transit unless rendered necessary by *force majeure* or by distress.

While the right of transit passage seems to imply a continuous and expeditious voyage, the right of innocent passage includes stopping and anchoring incidental to ordinary navigation. Vessels enjoying the right of transit passage are required to comply with accepted international regulations and practices for safety at sea and for the prevention and control of pollution from ships. As to aircraft, civil flights are to comply with Rules of the Air established by the International Civil Aviation Organization, while state aircraft will normally comply with such measures and will at all times pay due regard to the safety of navigation. All aircraft are to monitor the radio frequency assigned by the appropriately internationally designated air traffic control authority or the appropriate international distress frequency. As in the case of innocent passage through the territorial sea, a strait state may designate sealanes and prescribe traffic separation schemes for navigation where this is necessary to promote the safe passage of ships, and, when circumstances require, such state may substitute other sealanes or schemes. Even though strait states may be inclined to act in accordance with these provisions in order to regulate the passage of supertankers, the draft stipulates that the strait state is not free to designate such lanes solely at its own discretion. Any proposals to this end must be submitted to the "competent international organization" — presumably the Intergovernmental Maritime Consultative Organization — with a view to their adoption, but the Organization may adopt them only with the agreement of the strait state. The remaining regulations that the strait state is permitted to make are far narrower in their scope than those relating to control of innocent passage through the territorial sea: namely, for the prevention of pollution, "giving effect to applicable international regulations regarding the discharge of oil, oily waste and other noxious substances", to prevent fishing by fishing vessels, including regulations concerning the stowage of gear, and, finally, "the taking on board or putting overboard of any commodity, currency or person in contravention of the customs, fiscal, immigration or sanitary regulations of the strait State". In applying such regulations, the strait state must operate on a non-discriminatory basis and so as not to have "the practical effect of denying, hampering or impairing the right of transit passage". Does this mean that Indonesia, Malaysia and Singapore would have to dredge the Malacca Strait rather than close it to the passage of Japanese supertankers?

It would seem from these provisions that the right of transit passage through the strait is wider than the right of innocent passage through the territorial sea, and that the littoral state is consequently less free to regulate such passage. However, the draft does provide for the right of innocent passage in straits used for international navigation between "one area of the high seas or an exclusive economic zone and another area of the high seas or an exclusive economic zone, other than those straits in which the regime of transit passage applies, and between an area of the high seas or an exclusive economic zone and the territorial sea of a foreign state." It may well be that at the next session of the Law of the Sea Conference attempts will be made to co-ordinate and simplify these regulations so as to achieve a common system for all straits used for international navigation.

From a purely geographic point of view it is clear that not all coastal states possess a continental shelf and this fact was to some extent recognized by the 1958 Convention with its definition based on exploitability rather than simple distance. Even when a continental shelf is present there is no uniformity of extent and some countries, including Canada, have expressed the view that a coastal state's sovereignty should in any case go to the limit of the continental margin. Claims of this kind involve an assertion of exclusive rights over resources and are bound to be opposed by landlocked states, who have in fact played a perhaps unnecessarily large role in the development of the conventional law of the sea. In addition, such extensive claims would be opposed by all coastal states which lack a continental shelf — even as early as 1948 some Latin American states had claimed sovereignty and exclusive jurisdiction over a belt of sea 200 miles from their coasts and regardless of depth. Moreover, and perhaps this fact is of greatest significance, opposition would come from developing countries which would contend that their economy and growth potential, when compared with developed countries, would become even more unbalanced if littoral states were able to assert exclusive authority over extensive areas of what is now described as "the common heritage of mankind", which begins at the limits of national jurisdiction:[35]

> The sea-bed and ocean floor, and the subsoil thereof, beyond the limits of national jurisdiction . . . , as well as the resources of the sea, are the common heritage of mankind.
> The area shall not be subject to appropriation by any means by States or persons, natural or juridical (— thus, the purported claims put forward by some oil and mineral ex-

ploration companies lack all validity —), and no State shall claim or exercise sovereignty or sovereign rights over any part thereof. . . .

All activities regarding the exploration and exploitation of the resources of the area and other related activities shall be governed by the international regime to be established.

The area shall be open to use exclusively for peaceful purposes by all States whether coastal or land-locked, without discrimination, in accordance with the international regime to be established. . . .

The exploration of the area and the exploitation of its resources shall be carried out for the benefit of mankind as a whole, irrespective of the geographical location of States, whether land-locked or coastal, and taking into particular consideration the interests and needs of the developing countries.

As has been noted, when Latin American states which lacked a continental shelf first put forward "compensatory" claims, they tended to regard a 200-mile belt as one that would satisfy them, even though other states, including some which had made declarations of sovereignty over their continental shelves, and especially the United States, rejected such claims as predatory.[36] In 1975, at Geneva, there appeared to be general agreement that a coastal state should enjoy some measure of exclusive economic sovereignty over an expanse of sea beyond the absolute sovereignty it would enjoy over its territorial sea. This principle finds acceptance in the draft and the exclusive economic zone is fixed at 200 miles, measured not from the outer territorial limit but from the baseline itself. Presumably, if the Latin American countries persist with their 200-mile sovereignty claim they would be precluded from enjoying any further exclusive economic zone. By restricting the exclusive economic zone to 200 miles and rejecting the line of the continental margin, the extent of the zone in Canada's case is cut back by anything up to 500 miles and the total area lost is about 400,000 square statute miles. Within the exclusive economic zone, the coastal state shall enjoy limited sovereignty, for the area will remain high sea in so far as rights of navigation and immunity from jurisdiction are concerned. The coastal state will have

sovereign rights for the purpose of exploring and exploiting, conserving and managing the natural resources, whether renewable or non-renewable, of the bed and sub-soil and the superjacent waters;

exclusive rights and jurisdiction with regard to the establishment and use of artificial islands, installations and structures (— around which safety zones may be established to a distance of 500 metres):

exclusive jurisdiction with regard to

i) other activities for the economic exploitation and exploration of the zone, such as the production of energy from the water, currents and winds; and

ii) scientific research;

jurisdiction with regard to the preservation of the marine environment, including pollution control and abatement.

In exercising such rights the coastal state is required to have due respect for the rights of other states which, whether landlocked or not, shall "enjoy in the exclusive economic zone the freedom of navigation and overflight and the laying of submarine cables and pipelines and other internationally lawful uses of the sea related to navigation and communication", so long as such states "shall have due regard to the rights and duties of the coastal State and shall comply with the laws and regulations enacted by the coastal State" in conformity with international law.

Perhaps for the first time in an international document, recognition is afforded to the international character of scientific research. Although the coastal state is to enjoy exclusive jurisdiction from this point of view and other states would have to request permission to conduct such research, the coastal state is enjoined not to withhold such consent from a qualified institution seeking to carry out "purely scientific research, subject to the provision that the coastal State shall have the right . . . to participate or to be represented in the research, and that the results shall be published after consultation with the coastal State concerned." This in fact coincides with the normal practice concerning such scientific research between Canada and the United States.

While the coastal state enjoys exclusive jurisdiction over its economic zone, its right to exploit the natural resources of the zone is not as complete as might be thought. Although it is for the coastal state alone to determine the allowable catch of the living resources of the zone, it is under an obligation to prevent over-exploitation through proper conservation and management measures which are to be taken in co-operation with the appropriate subregional, regional or global organizations. These conservation and maintenance measures are not merely intended to prevent exhaustion of the resources in question, for they are to take into account "the economic needs of coastal fishing communities (a matter which is constantly put forward by Iceland in its conflict with the United Kingdom and other European countries which had formerly fished off her coasts) and *the special requirements of developing countries*" (italics added). This special position of the developing countries is a constant feature of the draft articles as the representatives of those countries had, over the preceding years, indicated would be the case. There is of course nothing to prevent a coastal state allowing others to enter the exclusive economic zone for the purpose of exploitation, but in determining the right of access the coastal state must, in order "to promote the optimum utilization of the living resources", take into account "the requirements of developing countries in the subregion or region in harvesting part of the surplus."

This same concern is evident in the articles on the resources of the seabed and ocean floor beyond the limits of national jurisdiction. The development and use of this area, the resources of which are "the common heritage of mankind", is to be conducted so as to

> foster the healthy development of the world economy and a balanced growth in international trade; and
> avoid or minimize any adverse effects on the revenues and economies of the developing countries, resulting from a substantial decline in their export earnings from minerals and other materials originating in their territory which are also derived from the Area.

Moreover, the proposed International Seabed Authority which would have the task of administering the Area which constitutes this natural heritage is expressly instructed to

> adopt, upon the recommendation of the Economic Planning Commission, programmes or measures to avoid or minimize adverse effects on the revenues of developing

countries derived from the export of minerals and other products originating in their territories which are also derived from the resources of the Area. The Council (of the Authority) shall ensure that developing countries importers of minerals or other products derived from the resources of the Area shall be given preferential access on favourable terms to such minerals and products.

The consequence of this would appear to be that if the exploitation of mineral nodules within the Area is likely to affect adversely the economic interests of a developing country which produces such minerals, the Authority would have to ensure that the exploitation of this part of the "heritage of mankind" was conducted in such a way as not to have any such adverse effect on that country's economy. No similar provision exists with regard to the preservation of the economic stability of any developed country which may equally be adversely affected by exploitation of the mineral resources of the Area which could result in a glut on the international market or undue competition with its own developed industry. Such a situation could easily arise for Canada in connection with copper and nickel. In fact, the whole emphasis of the great new concept of the common heritage of mankind and the need to have this exploited by an international authority to ensure equality of opportunity and enjoyment is oriented towards discrimination against the developed countries and in favour of the developing, for, reiterating the General Assembly Declaration,[37] all activities in the Area

shall be carried out for the benefit of mankind as a whole, irrespective of the geographical location of States, whether coastal or landlocked, and taking into particular consideration the interests and needs of the developing countries.

It may well be true that in the past excessive weight has been given in the development of rules of international law to the interests of those countries which are well-established, but which then, after all, constituted the entire society of states. However, a situation is rapidly developing where, as a result of the automatic majority enjoyed in the General Assembly, and other international gatherings by the new states, most of whom are still disadvantaged from an economic point of view, an entirely new emphasis is being given to international law and the relations of states *inter se*. In the name of friendly relations[38] it is becoming increasingly manifest that a majority of states maintain that economic equality is the supreme law of the world, that the developed countries must be held back to assist their less fortunate brethren and must atone for their past exploitations, and this attitude is to be seen in almost every international conference that takes place, as well as with monotonous regularity in some of the individual opinions of judges of the World Court.[39] The Law of the Sea Conference is no exception, and the matters discussed here amply illustrate the trend away from the rights of coastal states towards the interests of the landlocked and of those who consider themselves so disadvantaged that the rest of the world owes them a living. This trend reminds one of the question put by Elizabeth I when controverting the unilateral assertions of Spain on the basis of the Pope's division of the undiscovered world: "Was the Pope present when Adam wrote his will?"

Since we have not yet seen the ultimate conclusion of the Law of the Sea Conference it is perhaps too soon to comment further on issues concerning sovereignty or resources. Enough has been said to indicate the trend and to emphasize that Canada, like other developed states, will have to compromise some of its basic desires in order to achieve some measure of agreement and to avoid being condemned as a self-interested predator. She must, therefore, show patience and, despite the pressures of various vested interests to take unilateral action with regard, for example, to a 200-mile territorial sea or economic zone, she must still abstain from taking such action as will not merely foretell complete failure when the Conference resumes in 1976, but will only presage similar individual action by others, much of which will militate against Canadian interests. Should the Conference fail in any case, then a new situation will present itself. On the other hand, we cannot ignore that we appear to be entering an era when the so-called advantaged states, including Canada, will find themselves among the new disadvantaged and compelled to proceed unilaterally if their interests are to be protected adequately, or else will have to enter into arrangements with their friends which will portend two international laws — the one that we sign because we all believe in motherhood, and the one that we actually observe and apply.

147

Notes

1. See 'Is International Law Law?'', in L. C. Green, *Law and Society* (1975), at p. 174.
2. See, e.g., judgments of World Court (Permanent Court of International Justice and International Court of Justice) in *S. S. Lotus* case (France v. Turkey) (1937) P.C.I.J., Ser. A, No. 10, p. 18, and *Asylum Case* (Colombia v. Peru) (1950) I.C.J. 266, at 276-7.
3. 1609 (Eng. tr., *On the Freedom of the Seas,* Carnegie Classics, 1916).
4. 1635 (Eng. tr., *The Right and Dominion of the Seas,* by J. H., 1663).
5. 1744 (Eng. tr., *On the Sovereignty of the Sea,* Carnegie Classics, 1923).
6. *Ibid.,* pp. 43, 44.
7. (1805) 5C Rob, 373, at 385c.
8. Bynkershoek, Latin text, *op. cit.,* p. 364.
9. Convention on the Territorial Sea and Contiguous Zone 1958 (516 U.N.T.S. 205), Articles 1 and 24.
10. Article 36
11. *I.C.J. Yearbook 1972-1973,* p. 56.
12. Press Conference, 8 April 1970 *International Legal Materials,* Vol. 9 (1970), 600, at 602-3, 604.
13. See, e.g., S. A. Swartztrauber, *The Three-Mile Limit of Territorial Seas* (1972).
14. It would be interesting to know why Mr. Trudeau referred to courts, and what tribunal other than the World Court he had in mind.
15. UN Doc. A/AC. 138/SC.II/SR.31 (1973) 13.
16. See chapter on "The Impact of the New States in International Law", Green, *op. cit.,* n. 1 above, 183.
17. UN Doc. A/AC138./SC.II/SR.67 (1973) 15.
18. (Belgium v. Spain) (1970) I.C.J. 3, at 310.
19. 499 U.N.T.S. 311, Article 1.
20. See *loc. cit.,* n. 16 above.
21. *Loc. cit.,* n. 18 above, 303-4, 329.
22. This may be translated as "commonly accepted view of the law". As to the specific legal question referred to, see, e.g., F. V. Garcia Amador, and Others, *Recent Codification of the Law of State Responsibility for Injuries to Aliens* (1974).

23. *Loc. cit.,* n. 17 above.
24. UN Doc. A./CONF.62/WP.8/Parts I, II, III, 7 May 1975.
25. Perhaps two of the best examples of such a state are Indonesia and the Philippines.
26. See, e.g., L. C. Green "International Law and Canada's Anti-Pollution Legislation", *Oregon Law Review,* Vol. 50 (1971), 462; "Canada's Jurisdiction over the Arctic and the Littoral Sea", in Yates and Young, *Limits to National Jurisdiction over the Sea* (1974), 207.
27. U.S. Statement on Canada's Proposed Legislation, 15 April 1970 *International Legal Materials,* Vol. 9 (1970), 605.
28. (1949) I.C.J. 4, at 28.
29. *Ibid.,* at 46-47.
30. *International Legal Materials,* Vol. 11 (1972), 1416.
31. See, e.g., N. Mostert, *Supership* (1974).
32. See, e.g., L. C. Green "Canada and Arctic Sovereignty", *Canadian Bar Review,* vol. 48 (1970), 740; D. Pharand, *The Law of the Sea of the Arctic* (1973), 55 *et seq.*
33. Pharand, *op.cit.,* 60.
34. For Canadian views on Arctic Sovereignty, see, e.g., I. L. Head, "Canadian Claims to Territorial Sovereignty in the Arctic", *McGill Law Journal,* Vol. 9 (1963), 200; Green, *loc.cit.,* n. 26 and 32; Pharand, *op.cit.,* n. 32, and his Selected Bibliography.
35. G.A. Res. 2749 (XXV), 1970, Declaration of Principles Governing the Seabed and Ocean Floor, and Subsoil thereof, Beyond the Limits of National Jurisdiction.
36. See, e.g., R. Young, "Recent Developments with respect to the Continental Shelf", *American Journal of International Law,* Vol. 42 (1948) 849; L. C. Green, "The Continental Shelf", *Current Legal Problems,* Vol. 4 (1951), at 71 *et seq.*
37. Note 35 above.
38. See G.A. Res. 2625 (XXV), 1970, Declaration on Principles of International Law concerning Friendly Relations and Cooperation among States. .
39. For some examples of this, see Green, *loc.cit.,* n. 16 above.

CHAPTER 7

CANADA
IN THE
UNITED
NATIONS

Garth Stevenson

"The confidence of the Western world in the United Nations has never been lower." With these words the Toronto *Globe and Mail* began a lead editorial entitled "The Weakening of the UN," which appeared shortly after the United Nations General Assembly concluded its twenty-ninth regular session.[1] The editorial accused the Eastern European, Arab and Third World member states of misusing the General Assembly and of introducing political bias into the workings of the specialized agencies. It described the General Assembly itself as "an arena for power plays." The editorialist did not pursue this unconsciously Canadian metaphor to the point of attributing the success of the winning team to South Africa's presence in the penalty box, although he did refer to the suspension of that state from the session as an abuse of the majority's power. He was forced to admit as well that the Western team had enjoyed a number of successful seasons in the past, and that its victories had been accompanied by some rough body-checking, notably on the question of Chinese representation. He concluded, however, that if the newly successful team failed to mend its ways, the losers might be tempted to hang up their skates after a few more seasons.

Just as the spread of professional teams as far south as Atlanta and the Soviet victories in intercontinental competition have caused some Canadians to lament the decline and fall of their national game, so the changing distribution of expertise in multilateral diplomacy, another game at which Canadians were once thought to excel, has caused others to lament the decline of the United Nations. Even before the twenty-ninth session, a Canadian Gallup poll showed that only 36 per cent of those questioned thought the United Nations was "doing a good job", down from 42 per cent in 1967 and 54 per cent in 1961.[2] Policy-makers, as well as the general public, seem to express greater reservations about the organization's performance, both publicly and privately, than would have been the case a decade or more ago. Few Canadians are really hostile to the United Nations, but expressions of strong enthusiasm for it have become almost equally infrequent.

Whatever reservations they may have about it today, there can be no doubt that for two decades Canadian policy-makers found the United Nations a useful instrument for the achievement of national purposes, and were in the happy position that they could use it as such without appearing to manipulate the Organization or to subordinate the goals of its charter to narrow definitions of national interest. A whole generation of Canadians absorbed with their mothers' milk the notion of inevitable congruence between Canadian goals and those attributed to the United Nations, which by definition were viewed as those of humanity in general. Related to this notion was a belief that Canada surpassed most if not all other member states in its contribution to the work of the organization.

The small Canadian policy-making elite were predisposed from the outset by ideology and background to think well of the United Nations, which was viewed accurately enough as a visible expression of Anglo-American liberalism and of Anglo-American predominance in world affairs. These sentiments were reinforced by a sense of guilt about Canada's pre-war "isolationism" and its failure to give sufficient support to the League of Nations. It is unlikely that Canadian policy-makers ever viewed the United Nations as a guarantee of national security, although in justifying their later adherence to NATO they took great pains to insist that they had done so, and had been disillusioned only by the iniquity of the Soviet Union.[3] However, the United Nations was certainly viewed as contributing significantly to other goals of Canadian foreign policy, both generally and on specific occasions such as the Korean war and the Suez crisis.

A number of assets, it was soon discovered, made Canada influential in the councils of the United Nations. Without colonies, border disputes, or a history of military intervention in the affairs of weaker neighbours, it could appear disinterested, moderate, and impartial. As a rich country it contributed extensively to voluntary programmes and to the regular budget. Its professional army, maintained more as a diplomatic asset than for any genuine reasons of national security, was easily adaptable to "peacekeeping," a role that particularly captured the attention of the Canadian public. Especially during the 1950s, when the Security Council was in eclipse and the General Assembly consisted mainly of states whose conservative policies were in harmony with Canadian objectives, Canada could operate. effectively in the congenial milieu of conference diplomacy. The proximity of Ottawa to New York facilitated attendance by ministers and senior officials, and English and French were the major working languages of the Organization.

Time, however, brought changes to the United Nations. With the influx of new members in the 1960s, problems of racism, colonialism, and underdevelopment began to dominate the agenda. The General Assembly began to adopt resolutions, particularly on African questions, that the major western states could not support. This fact, as well as the controversy over expenditures on peacekeeping in the Congo, lessened the tendency of western states to seek solutions to political problems through the United Nations. Canada's role as a seeker of compromise between the western camp and the non-aligned, or between Western Europe and the United States, became largely irrelevant.

The centennial year of Canadian Confederation, 1967, was a year of disappointment at the United Nations. The peacekeeping force established a decade earlier through the efforts of Lester Pearson, a monument to the effectiveness of Canadian diplomacy, was forced to withdraw from the Middle East. The Security Council, of which Canada was then an elected member, failed to prevent the six-day war or to resolve the political deadlock that followed the ceasefire. As in 1956 an emergency session of the General Assembly was called together, but this time no resolution of substance could secure the necessary two-thirds majority. Earlier in the year another special session had considered, without success, the intractable problem of the Organization's finances, and had established a Council for South-West Africa with all of the great powers abstaining on the vote. The Special Committee on Peacekeeping Operations, which included Canada, continued its interminable and fruitless discussions. Meanwhile, Rhodesia continued to defy the economic sanctions imposed on it by the Security Council in the preceding year.

With the replacement of Lester Pearson by Pierre Trudeau in April 1968, a reassessment of Canadian foreign policy was promised. The new Prime Minister had little experience of the United Nations, and the little he had, according to one well-informed observer, had impressed him unfavourably.[4] Even Paul Martin, a long-time supporter of the Organization, expressed dissatisfaction with its recent metamorphosis in a speech delivered shortly after he exchanged the portfolio of External Affairs for the post of Government Leader in the Senate:

> . . . the opportunities for diplomacy have to some extent been restricted by the ease of achieving a two-thirds majority for resolutions which are supported by member states from Africa, Asia and Latin America . . . . Now it is possible for resolutions on certain subjects, particularly resolutions relating to colonial issues and to issues of economic development, to be passed by a large majority without prior negotiation with the minority . . . . If I am right, the diplomatic function of the Organization has suffered damage and there may be some cause for apprehension about the Assembly's future role in this respect.[5]

Foreign Policy for Canadians, the series of white papers that resulted from the new government's foreign policy "review," argued for a closer integration between domestic and foreign policies, emphasized economic growth as an objective of the latter, expressed a modest view of Canada's diplomatic influence, and implied that previous governments had involved themselves too frequently in controversies not directly related to Canadian interests. In addition, the Trudeau government's 1970 white paper on national defence was notably more sceptical about the importance of United Nations peacekeeping than the one published by the previous government six years earlier. Another straw in the wind was the Prime Minister's decision not to appear at the twenty-third session of the General Assembly, or at any other session over the next six years. Prime Ministers Pearson, Diefenbaker, St. Laurent and King had all spoken in at least one of the Assembly's general debates during their respective periods of office.

On the other hand, there were indications under the Trudeau government of continuing Canadian interest in the United Nations. When *Foreign Policy for Canadians* was published, an entire booklet was devoted to the Organization, and it rejected as unrealistic the option of playing "merely a passive and disengaged role" in its activities. When the Department of External Affairs reorganized its internal structure in 1972, a Bureau of United Nations Affairs was established, and the old United Nations Division was divided in two: one for economic and social and the other for political and institutional questions. Considerable diplomatic effort was devoted to ensuring that a Canadian contingent would be included when UNEF was re-established after the Yom Kippur war in 1973, and the Canadian contingent on Cyprus was also reinforced the following year. Canada was re-elected to the Economic and Social Council at the end of 1973 after a five-year absence, and at the time of writing was considering whether to seek another term on the Security Council, despite the fact that the election of Canada to represent the "Western Europe and other" group could no longer be taken for granted. It is also worth noting that Canada has continued without complaint to contribute more than three per cent of the regular budget, even after the United States was successful in demanding a twenty-five per cent ceiling on its contribution.

Canadian perceptions of the United Nations may have changed, but the change was far less dramatic than in the United States, which appears to have suffered an abrupt and bitter disillusionment with the organization it was instrumental in founding.[6] Although both countries in the past perceived a broad similarity between their own purposes and those of the United Nations, and although both found such an assumption increasingly implausible as the organization changed, their experience otherwise differed. Since the United States had virtually controlled the organization at one time, the sudden reversal of its fortunes has been a shock and a humiliation. Since Canada on the other hand had never aspired to more than a modest influence in the United Nations or elsewhere, and since it has no global hegemony to defend, its national interests are not directly threatened by the changes that have taken place. With few exceptions, Canadians have responded more with declining interest than with outrage.

As countless observers have pointed out, the United Nations is partly a reflection of the real world of international politics, and partly an influence, however modest, on that world. There is a temptation now perhaps for Canadians to underestimate its importance in both respects, just as much as the Canadians of an earlier day tended to overestimate its importance. The reality that the present-day United Nations both reflects and reinforces is the revolt of the so-called "developing" countries against the present system of international stratification. In one form or another, that fundamental issue pervades the politics of the organization. The behaviour of member states at the United Nations and their orientations towards the United Nations itself are strongly influenced by their positions on this question. Those member states that rigidly oppose the revisionism of the developing countries have the most to lose by increasing the effectiveness and prestige of the United Nations, if only because their isolation is painfully advertised and reinforced by every roll call. Insofar as the organization's own bureaucracy pursues consistent goals in a purposeful manner (an assumption that some may find questionable) those goals themselves increasingly reflect the objectives of the developing countries. It could hardly be otherwise.

This chapter will discuss Canadian policy in the United Nations in terms of three major issue-areas that illustrate the current politics of the Organization. Canadian readers whose image of the United Nations is dominated by the national obsession with peacekeeping may find it surprising that the subject is hardly mentioned in the following pages, but the omission is deliberately intended to promote a more balanced picture of Canada's United Nations activities in the 1970s than the one most Canadians retain. The areas that will be discussed are firstly the structures and procedures of the United Nations itself, secondly United Nations efforts to promote economic development, and lastly questions related to multinational corporations. All of these matters have recently been prominent on the United Nations agenda, and all have produced some degree of polarization between developing and industrialized countries. Aside from their intrinsic interest, they illustrate the diverse patterns of foreign-policy-making in Canada. Responsibility for structural and procedural questions rests largely with the Political and Institutional Division in the United Nations Bureau of the Department of External Affairs, but the Department's Bureau of Legal Affairs is also involved. Policy concerning development programmes is made primarily by the Canadian International Development Agency, especially the Multilateral Programmes branch, but External Affairs is involved through the Aid and Development Division in its Bureau of Economic and Scientific Affairs. The United Nations Bureau plays a minimal role in this area. Because of its economic implications, aid and development policy also involves the Department of Industry, Trade and Commerce and the Department of Finance. Canadian positions at the U.N. concerning multinational corporations are largely formulated by the Commercial Policy Division of External Affairs, although Industry, Trade and Commerce plays an important role in this area as well. In general, substantive positions expressed by Canada at the United Nations originate outside the United Nations Bureau, which acts as a link between the functional or geographical divisions responsible and the Canadian permanent missions at New York and Geneva. Canadian delegations to United Nations conferences, and to the General Assembly, include personnel from various departments, as required.

Organization and structure

Although amendments to the United Nations Charter have been minimal in the three decades of its existence, a number of informal changes in the procedures and even structures of the Organization have taken place, and discussions of such matters among member-states have been more or less continuous.[7] Demands for the revision of the Charter have become widespread from time to time, and have normally been associated with demands for greater emphasis on the principles of international majoritarianism and egalitarianism. By majoritarianism is meant the view that the collective wishes of a majority of member-states expressed through United Nations resolutions should in some sense create obligations for the dissenting minority. Egalitarianism is the principle according to which the views of all member-states should have equal weight in arriving at collective decisions, and implies that organs in whose voting arrangements this principle prevails (e.g. the General

Assembly) should take precedence over those in which it does not (e.g. the Security Council).

The practical implications of these principles depend of course on the composition of the majority, and also on the kinds of substantive questions concerning which the views of "small" member-states differ from those of some or all of the major powers. In the first decade of the United Nations, majoritarianism and egalitarianism operated to the benefit of the United states and its allies in Greece, Korea and elsewhere. By the so-called "uniting for peace" resolution of 1950 the western-controlled General Assembly assumed the right to substitute itself, in emergency situations, for the Security Council, which could only act with the concurrence of the U.S.S.R. This resolution was used as the basis for the Assembly's action in establishing UNEF during the Suez crisis of 1956, although the admission of sixteen new member-states in the previous year had already begun the process which was to result in the erosion of western dominance in the General Assembly. Even subsequent to this, and as late as 1965, the United States and other western members invoked the principles of majoritarianism and egalitarianism to argue that the U.S.S.R. was obligated to contribute funds for peace-keeping in the Congo, regardless of its views on the legality or morality of the operations concerned.

Canada consistently supported the position of the United States in applying the principles of majoritarianism and egalitarianism to peacekeeping and pacific settlement for as long as it served American purposes to do so. The western European colonial powers were always less convinced of the wisdom of such a strategy, and France moved to a position of open hostility after the Suez crisis. The moment of truth for both Canada and the United States came in the late sixties when the General Assembly not only proved unwilling to suspend the voting rights of non-contributors to peacekeeping expenses but proceeded to adopt increasingly uncongenial resolutions in regard to southern Africa, the Middle East, and a variety of economic and social questions. Paul Martin's speech to the United Nations Institute for Training and Research, already quoted in this chapter, indicated that Canada's support for international majoritarianism and egalitarianism had for all practical purposes come to an end.

Canada's increasing disillusionment with the General

Assembly took a more concrete and practical form in the following year when Martin's successor, Mitchell Sharp, proposed during the twenty-fourth annual general debate that the Assembly undertake a major review of its own structures and procedures. The idea was pursued by the Canadian permanent representative in New York and in 1970, after Sharp had referred to it at another of his annual appearances, the twenty-fifth General Assembly at Canada's request established a committee of thirty-one member-states, including Canada, to study and report on "rationalization of procedures and organization." Interestingly enough, the original proposal had been to entrust the study to a committee of three "distinguished persons with long experience of the General Assembly," rather than a large intergovernmental committee that would inevitably be dominated by representatives of developing countries.[8] Such a proposal had no chance of success; persons of "long experience" would almost by definition share the nostalgic memories of the Hammarskjold era that seemed to animate Canada's concern, and the egalitarian principle of giving "geographical distribution" priority over personal or national eminence had long been accepted practice at the United Nations.

In requesting that the study be undertaken, Canada's permanent representative argued that the practices of the General Assembly had not adapted to its increasing size and the diversity of its agenda. A number of Canada's subsequent suggestions to the committee were designed to save time by such means as reducing the number of roll calls, ceremonial statements, and speeches explaining a state's voting position or responding to allegations by another delegate. Others were intended to save money, reflecting a growing unease by states that contributed substantially to the budget at the cost of servicing an increasing roster of penurious members. In this category could be placed proposals to reduce the output of United Nations documents, to eliminate verbatim records of debates, and to require that draft resolutions with "substantial financial implications" be submitted to the administrative and budgetary organs before being voted upon in the Assembly. Canada also wanted to restrict the annual session to a maximum of twelve weeks (the United States suggested eight weeks), to have more resolutions drafted in the secretariat rather than by representatives of member states, and to re-assign a number of agenda items such as housing, narcotics and refugees from the social committee to the economic committee of the Assembly. The social committee would have been left with responsibility only for human rights and "certain other questions."[9] In view of the increasing importance of economic issues over the next few years, delegates assigned by their governments to the economic committee may be thankful that this suggestion was not adopted.

In the end Canada's recommendations were discarded by the committee, as were more extreme suggestions of the same general character contributed by the United States, Japan, and a number of western European members. The committee made only the most minimal suggestions for change in a massive report that ranks among the more tedious documents ever produced by the United Nations. The resolution accepting this report was adopted without a vote by the twenty-sixth General Assembly and the report was quickly forgotten. Commenting on the work of the committee, the Department of External Affairs expressed a philosophical view:

> If no spectacular success can be claimed for this Canadian initiative, reasonable satisfaction can be taken in its workmanlike result . . . . It is true that none of the more far-reaching proposals have been adopted (including some of Canada's) but it was never really in the cards that such ideas as dividing or reducing the length of Assembly sessions, electing the General Committee in advance, or altering the responsibilities of the main committees would command broad enough support.[10]

The attempt to alter procedures and organization within the framework of the existing Charter was soon overshadowed by more ambitious efforts to modify the Charter itself. Whereas the first effort was apparently designed to lessen the impact of egalitarian and majoritarian tendencies in the United Nations by relegating the General Assembly to a less prominent position, the initiative for amending the charter came from the developing countries and was designed to make the United Nations more egalitarian than before. In this respect it followed the pattern of previous efforts to amend the Charter. During the Organization's first decade a number of member states, particularly in the Latin American group, had called unsuccessfully for amendments to restrict or even eliminate the "veto" power enjoyed by permanent members of the Security Council. During the second decade pressure from developing countries was eventually successful in bringing about amendments which increased the number of non-permanent seats on the Security Council and the Economic and Social Council, thus diluting the influence of the major powers and providing more representation for developing countries. A further enlargement of the Economic and Social Council was agreed upon in 1971, with the United Kingdom and France voting against the proposal and the United States abstaining. Although any one of these states could have vetoed the necessary amendment by refusing ratification, they subsequently bowed to the will of the majority and the Council was increased to fifty-four members effective 1 January 1974.

Meanwhile, the General Assembly in 1970 had requested the Secretary-General to canvass the views of member states on possible amendments to the Charter, and to report his findings after two years.[11] Relatively few states made suggestions, but by 1972 demands for the curtailment of great-power influence had been sharpened by the confrontations over southern Africa and the Middle East. Another factor was the arrival in 1971 of the People's Republic of China, which attempted to assume the leadership of egalitarian revisionism by denouncing Soviet-American "hegemony." Soviet and American efforts at the twenty-seventh session were nonetheless successful in sidetracking a resolution which would have established a special committee to review the Charter. Canada assisted in these efforts and a resolution was adopted postponing further consideration of the subject until 1974.[12]

Canada voted in favour of enlarging the Economic and Social Council in 1971, just as it had voted to enlarge both councils in 1963. On both occasions its position placed it in agreement with the developing countries, and in opposition to the United States, the United Kingdom, and France. Subsequently, however, Canada did not see any reason to move further in the same direction. In a document submitted to the Secretary-General in 1972 Canada stated that the effectiveness of the United Nations depended on the political will of its members, rather than on the precise terms of the Charter, that improvements could be made without amending the Charter, and that amendments would in any event be very difficult to achieve because of the requirement that they be accepted by the five permanent members of the

Security Council. Referring specifically to the "veto" in the Security Council, a provision of the Charter which many developing countries resented, Canada argued that "the principle of unanimity of the five permanent members of the Security Council must be accepted as an indispensable mechanism to prevent intolerable strains in the fabric of the Organization." A long section of the Canadian submission was devoted to arguments against weighted voting in the General Assembly which appears, since no member state had actually proposed this, to be something of a red herring.[13]

The question of Charter review returned to the General Assembly at its twenty-ninth session in 1974. As it had done two years previously, Canada again co-operated in efforts to postpone consideration of the question for two more years, on the by now somewhat implausible pretext that member states had not had adequate time to present their views. This time the combined efforts of east and west were unsuccessful and a resolution setting up an *ad hoc* committee on the Charter was adopted by a vote of 82 to 15, with 36 abstentions.[14] In general the voting reflected a polarization between developing and developed countries, although Italy, Japan, Australia and New Zealand broke ranks to vote with the majority. Britain, France, the U.S.S.R. and the United States all opposed the resolution, while Canada abstained. Subsequently, Canada did not seek appointment to the *ad hoc* committee, being convinced of the futility of efforts to amend the Charter. There is little likelihood that Canada will be proved wrong in its evaluation of the committee's usefulness.

Canada's position in the recent discussions of the Charter has closely resembled its position at the founding conference of the United Nations in 1945. At that conference the alignments of the Cold War had not yet emerged and the major disagreement over the Charter was between the great powers, defending the hierarchical features of the draft charter produced by their representatives at Dumbarton Oaks, and a group of smaller states, including Australia, New Zealand, and most of the Latin Americans, which argued for a more egalitarian organization. At that time Canada adopted a position of moderation, rejecting proposals to curtail the veto power and increase the powers of the General Assembly as unrealistic and undesirable.[15] By a circuitous route through the vicissitudes of Cold War politics, the old alignments have re-emerged, and Canada has retained essentially the same position.

Canada's support for Soviet-American detente and its moderately conservative position on economic and social questions (of which more below) both contribute to its rejection of the egalitarian revisionism promoted by China and the more radical developing countries. Canada considers that the Security Council is returning to the pre-eminent peacekeeping role envisaged by the Charter, a contention supported by the arrangements under which the second UNEF was established in 1973.[16] This trend is considered encouraging both as evidence of detente and in view of the increasingly intransigeant and one-sided position of the General Assembly in regard to the Arab-Israel question. At the same time, Canada recognizes that economic and social questions now dominate the United Nations agenda. The Charter provides no veto to protect minority interests on these questions. Western industrialized countries have another weapon, however, since the United Nations still depends on them for most of its funds.

Economic Development

The United Natons has been directly involved in economic development ever since it established the Extended Programme of Technical Assistance in 1949, but only recently have its activities become extensive enough to have a significant impact. In 1958 the Special Fund was established, with responsibility for pre-investment projects, and in 1965 the two programmes were combined into the United Nations Development Programme. The growth of these programmes has been restricted throughout their history by reservations on the part of the industrialized states upon whose voluntary contributions the programmes largely depend. The industrialized countries have argued that large-scale capital disbursements should be made through the International Bank or through regional and bilateral agencies rather than through the United Nations. Although this view is usually defended in public on the grounds of the International Bank's greater experience and allegedly greater administrative expertise, the real reason for it is their distaste for the more egalitarian structure of the United Nations, which gives the developing countries themselves considerable influence over the allocation of funds. Thus UNDP has remained relatively modest in resources, while aid-givers and aid-recipients have disagreed concerning the appropriate size of the programme, its place in the overall picture of global development efforts, and the relative influence that the two groups of states should have over its decisions.

TABLE I
CANADA'S CONTRIBUTION TO UNDP
FROM 1968 THROUGH 1974

	Total UNDP Contributions (U.S. dollars)	Canada's Contribution	Canada's Contribution as % of total	Canada's Rank as Contributor
1968	182,783,308	9,953,704	5.5	5
1969	195,891,664	12,500,000	6.4	5
1970	225,387,014	15,000,000	6.7	4
1971	239,241,505	16,000,000	6.7	4
1972	269,862,073	18,000,000	6.7	5
1973	307,628,491	19,800,000	6.5	6
1974	362,457,917 (est.)	21,700,000	6.0 (est.)	7

Source: United Nations Yearbooks, and U.N. document
DP/48/Annex I

As Table I shows, Canada has been among the most generous contributors to UNDP in recent years. The amount of Canada's contribution more than doubled from 1968 to 1974 and more than kept pace with the increase in the overall size of the programme. During the same period the United States' share of contributions fell from about two fifths to one quarter of the total, and on a per capita basis is now far inferior to Canada's contribution. Only three contributors, the United States, Sweden and Denmark, have consistently exceeded Canada in the size of their contributions. The United Kingdom contributed more than Canada in all but two of the seven years, as did the Federal Republic of Germany in the last two years, and the Netherlands in 1974, but as a percentage of GNP Canada's contribution was always higher than that of the United Kingdom or the Federal Republic.

TABLE II
CONTRIBUTIONS TO UNDP AND EQUIPMENT ORDERS RECEIVED BY SELECTED CONTRIBUTORS

	1973 contribution (U.S. dollars)	1973 equipment orders (U.S. dollars)
Canada	19,800,000	848,000
Denmark	29,271,000	790,000
France	6,492,000	2,121,000
Germany (Federal Republic)	21,324,000	3,514,000
Japan	10,000,000	2,618,000
Netherlands	15,867,000	878,000
Sweden	29,000,000	1,246,000
Switzerland	5,000,000	1,328,000
United Kingdom	21,314,000	5,671,000
United States	90,000,000	9,039,000

Source: U.N. document DP/48/Annex I

Canada's performance looks even better when contributions to UNDP are compared with returns to the contributing states in orders for equipment, as shown in Table II. Most major contributors, particularly France, Japan, Switzerland, and the United Kingdom, effectively take back a large proportion of what they contribe in the form of payments by UNDP for their exports. The return to Canada in this respect is negligible, although proportionately no more negligible than the returns to Denmark, the Netherlands, and Sweden. Canadian policymakers are justified in believing, as they do, that Canada has a good record of contributing to UNDP and that a number of larger industrialized countries are not pulling their weight in the programme. On the other hand Canada lags substantially behind Denmark and Sweden, whose populations are smaller than those of Quebec and Ontario respectively. The reason for this is that Canada contributes a much smaller share of its total aid through multilateral programmes than do Denmark, Sweden or the

Netherlands. For domestic political reasons Canada must maintain extensive bilateral programmes in both francophone and Commonwealth countries, and the fact that Canada's official languages are widely spoken in the developing world makes bilateral programmes easier for Canada to undertake than for most European countries.

Despite its substantial support for UNDP, Canada shares in part the reservations about the programme held by other industrialized states, and it has often found itself in disagreement with the aid recipients on questions related to UNDP. One question on which Canada found itself almost isolated was the enlargement of the Governing Council of UNDP, a measure desired by developing countries as a means of increasing their own representation, and thus their influence over decision-making in the programme. When a proposal to enlarge the Governing Council was introduced at the twenty-sixth General Assembly, Canada expressed its predictable reservations concerning the "efficiency" of a larger decision-making body. A Canadian amendment to the draft resolution, inviting the enlarged Governing Council to establish "mechanisms" which would ensure efficient and rapid conduct of its business, received only twenty-five votes in the Economic Committee, with fifty opposed and thirty-seven abstentions. Almost all the supporters of the amendment were industrialized market economies. The resolution to enlarge the Governing Council was approved in plenary session by a vote of 86 to 2, with 25 abstentions.[17] Canada and the United States cast the only two opposing votes, while even Belgium, France, Japan and Caetano's Portugal voted with the majority. The reasoning that led to this landmark of Canadian diplomacy remains obscure, and in fact Canadian officials now concede that the enlargement of the Governing Council has not been followed by any deterioration of its performance.

At the same session of the General Assembly Canada opposed a resolution, sponsored by several developing countries, that called for the financial resources of UNDP to be doubled over the next five years.[18] On this occasion Canada was joined by Australia, Japan and the United Kingdom, as well as the United States, in voting against the resolution. Canada took this position on the grounds that it had no intention of doubling its own contribution over five years, and that an affirmative vote might have implied a commitment to do so. As already noted, Canadians involved with multilateral aid consider that Canada is doing more than its share and that larger industrialized countries such as Japan and France should be carrying a larger share of the burden. There is also a general reluctance on the part of Canadians to promise more in statements or in roll call votes that Canada is willing or able to deliver in actual performance, and this attitude is by no means confined to the field of multilateral aid. If there are political, economic or constitutional reasons why Canada cannot undertake actions that would be popular with a majority of United Nations members, it is considered more honest, and ultimately less harmful to Canada's reputation, to say so frankly at the outset. Canadian officials tend to contrast this "boy scout approach," as one of them described it, with that of certain other industrialized middle powers, which are alleged to be stronger on idealistic rhetoric than on actual performance.

As regards UNDP itself, there seems to be a lack of consensus among Canadian policy-makers concerning its performance and prospects. The UNDP made a significant innovation in recent years by introducing "country programming," a system by which projects in each recipient country are related to one another and to an overall five-year plan submitted by the recipient state and approved by the Governing Council. Other significant changes include the enlargement of the Governing Council itself, the increasing proportion of personnel drawn from developing countries, and the diminishing reliance on the United States as a financial contributor. All of these changes mean that UNDP will more and more reflect priorities and criteria for evaluation established in the developing countries themselves, rather than in the industrialized market economies. These trends tend to be favourably viewed in the Canadian International Development Agency, which in a sense is the advocate of developing-country interests in the bureaucratic politics of official Ottawa. In External Affairs on the other hand there seem still to be certain reservations about the efficiency and effectiveness of UNDP, and a tendency to compare it unfavourably with the International Bank and its affiliates. In a statement read to the Twenty-ninth General Assembly's Economic Committee by Senator Harry Hays, a former Liberal cabinet minister, criticism of UNDP administration was expressed, and reference was made to "undue pressures" on United Nations representatives by the governments of aid-receiving countries.[19] The fact that CIDA, which has operational responsibility for Canada's participation in UNDP, is not represented on Canadian delegations to the General Assembly may explain in part why Canada's public stance concerning UNDP sometimes appears less favourable than its actual performance.

In general, Canada has not favoured efforts by developing countries to establish new international machinery with the aim of redistributing wealth in their favour. The United Nations Conference on Trade and Development, the most grandiose of such efforts, is regarded by Canadian officials as contributing by its very structure to sterile confrontations between rich and poor. Canada also reacted unsympathetically in 1966 when the General Assembly with the support of most developing countries established the United Nations Capital Development Fund. Developing countries saw this as a useful supplement to UNDP, while the industrialized market economies resented it as an effort to compete directly with the International Bank. Over the next five years Canada voted against every General Assembly resolution concerning the fund, along with a small group of industrialized states that invariably included France, Japan, the United Kingdom and the United States. Refusal by rich countries to contribute to the fund meant that it existed only on paper for several years. Recently it has apparently developed a *modus vivendi* with the International Bank by concentrating on small-scale projects, particularly in the countries designated by the General Assembly as the twenty-five poorest. As a result the industrialized states have somewhat softened their attitude towards the fund. A few have even made financial contributions but Canada as yet has not done so.

A somewhat similar history has characterized the United Nations Industrial Development Organization, which also dates from 1966. Intended as an agency to promote industrialization in developing countries, it is one of the very few United Nations voluntary programmes to which the U.S.S.R. is a substantial contributor, and in fact about half its funds have come from Eastern Europe. Canada has taken little interest in UNIDO, makes no contributions to it, and by choice is not a member of its governing body, the Industrial Development Board. The traditional specialized agencies such as WHO and FAO work closely with the corresponding government departments in Ottawa, and Canadian contributions to them appear in those departments' estimates. UNIDO, which is actually a subsidiary organ of the General Assembly rather than a fully autonomous agency, has apparently forged no link with the Department of Industry, Trade and Commerce, although CIDA regards it with more enthusiasm. Contrary to Canadian expectations, UNIDO is proving to be among the more vigorous of United Nations agencies, and this fact may eventually overcome the scepticism of Canadian officialdom.

Multinational Corporations

Efforts by developing countries to redistribute wealth and economic power through the United Nations have moved beyond the traditional concept of "aid" into notions of restructuring fundamentally the economic relationships between the industrialized market economies and their southern hinterlands. The first United Nations Conference on Trade and Development in 1964 was a milestone in the mobilization of developing countries to support their common objectives. The creation of UNCTAD as a permanent subsidiary organ of the General Assembly, and the subsequent conferences at New Delhi in 1968 and at Santiago in 1972, continued the process. In the General Assembly itself economic issues became increasingly prominent.

Inevitably, foreign-controlled enterprises attracted attention as a conspicuous and significant aspect of the unequal economic relationship between north and south, and also because of their political implications. In the early 1960s the United Nations was directly involved in a situation created by the political activities of one foreign-controlled enterprise, the secession of Katanga province from the Congo with the support of the European owned Union Miniere. Not long afterwards the United Nations became interested in the role of foreign-controlled enterprise in reinforcing colonialism and apartheid in southern Africa and the General Assembly began in 1969 to adopt an annual resolution on this topic.[20] However, the major factor in bringing the whole question of foreign-controlled enterprises to the attention of the United Nations was their intervention in the politics of Chile while Salvador Allende was President of that country from 1970 to 1973. At the third UNCTAD, which took place in Chile during this period, the question was considered at the request of the host country and of Mexico. President Allende appeared at the twenty-seventh General Assembly to denounce the efforts by foreign-controlled enterprises to overturn his administration. In the same year the Economic and Social Council set up a "group of eminent persons" to study the political and economic implications of foreign-controlled enterprises, especially in developing countries. Meanwhile, the General Assembly was considering a closely related subject, permanent sovereignty over natural resources, concerning which important resolutions were adopted at the twenty-seventh and twenty-eight sessions.

These topics are of considerable interest to Canadians, and they draw attention to Canada's unusual and somewhat ambiguous position in the international system of economic relationships. On the one hand Canada is a rich country with a market economy, the headquarters of several corporations that operate in developing countries, and a close associate of the United Kingdom and the United States. On the other hand foreign-controlled enterprises play a massive role in the Canadian economy, and Canada's trade pattern resembles that of a developing country, since it exports raw materials to the United States, Europe and Japan while importing manufactured end products from the same areas. Thus Canada has a foot in both camps, its government is subjected to conflicting domestic pressures, and its policy on these questions inevitably betrays a certain ambivalence.

The Canadian government had of course been concerned with the problem of foreign-controlled enterprises for years before the United Nations began to consider it. Canada had even raised the question in the multilateral framework of the OECD, but the other members of that organization had no interest in pursuing it since most were net exporters of direct investment. When the question came before the United Nations in 1972, Canadian efforts were directed towards ensuring a more "moderate" approach would be taken than that favoured by Allende's Chile. Canada's second objective was to draw attention to the fact that foreign-controlled enterprises created problems for industrialized host countries such as Canada as well as for developing countries. After the Economic and Social Council voted unanimously to set up the "group of eminent persons," the Secretary-General asked the Canadian government, among others, to suggest possible nominees. From the names provided he selected John J. Deutsch, economist and Principal of Queen's University, to serve on the twenty-member commission. France, Japan, the United Kingdom and the U.S.S.R. were also represented by academic economists, while the United States provided a corporation executive and a senator. Most of the nine members from developing countries were politicians or civil servants. Stephen Hymer, a Canadian economist teaching in New York, and Albert Thornbrough, the president of Massey-Ferguson, were among the forty-seven witnesses who appeared before the group at its hearings in the fall of 1973.

The group's report, entitled "The Impact of Multinational Corporations on Development and on International Relations," was submitted to the Economic and Social Council in 1974.[21] It discussed most of the problems encountered by host countries in dealing with foreign-controlled enterprises and suggested ways in which the United Nations might strengthen the bargaining position of developing countries in dealing with foreign-controlled enterprises. Recommendations were addressed to home countries, to host countries, to multinational enterprises, and to the United Nations. The report was by no means radical, although several members of the group from industrialized countries submitted lengthy individual comments that amounted to dissenting opinions.

Governments were invited by the Economic and Social Council to submit their comments on the report, and Canada was one of the first to do so. The Canadian submission, drafted mainly by the Commercial Policy Division of External Affairs, was generally favourable to the report, although there were critical comments concerning a number of individual recommendations. Canada was particularly wary of recommendations directed to home governments of multinational enterprises, arguing that these governments should neither be regarded as parties to controversies between the enterprises and the governments of other countries in which they operate nor encouraged to impose their own directives on the foreign subsidiaries of their enterprises. This view reflected Canada's long struggle against the extraterritorial application of United States law to subsidiaries operating in Canada.[22]

On the other hand Canada favoured a "balanced approach" and argued that "The Report does not give sufficient weight to

170

the very real advantages that MNE's can confer."[23] The report was also criticized for its "very limited understanding of how technology is developed, acquired, or exchanged in a free enterprise system."[24] The recommendations dealing with technology transfers were indeed considered generally unworkable and simplistic. Canada also took issue with a statement that "international agencies" should not be used to "exert pressure" against governments that were having difficulty with multinational enterprises. This statement was obviously directed against the International Bank and the International Monetary Fund, two of official Ottawa's favourite institutions. Canada warned against "imposing any restrictions that might impede the progress of agencies in solving financial problems in host countries."[25]   In summary, the Canadian submission revealed the ambivalence of a country concerned about foreign control of its economy but one that was also conservative, market-oriented and industrialized. Despite its reservations, the Canadian statement differed significantly from those of the United States, the Unkted Kingdom and the Federal Republic of Germany, which were almost completely hostile to the report.

The task of the Economic and Social Council was to set up institutional machinery which could follow up the report and assist in implementing its recommendations. Canada introduced a resolution to establish a Committee on Multinational Enterprises, which would report to the Economic and Social Council every two years. The committee would consist of experts appointed by the Secretary-General. Its tasks would include collecting and disseminating information as well as promoting technical co-operation which would strengthen the capacity of host countries to deal with multinational enterprises.[26] This proposal was withdrawn when it became apparent that it lacked sufficient support to be adopted. Instead, the Council at the suggestion of several developing countries directed the Secretary-General to establish an information and research centre on multinational corporations within the Secretariat, and postponed the establishment of further machinery until its resumed session at the end of the year. In effect the information and research centre already existed, since the Secretariat had assisted the Group of Eminent Persons and had prepared an extensive working paper of its own entitled "Multinational Corporations in World Development."[27]

A special intersessional committee of the Economic and Social Council considered further courses of action in the fall of 1974. Canada persisted with its idea of a permanent committee of experts, but the preference of most member states, industrialized as well as developing, was for a commission of government representatives. Canada again abandoned its own proposal and accepted the will of the majority. On the recommendation of its intersessional committee the Council decided to establish a commission of forty-eight states, elected for three year renewable terms on a basis of equitable geographical distribution. Each state would appoint an expert representative. The commission would work closely with the information and research centre of the Secretariat, and would recommend priorities and programmes of work on multinational corporations to the Council's sixtieth session in early 1976.

Canada was elected to the Commission as one of ten representatives from the "Western European and other" group of member states. A continuing unwillingness to view this as an intergovernmental commission rather than a functional committee was suggested by Canada's decision to appoint its "expert" from the Department of Industry, Trade and Commerce while leaving External Affairs responsible for formulating Canada's representations "to" the commission. What the commission would recommend remained to be seen at the time of writing, but the developing countries appear generally convinced of the need to draft a "code of conduct" for multinational corporations, a project that Canada considers would be valueless.

Questions relating to foreign-controlled enterprises have also arisen in the course of the General Assembly's consideration of the agenda item "Permanent Sovereignty over Natural Resources." As early as 1952 the Assembly proclaimed, with the United States opposed and Canada abstaining, that sovereign states had the right freely to exploit their natural wealth and resources.[28] Ten years later, at a time when events in the Congo made the subject particularly timely, the Assembly adopted the Declaration on Permanent Sovereignty over Natural Resources.[29] A further resolution in 1966 affirmed the right of the host country to a share in the management and the profits of foreign-controlled firms engaged in the extraction of natural resources.[30]

At its twenty-eighth session, which coincided with the overthrow of Allende's government by the Chilean armed forces, the Assembly confronted the problem of compensation for the nationalized properties of foreign-controlled resource enterprises. Earlier resolutions on natural resources had attempted to strike a balance between the interests of national sovereignty and of private property. The 1962 Declaration for example, stated that in case of nationalization the amount of compensation to the former owners should be determined "in accordance with international law". By 1973 most developing countries argued that the existing framework of international law was biased in favour of capitalist interests. Instead they wished to affirm the principle that compensation should be determined in accordance with the domestic law of the host country concerned.

When the draft resolution came to a vote the paragraph on compensation was voted upon separately, and Canada was one of twenty-eight states that abstained. About half of these were developing countries while the rest were mainly industrialized countries with significant foreign-owned mining industries. The United States, Japan, Israel and eight Western European members voted against the paragraph. When the resolution as a whole was put to a vote, including the paragraph on compensation, Canada voted in favour. Only the United Kingdom cast a negative vote, while the United States, Japan and most of Western Europe abstained. Nicaragua was the only developing country to do so.[31]

On 12 December 1974 the General Assembly adopted the Charter of Economic Rights and Duties of States, which included in the second of its thirty-four articles the following statement:

> Each State has the right . . . to nationalize, expropriate or transfer ownership of foreign property in which case appropriate compensation should be paid by the State adopting such measures, taking into account its relevant laws and regulations and all circumstances that the State considers pertinent. In any case where the question of compensation gives rise to a controversy, it shall be settled under the domestic law of the nationalizing State and by its tribunals . . .[32]

The question of whether Canada's objection to this principle should cause it to abstain in the vote on the document as a whole was not resolved without the involvement of several members of Cabinet. In the end caution prevailed and Canada abstained, along with Israel, Japan, and seven states of Western Europe. Five Western Europeans joined the United States in voting against the resolution; one hundred and twenty votes were cast in favour.

Conclusion

Like the world which it reflects, the United Nations has changed fundamentally, and irreversibly, since the days of Pearsonian diplomacy. To many Canadians the new United Nations may seem less cosy and familiar than the old, the issues more obscure, and the opportunities for Canadian diplomacy less evident. Yet it would be wrong to assume that opportunities no longer exist, or that Canada as an industrialized capitalist state is inevitably isolated and deprived of influence by the "tyranny of the majority." In actual fact Canada voted with the majority on slightly more than two-thirds of General Assembly resolutions adopted by roll call vote between 30 April 1968 and 30 April 1975. On most of the others it abstained, so that only forty-nine negative votes were cast out of 725 roll calls.[33] These proportions are little different from those of earlier years.[34]

With its resource-based, foreign-dominated economy and its freedom from "commitments" (a euphemism for spheres of influence) Canada has much more in common with the developing countries than do the United Kingdom or the United States. With many developing countries, particularly Commonwealth members, francophone states, and certain of the Latin Americans, Canada enjoys good working relationships at the United Nations. Since Canada by virtue of its wealth is also a major contributor to voluntary programmes and to the regular budget, one might even conclude that it enjoys the best of both worlds, and that its opportunities for pursuing its national purposes through the United Nations are usually great.

Canadian policy-makers, whose work brings them into contact with the United Nations, seem to have adapted reasonably well to the changes in the Organization, but the same can probably not be said about Canadian public opinion. Probably no more than a handful of Canadians could describe even vaguely anything that their country's representatives do in the United Nations, aside from peacekeeping in Cyprus and the Middle

East. There are a number of reasons for this. The United Nations has no information office in Canada, apparently on the theory that Canadians are close enough to the one in New York. The Canadian media do not maintain permanent correspondents at United Nations headquarters, and depend heavily on American sources for the little information they provide about United Nations activities. A few members of Parliament, such as Andrew Brewin, Heath Macquarrie, and Douglas Roche, maintain a well-informed interest in the United Nations, but the number is surprisingly small, considering the fact that an all-party delegation has been sent to every session of the General Assembly.[36] To most Canadians the United Nations must be little more than a vague blur of incomprehensible meetings and resolutions, and the widely-published photograph of Yasser Arafat packing his pistol on the General Assembly podium probably provided a more lasting impression of the Organization than any event since the Suez crisis.

Canadian policy-makers are aware that public opinion provides neither effective support nor well-informed criticism of Canadian policy at the United Nations and that its more irrational manifestations, which reflect the influence of the American media, could limit Canada's ability to pursue constructive policies. On the other hand there are a number of voluntary organizations with at least a potential interest in various areas of United Nations activity, and the United Nations Bureau in the Department of External Affairs is now making efforts to involve them in formulating Canadian policy concerning questions that come before the Organization. Besides contributing to the education of the public, these efforts will presumably strengthen the United Nations Bureau vis-a-vis other sectors of the policy-making community on which it now depends for information and expertise.

For the rich countries which brought the United Nations into being, only to lose control of its machinery and to find their own policies examined critically in the light of its principles, the Organization may offer the last best hope of coming peacefully to terms with the poor and non-white majority on this planet. Just as the United Nations once facilitated the dismantling of a weakened European colonialism, so it may contribute to the harder task of replacing the informal structures of neo-colonial domination with a more generally acceptable economic and social order in the last decades of the twentieth century. To what extent Canadian foreign policy will rise to this challenge is not yet clear, but the prospects may be more hopeful here than in the United States or the European Community.

Notes

1. *The Globe and Mail,* 10 February 1975.
2. Canadian Institute of Public Opinion, *The Gallup Report,* 9 January 1974.
3. For evidence that Canada was sceptical about Chapter VII of the Charter even in 1945, see the statement of a Canadian delegate summarized in United Nations Conference on International Organization, Documents, Volume 12, p. 297.
4. Peter Dobell, *Canada's Search for New Roles* (London: Oxford University Press, 1972), pp. 10-11.
5. Canada Department of External Affairs, Statements and Speeches, no. 68/12. "The United Nations Political Organs and Multilateral Diplomacy."
6. See Hollis W. Barber, "The United States vs. The United Nations," *International Organization,* Vol. XXVII, No. 2 (Spring 1973), pp. 139-164.
7. For an extended treatment of these discussions, see the author's unpublished doctoral dissertation, Constitutional Change in the United Nations (Princeton University, 1971).
8. UN document A/7992.
9. The suggestions of member states are included in the Committee's report, UN document A/8426, pp. 161-219.
10. *External Affairs,* Vol. XXIII, No. 9 (September 1971), p. 340.
11. UNGA Res. 2697 (XXV).
12. UNGA Res. 2968 (XXVII).
13. The Canadian statement can be found in UN document A/8746, pp. 7-11.
14. UNGA Res. 3349 (XXIX).
15. See F. H. Soward, *Canada in World Affairs, 1944-1946* (Toronto: Oxford University Press, 1950), pp. 134-144, and Lester B. Pearson, *Mike,* Volume I (Toronto: University of Toronto Press, 1972), pp. 273-278. Pearson's comments on the Australian delegation are particularly illuminating.
16. See the Canadian statement in UN document A/8563.

17. UNGA Res. 2813 (XXVI) The discussions of the resolution and of the Canadian amendment are summarized in UN document A/8563.

18. UNGA Res. 2811 (XXVI).

19. *International Canada,* Vol. V, No. 10 (October 1974), p. 195.

20. Canada opposed this resolution for the first four years, abstained in 1973, and supported it in 1974, when there were no votes against and only eleven abstentions.

21. UN document E/5500/Rev. 1. Sales number E.74.II.A.5

22. Government of Canada: "Canadian statement on the (ecosoc) report of the group of eminent persons to study the role of multinational corporations on development and on international relations," September 1974.

23. "Canadian statement," p. 1.

24. "Canadian statement," p. 20.

25. "Canadian statement," p. 6.

26. The text can be found in UN document A/9603, pp. 30-31.

27. UN document ST/ECA/190. Sales number E.73.II.A.II.

28. UNGA Res. 626 (VII).

29. UNGA Res. 1803 (XVII). Only France and South Africa opposed the resolution. The Eastern Europeans and Ghana, who would have preferred a more forceful resolution, abstained.

30. UNGA Res. 2158 (XXI).

31. UNGA Res. 3171 (XXVIII).

32. UNGA Res. 3281 (XXIX).

33. Canada, House of Commons Debates, 30 April 1975, p. 5335.

34. Catherine Senf Manno: "Majority Decisions and Minority Responses in the UN General Assembly," *The Journal of Conflict Resolution,* Vol. X, No. 1 (March 1966), pp. 1-20.

35. For a depressing display of ignorance and ill-will towards the United Nations, see the speech by Robert Kaplan (Liberal, York Centre) in Canada, House of Commons Debates, 17 June 1975, pp. 6851-6856.

CHAPTER 8

CANADA'S ROLE IN AFRICA

Steven Langdon

Africa seems to impinge on Canada in remarkable ways — more at the level of imagination than of mundane political economy. Some of our best authors, Margaret Laurence and Dave Godfrey, for instance, have been spurred to write by African experience. Canadian politicians have felt sufficiently moved to fly romantically into dangerous airstrips in rebellious Biafra. Canadian citizens seem to have been specially touched, not just by that war and its humanitarian issues, but by the drought in the Sahel regions of Africa in 1973/74, and by the Southern African question. Shareholders meetings of Canadian-based companies have become the forum within which Canadian church people, students and others have raised detailed questions about contracts, wages and investment policies operative thousands of miles away.

There is, however, more to Canada's emerging relationships with Africa than these emotional ties. Developing economic links mark the Canadian role in the continent, and these links raise some important questions about Canadian foreign policy in Africa in particular, and about this country's relations with the poor majority of the world generally. This chapter will first outline Canada's developing economic relationship with Africa; it will then explore some of the central questions which emerge for Canadian foreign policy in the continent — questions about foreign aid and African income distribution, about trade strategy and economic development, about Canadian direct investment's impact, and about Southern African policy; finally, the chapter will assess Canada's current foreign policy in Africa, asking if it represents a positive response to poor countries' demands for a New Economic Order in the world, or a developing pattern of new style colonialism.

Canada and Africa: The Developing Economic Relationship
The Canadian relationship with Africa remains in some respects marginal. The bulk of Canadian trade and investment abroad involves the United States, with European links of secondary significance, and commercial ties with the Commonwealth Caribbean representing Canada's most prominent economic relationship with the less developed countries; in 1974, for example, only 1.21 percent of Canadian domestic exports went to African markets, and only 1.41 percent of Canadian imports came from that source.[1] Such statistics, though, do not capture the emerging dynamic of an economic relationship. Examination of detailed figures, which show how Canadian foreign links are changing, suggests more significant Canada-Africa economic ties.

Canadian development aid represents the focus of these emerging ties. As Table I shows, Africa has become a point of increasing concentration for official Canadian assistance, through the Canadian International Development Agency (CIDA). The drive in the 1960s to build ties with French-speaking African countries, as a reflection of official Canadian bilingualism, has been a factor in this concentration; but as the table illustrates, Commonwealth African countries have experienced almost as dramatic an increased concentration in the early seventies; the largest African aid recipient in 1973/74, for example, was Tanzania with almost 5 percent of total Canadian bilateral aid. Overall, this new concentration has taken Canadian bilateral aid in Africa from $29.9 million in 1968/69 to $130.8 million in 1973/74, an annual average increase of 34.3 percent.

These statistics reflect only bilateral official aid to Africa. The Canadian government also devotes increasing resources through multilateral aid agencies such as the various U.N. and World Bank development bodies; and much of this reaches Africa. External Affairs Minister Allan MacEachen estimated in 1975 that such disbursements channelled another $26 million into Africa from Canada. Beyond that, various non-governmental agencies convey Canadian aid to Africa; Canadian University Service Overseas (CUSO) and its Quebec equivalent, for instance, support some five hundred volunteers in Africa, helped by official

TABLE I
CANADIAN DEVELOPMENT AID TO AFRICA

a) Percentage of Bilateral Aid Allocations by Year:

	1968/69	1969/70	1970/71	1971/72	1972/73	1973/74
to Africa	20.41%	18.94%	20.86%	35.53%	35.74%	36.05%
Francophone Africa	9.84	10.97	11.30	16.87	18.68	18.37
Commonwealth Africa	10.53	7.96	9.54	18.63	16.90	17.27

b) Percentage of Personnel Exchanges by Year:

	1970	1971	1972	1973	1974
CIDA Advisors & Educators: Pct. in Africa	75.14	70.44	81.50	84.50	85.71
Trainees in Canada: Pct. from Africa	36.53	43.01	53.31	58.37	61.97

Source: Canadian International Development Agency, *Annual Reports*, 1970/71 to 1973/74

government funding (of over \$7 million in 1973/74).[2] The government-supported International Development Research Centre (IDRC) funds major research efforts in Africa, too. There are also private church missionary activities run by Canadians that represent development assistance in part; a recent survey suggests that there were almost 3,300 Canadian missionaries in Africa in 1973.[3]

Since at least two-thirds of any Canadian bilateral aid must be spent on Canadian goods or services,[4] this emerging aid concentration underlies a notable expansion of Canadian exports to Africa. Such exports expanded at an annual average of 23.2 percent over 1968/74, compared to a growth rate of 15.4 percent for all exports for the same period. Much of this export trade remains with white-run South Africa (24 percent of the total in 1974); but it is significant that exports to fourteen black African states (most of them prominent recipients of Canadian aid)[5] have increased at an annual rate of 32.6 percent over 1968-74 and now exceed exports to South Africa by a comfortable margin. Canadian imports from Africa are also increasing markedly — at an annual rate of 26.5 percent over 1968-74, compared to 16.9 percent for overall imports.

This trade is taking on a particular character as it emerges. Africa remains an important source of tropical agricultural commodities for Canada, but the most dramatic change in the last six years has been the emergence of Africa as a key source for some important mineral resources imported into Canada. No bauxite or copper ore, for instance, were imported from Africa in 1968 and very little as late as 1971, but by 1974 38.3 percent of Canadian bauxite imports came from Guinea and Sierra Leone, and 12.1 percent of Canadian copper ore imports from Mauritania; also, some 49.0 percent of manganese ore imports came from Gabon, Zaire and South Africa in 1974. In return for this raw material input, Canada is developing African markets for sophisticated machinery and equipment output; and though Africa remains a marginal market overall for Canadian manufacturers, African demand for a number of sophisticated products has become quite significant: 13.3 percent of Canada's 1974 exports of excavating/dredging machinery, for instance, went to five African countries, 15.4 percent of 1974 construction machinery exports were sold in eleven African countries and 10.6 percent of earthdrilling and related machinery exports went to six African countries. Such sales of advanced manufactured goods (important to the Canadian strategy of developing export industrial abilities beyond the U.S. market) were major components of Canadian 1972-74 trade with such aid recipients as Kenya, Nigeria, Zambia, Zaire, Gabon, and especially Tanzania. This growing importance of Canadian exports to Africa also shows up in details of government export credits; in 1971 Africa received only 2.6 percent of such credits (worth $11 million), but by 1974 over 10 percent of such credits were going to Africa.[6]

The relationship of this equipment trade to aid should be stressed. In an interesting paper, for instance, Glen Bailey has examined the detailed Canadian trade returns for six African countries, over six years, and shown that it is possible to account for nearly every year-to-year variation in the individual machinery/equipment export categories by reference to CIDA disbursements for given projects. Bailey underlines this trade-aid relationship by noting interviews with CIDA personnel in which respondents stressed how they felt CIDA's development efforts could be and sometimes were distorted by government export-generating priorities. Locomotive manufacturers and the electrical industry were mentioned as specific examples; both worked through the Department of Industry, Trade and Commerce to pressure CIDA to allocate more funds to those better-off countries willing to purchase their expensive products, while CIDA was attempting to allocate its assistance, on the basis of need, to the poorer countries in Africa.[7]

Increased Canadian direct investment in Africa is in part related to these emerging trade patterns. Canadian reliance on Africa for bauxite, for instance, reflects Alcan's investment in a large Guinea development project (and Alcan's loss, through nationalization, of its South American bauxite source). However, Canadian direct investment in Africa has a dynamic of its own, too. Again, in absolute terms Canada's investments in Africa seem insignificant, only 2.86 percent of overall book value of investment abroad by the end of 1971; at the margin, though, this African investment *does* seem important, as Table II suggests. In 1970 and 1971, in particular (these are the latest data available), Canadian investment in Africa was clearly accelerating; and though direct investment in South Africa was the most significant element in the increase over 1965-71, by

TABLE II
CHANGES IN BOOK VALUE OF
CANADIAN DIRECT INVESTMENT ABROAD

	1965-71 (Year Ends)	1970 & 1971
Absolute Net Change (excluding South and Central America)[a]	+ $2,428 million	+ $726 million
Pct. of Net change Accounted for by investment in:		
United States	+ 55.47%	+ 56.34
United Kingdom	+ 4.45	- .69
EEC countries	+ 7.25	+ 1.52
Australia	+ 7.00	+ 10.74
Caribbean	+ 10.79	+ 10.88
Asia	+ 3.58	+ 4.96
Africa	+ 4.74	+ 11.29
-South Africa	+ 3.25	+ 6.34
-Other Africa	+ 1.48	+ 4.96
Average Annual Increase in net book value of Canadian Direct Investment:		
Overall (excluding South and Central America)[a]	+ 9.7%	+ 7.0%
in Africa	+ 17.2	+ 33.5
-South Africa	+ 23.0	+ 30.7
-Other Africa	+ 11.3	+ 37.9

Source: *Direct Investment Abroad by Canada, 1946-1967,* Ottawa, 1971, p. A10; *Statistics Canada Daily,* Apr. 3, 1975, p. 4.

[a] South and Central America are excluded from the analysis because of a statistical discontinuity in 1970, when certain Canadian investments were redefined as direct rather than portfolio.

1970-71, the rest of Africa was sharing fully in the new capital inflows.

By the early seventies, Canadian-based multinational firms were shaping a notable role in the African political economy, with Massey-Ferguson, Alcan, Consolidated Bathurst, International Nickel, Falconbridge and Bata Shoes, among those heavily committed to investment in the continent. It is likely that this Canadian role has increased since then, too, not least because of a new (since 1971) CIDA program of pre-investment incentives, aimed at accelerating Canada's direct investments in developing countries. The focus of African investments for Canada remains South Africa; but that also ties this country's economic interests into increasing trade with black Africa, since South Africa's present strategy on the continent aims at capturing the manufactured export markets north of it.

Overall, then, Canada's economic relationship with Africa is taking on significant dimensions. Especially in recent years, marked Canadian aid accelerations and export sales in Africa are evident. These are reflected in increased export credits to that continent, and paralleled by emerging reliance on certain African mineral resource sources. Increased Canadian direct investment in Africa also seems to be taking place. In short, Canada seems to be building economic links with poor African countries similar to those which critics of other industrial capitalist nations have labelled neo-colonialism, namely, establishing relationships in which the less developed countries supply raw materials in return for finished industrial goods, in which aid is used to enforce these economic ties, and in which direct investment leads to foreign control of key parts of the poorer economies.[8] Should Canada's role in Africa be perceived in this neo-colonial light? If so, what alternatives are there to such a role? Section III returns to these questions after a more detailed examination of four facets of Canada's policies in Africa.

Canadian Foreign Policy in Africa: Issues and Ambiguities
In a speech to the 1975 Conference of the Canadian Association of African Studies, External Affairs Minister Allan MacEachen identified two special concerns of Canada in its relationship with Africa: first, concern for "social justice" for "the impoverished and the deprived" in Africa; and second, "our concern for human rights and dignity". The first perception is "pursued

largely through development assistance;" the second has meant that "successive Canadian governments have condemned racial injustice and colonialism as they have been practised in Southern Africa".[9]

The implementation of Canadian foreign policy in Africa, however, as distinct from this high-minded articulation, has experienced certain ambiguities, in part a result of the realities of contemporary African political economy, in part of the contradictions implicit in Canada's policy stance. These ambiguities emerge keenly in four facets of the relationship, each of which is explored briefly in this section.

a) Development, Foreign Aid and "Social Justice":

In the heady days of the First Development Decade, as the 1960s were designated, a concept of development was widely prevalent that suggested, first, that economic growth was development, and, second, that such growth in poor countries required foreign aid inflows to cover foreign exchange constraints, and permit the importation of essential capital equipment and the provision of necessary local infrastructure. Foreign aid would help establish the preconditions for W. W. Rostow's famous "takeoff into self-sustained growth".[10] And that growth would take care of MacEachen's "impoverished and deprived", in Africa and elsewhere.

That view of development is now widely rejected as being naive in its simple capital-centred model of economic growth, shallow in its abstraction from dominance-dependence relations in the international economy, and misguided in its direct identification of economic growth with development and social justice. It has, for instance, become quite clear that economic growth in poorer countries may leave many of the poor as badly off as ever. In fact, a recent study for the World Bank suggests that most patterns of LDC economic growth lead to "an absolute as well as a relative decline in the average income of the very poor", comprising some 40 to 60 percent of most populations.[11] Such processes are reflected in the very gross inequalities in income distribution reported in various African countries, as shown in Table III. In most of the countries covered, the top 5 percent of household income recipients obtain significantly more of overall national income than the bottom 60 percent of recipients, a much more unequal pattern than in Canada or the United States.

185

TABLE III
INCOME DISTRIBUTION IN
AFRICAN LESS DEVELOPED COUNTRIES

Percentage of Pre-Tax National Income Received by:	(a) Lowest 40% of Households	(b) Lowest 60% of Households	(c) Top 5% of Households	(d) (c) (b)
Nigeria	14.00%	23.00%	38.38%	1.67
Ivory Coast	18.00	30.00	29.00	.97
Gabon	8.00	15.00	47.00	3.13
Tanzania	19.50	29.25	42.90	1.47
Zambia	15.85	26.95	37.50	1.39
Senegal	10.00	20.00	36.00	1.80
Sierra Leone	10.10	19.20	33.80	1.76
Niger	23.00	35.00	23.00	.66
Canada (1972)	14.4	32.3	16.2	.50
United States (1970)	17.5	34.9	14.4	.41

Sources: Adelman & Morris, *op. cit.,* 1973, p. 152; Statistics Canada, *Income Distributions by Size in Canada, 1972;* Thurow, *Public Interest,* Spring 1973.

Development aid motivated by concern for the impoverished and deprived, then, must do more than just generate economic growth. It must somehow penetrate to the poor majorities of less-developed countries, providing them with economic opportunities and resources. That is in itself an extraordinarily difficult strategy to implement, and it becomes a virtual impossibility for Canadian aid in Africa because of the Canadian content requirement regulating bilateral aid.

This requirement means that the bulk of Canadian foreign assistance, taking the form of machinery and other expensive capital goods, serves to build up the small, capital-intensive "modern" sectors of African economies. It is the very prominence and growth of these sectors which are now widely seen as a basic *cause* of the increasing inequality in many poorer countries.[12] Urban, highly-mechanized industries and sophisticated resource-extracting operations not only direct their benefits to very restricted minorities of the African population; their growth may also directly hurt the rural and urban poor by increasing local price levels and by disrupting markets for local small-scale enterprises. One example of the latter effect sits in Dar Es Salaam, Tanzania: a new automated bakery (courtesy of Canadian foreign aid), which is destroying the economic base of many small-scale, labour intensive bakeries across the city.[13]

Recent development analysis, in fact, suggests that improving the lives of the poor majorities in less-developed countries will require policies discriminating against such modern sector growth, rejecting dependence on foreign "advanced" technology, and relying much more on small-scale indigenous, rural enterprise.[14] Though there are exceptions (such as Canada's rural honey harvesting project in East Africa), most Canadian aid in its present form works against such policies.

The second problem with Canadian development aid as an instrument for social justice is even less tractable. A restructured development strategy, aimed at social justice for the poor, requires commitments to income and asset redistribution from wealthy elites, as they reshape their nations' external economic links. Yet, as Tanzania's manifesto to the 1970 Lusaka Conference of Non-Aligned States noted, the developed-country ties of some poorer countries have "often led to the internal dominance of groups whose personal interests are linked to the interests of external economic forces, and who recognize that their continued internal power is dependent upon the power exerted by these forces".[15] New-style African dependence is thus established, based on the internal dominance of classes that maintain their local privileges over their *own* poor, by maintaining favourable local trade and investment opportunities for advanced capitalist countries. The internal dominance of such groups freezes out policies committed to aiding the African poor.

The second problem with development aid is that it can help keep such regimes in power. Inevitably, foreign aid inflows strengthen such dominant classes directly, by giving them more resources to allocate internally, and more chance to manipulate opportunities to their (political or economic) advantage.

The nature of African income distribution and development

priorities, then, and the reality of dependence ties, both make it unlikely that the large acceleration of Canadian bilateral aid to Africa is, in fact, serving primarily to generate social justice. This acceleration probably helps maintain certain wealthy, oppressive elites in power in some countries, while elsewhere it furthers the growth of small capital-intensive "advanced" economic sectors, to the (relative or absolute) detriment of poor majorities in the continent. This is a first, fundamental ambiguity in the Canadian policy stance.

b) Trade Policy: Cartels and Manufactured Exports:

What of Canadian trade policy? As Professor Helleiner of the University of Toronto stresses,[16]

> one cannot separate aid relationships from commercial ones. One cannot, on the one hand, pump finance described as "aid" into poor nations, and, on the other hand, pursue commercial policies which deprive these same nations of the better prices and the market access which are essential for their self-sufficient and self-sustained growth.

Two particular trade issues deserve attention: first, Canada's attitude toward poorer nations' efforts to raise their returns from raw material exports to this country; second, the nature of Canadian market access permitted less-developed countries—in particular the degree of access permitted their manufactured exports.

Raising raw material export returns can take a number of forms, Canada, for instance, levies import duties on a number of important African agricultural products, including coffee and cocoa (key exports to Canada from Ghana, Nigeria, Kenya, Tanzania, Cameroun, Zaire and the Ivory Coast). Such levies mean that some of the price Canadians pay for such commodities does not go to poor-country producers, as would be the case if either those duties were eliminated, or preferably, the revenue collected through the Canadian levies were automatically turned over to the producer countries.

Of more immediate importance to poorer countries, however, are co-operative efforts to raise international prices for their agricultural and resource exports. Generally speaking, over the relevant range of likely prices involved, developed country demand for such exports is price inelastic (i.e. demand changes comparatively little in response to comparatively large price changes). That means if producers can co-operate to cut back world sales a little, they will be rewarded with significantly higher per unit prices and increased total revenue from their export production. Such co-operation can follow one of two broad alternatives. Commodity agreements, involving both producer and consumer nations, can lead to longer-term price stability and somewhat higher prices for producers, as the International Coffee Agreement, first negotiated in 1962, has done. The essence of such agreements is that production cut-backs are negotiated, and arranged by quotas allocated to each producer country — with consumer nations then policing these quotas by reporting the sources of their imports of the commodity. Producer cartels, on the other hand, are unilateral arrangements, among producers alone, to cut back world sales and increase prices, as the OPEC countries have done in the case of oil. Such cartels, of course, are less stable than commodity agreements, since they have less effective means to police individual country production cut-backs; but cartels can also lead to much greater price increases on exports, since agreement to the prices by developed consumer countries is not necessary. (Conflict over price increases, for instance, complicated renegotiation of the International Coffee Agreement, as consumer countries resisted producer country pricing demands.)

Leaving aside OPEC, two emerging producer cartels are important in the Canadian-African relationship. The International Bauxite Association (IBA) involves the African producers of a significant Canadian import from the continent, while such African copper producers as Zambia and Zaire are involved in CIPEC, the copper equivalent of OPEC. The Coffee Agreement remains the most important commodity agreement in the Canadian-African relationship.

Canadian policy could make several positive responses to these efforts by poorer nations to increase their export revenues. The economics of producer cartel success are complex, but one clear factor is the percentage of overall world production of the particular commodity which members of the cartel control; thus, in the case of CIPEC, Canada's participation in the cartel, as an important copper exporter, could significantly improve poorer producers' chances of escalating their earnings. (Australia's participation in the IBA, for instance, has improved that cartel's chances of success). Canada could also co-operate with poorer producers in establishing higher commodity prices for Canadian imports. This could be especially important in commodity agreement cases, such as coffee, but a positive response from at least some consumer countries can also help producer cartels in other commodities, such as bauxite, succeed.

In fact, however, Canadian policy has been basically negative on these issues. The Departments of Industry, Trade and Commerce and External Affairs sources suggest that Canada has followed the United States' lead in resisting ICA coffee price increases, has refused to countenance participation in CIPEC, and has opposed, insofar as possible, the formation of new cartels, such as the IBA. In practice, Canada's role in policy areas critically affecting Africa has thus reflected concern to maintain low-cost raw material imports, rather than concern for social justice.

Over the longer run, even more important for less developed countries than higher commodity prices is easy access to developed country markets for manufactured goods, since such markets are growing much faster than commodity markets. In practice, Canada's trade policy has restricted such access very considerably; in 1972, only 3 percent of Canada's manufactured imports came from less-developed nations.

Canadian trade restrictions rest on both tariff and non-tariff barriers to manufactured exports. In the sixties, average Canadian tariff rates on goods manufactured mainly by poor countries were much higher than on manufactures of interest to developed country exporters (14 percent as opposed to 8 percent). When different tariff rates on raw input imports are taken into account, moreover, Canadian leather industries could produce at costs 49.9 percent above world market costs before poor country producers, after paying Canadian duty, could compete with them on price; similarly, Canadian textile industries could produce at 38.4 percent above world costs, knitting mills at 91.1 percent above, and clothing industries at 44.8 percent above.[17] Despite these tariff barriers, however, exports of such goods from poorer nations to Canada have grown, with the result that Canada has used non-tariff barriers to restrict market entry. Legislation has given the Canadian government power to impose import quotas on manufactued goods, if importation is "causing or threatening serious injury" to Canadian producers. The threat of using such quotas has, in turn, been used to persuade poor country producers to accept "voluntary" restraints on manufactured exports to Canada; as of 1974, eighteen countries, including at least twelve less-developed countries, had entered export restraint agreements with Canada, covering twenty products. Such restrictions are particularly prevalent in the textile and clothing sectors which, with footwear, comprise the bulk of Canadian manufactered imports from the Third World.

These Canadian non-tariff barriers have not so far had a notable effect on poor *African* countries; only Egypt, for instance, has been forced into voluntary restraints of exports to Canada. Moreover, in mid-1974, Canada introduced a generalized system of preferences into its tariff, lowering rates for less-developed countries to two thirds of the lowest existing developed country rates. That change will tend to offset existing Canadian trade policy discrimination against poor nations' manufactured exports.

Ambiguities remain, however; textile, clothing and footwear were exempted from these new preferences; and non-tariff barriers persist, constraining potential African manufactured exports to Canada. Overall, concern for inefficient domestic manufacturing industries, many of them concentrated in Quebec, has outweighed concern for international social justice in these aspects of Canada's foreign policy, too.

c) Canadian Multinationals in Africa:

Canadian policy encourages direct foreign investment in independent Africa, and there are ambiguities in that stance, too, given the "social justice" perspective articulated by Canadian spokesmen. This is not the place for a detailed discussion of the nature of multinational corporations and their impact on poorer economies.[18] Two problems associated with their spread in Africa deserve note, however.

First, in many respects, their impact on Africa reflects the ambiguities of foreign aid, discussed above. Their investment serves to build up a small, capital-intensive "modern" sector of the economy, to the potential detriment of poor majorities in African countries. Small numbers of workers may be hired, for production processes that often rely heavily on imported inputs, while larger numbers of small-scale producers, using local inputs, find their activities disrupted and undermined.[19] The difference between foreign aid and foreign direct investment is that the latter involves higher costs to the host country (in the shape of dividends and fees paid abroad), and may involve taste transfer efforts (such as advertising) that strengthen the disruptive impact of "modern" sector expansion.

A case study of Bata operations in Kenya, for instance, found that this Canadian-based company was much more capital-intensive than local shoe manufacturing enterprises, that it therefore imported much more machinery from abroad (much of it sold by other Bata subsidiaries), and that it imported relatively more raw materials because it made much of its footwear from plastic and rubber. The result was beneficial to its 2,000 employees, based in a comparatively wealthy region, but Bata's aggressive marketing of "modern" shoes undercut local, labour-intensive enterprises throughout the rest of Kenya. In one district alone (a poorer rural and town area seventy miles from Nairobi), eighteen of thirty-two shoe manufacturers interviewed reported significant disruption from Bata's expansion.[20]

Foreign direct investment therefore can further economic inequality in poorer countries. That is one problem. The second problem is the bargaining power multinational corporations carry into their activities in the Third World.

Multinational firms have many strengths in their negotiations with governments. They have long experience and skilled bargaining expertise to call on; they control some key items in the international economy, such as sophisticated technology and easy access to brand-name-conscious, developed country markets; and they have considerable financial resources and job opportunities to use in rewarding people. As a number of studies have stressed, these strengths lead to great inequalities in bargaining.[21] Multinationals also find it possible to develop local political influence in less developed countries and to shape advantages for themselves as a result — a central aspect of international dependency relations. As a senior civil servant described one Bata request for a favour in Kenya, "We are not happy about it; nor is the Treasury happy; but there's very heavy political pressure on my Minister."

The most important advantages multinational firms usually negotiate for themselves are high tariff and quota protection in local markets, and bargain-basement concessions in important export projects.[22] The latter cut down the nation's long-term earning prospects (though the concessions may be renegotiated later). The former give multinationals monopoly power in local markets, and force poor consumers to pay higher than necessary prices for formerly imported products. At the same time, high multinational company profits, either declared or surreptitious,[23] reflect and extend these concessions.

Some multinational investments, of course, can benefit poor African countries (by transferring certain essential technology or providing market access abroad, for instance), but the criticisms above suggest that most multinational enterprises will not make such contributions to long-run egalitarian development. The Canadian government's blanket encouragement of Canadian corporate enterprise in Africa is therefore exceedingly dubious in a policy approach committed to "social justice".

d) Canada and Southern Africa:

Perhaps the most glaring ambiguities in the Canadian policy stance, though, emerge in the context of articulated commitments to "human rights and dignity in Southern Africa". In 1970, in its foreign policy white paper, the government adopted a position which condemned South Africa's "apartheid" policies of racial domination, yet also recognized Canadian business interests in the better-than-normal trade and investment opportunities in the country. In doing this, as the superb 1970 *Black Paper* critique of Canadian Southern African policy put it, the government.

> consciously placed a price tag on the basic social and political values which Canadians might expect their foreign policy to reflect. . . It has entrenched the dichotomy between the strong affirmation of basic policies and the weak and inconsistent implementation of them.[24]

Since 1970, the political situation in Southern Africa as a whole has changed dramatically. Military revolt in Portugal has spurred colonial independence in Mozambique and Angola; the Pearce Commission gave Rhodesian Africans the chance to articulate their rejection of Ian Smith's white regime;[25] guerrilla warfare has expanded inside Rhodesia; and under South African pressure, the Smith government has moved in the direction of negotiations and concessions on the African role there. In the context of this general upheaval in the area, the Organization of African Unity has even expressed some willingness to negotiate directly with South Africa in the hopes of generating fundamental reforms inside that country.

In all this, the South African strategy has been fairly clear. It seeks to normalize its relations with black Africa, not just for security reasons, but because its own changing economic structure, based more around manufacturing now than mineral resource extraction, requires the sorts of export markets African countries could provide. However, at the same time, South Africa seeks to maintain intact its own internal racial structures, which in 1971 generated average per capita incomes for Africans of some $140, and for whites of over $2,400 and seemed to be widening the income gaps between the racial communities.[26]

Despite the dramatic changes in Southern Africa, Canadian policy has remained basically the same. Ottawa continues to condemn South African racism publicly, while encouraging Canadian business to share in the high profits that racism generates. Canadian trade promotion with South Africa has been stepped up; Canada maintains its Commonwealth Trade Preferences with South Africa (despite the latter's exit from the Commonwealth in 1961); as noted above, Canadian direct investment in South Africa has accelerated significantly, and this investment has included large investments in Namibia, the former South West Africa, which the U.N. has officially removed from South African control. Such investments are against U.N. policy, which the United States, for instance, has supported by officially discouraging U.S. investment in Namibia, and banning export credits for trade there.[27] Canada has taken no such position. The contradiction in Canada's stance remains as disturbing as it was in 1970, when the *Black Paper* made its critique:

> foreign policy cannot be considered apart from trade policy. In a very real sense, Alcan's and George Weston Limited's extensive investments in South Africa and Falconbridge's copper and silver explorations in Namibia are at least as important an aspect of Canada's foreign policies as the rhetoric or the voting record of our representatives at the United Nations. If we do nothing, we are not thereby neutral. The Canadian economic involvement which such a "doing nothing" stance permits, reinforces these regimes by its contribution to the strength of their economies . . . . [28]

What of the argument that Canadian investment and trade help break down South African racism, since our companies will not be committed to apartheid policies? Two 1973 reports have surely demolished that apology definitively. In a detailed investigation of Canadian companies in South Africa, a YWCA Committee found " that foreign investment has not been and is not likely to become a liberalizing force in South Africa."[29] While an on-the-spot study of most large Canadian-owned subsidiaries in the country, by journalist Hugh Nangle, showed the majority of them paying many of their black workers below recognized subsistence levels, and all of them co-operating fully in the racial job classification systems that maintain apartheid. Nangle concluded that Canadian investment in South Africa "has been a reinforcing element in racism and repression".[30]

It is difficult to see Canadian government encouragement of such trade and investment, then, as anything other than a concern for short-term economic advantages. The problem with such a stance is cumulative, too, as the 1973 YWCA Report stressed: "The more Canadian economic interests become intertwined and aligned with the interests of the apartheid system the more reluctant will Canadians and their government become to initiate policies consistent with Canadian values and the principle of social justice."[31] Such reluctance is particularly unfortunate in the current fluid situation in Southern Africa, where some firm economic initiatives by a number of developed countries might help force South Africa into some major concessions in negotiations with Black Africa: in particular, independence for Namibia and immediate majority rule in Rhodesia.

Canada and Africa: Neocolonialism or New Economic Order.
This chapter has approached the Canadian role in Africa from two perspectives. Section one outlined the accelerating Canadian economic relationship with Africa. Section two examined Canadian policy stances in Africa, in the context of government emphasis on "social justice" and "human dignity" as its special concerns there. This second examination showed up serious ambiguities in Canadian policy, when evaluated in terms of those concerns; while the nature of accelerating Canadian economic interests in Africa was clearly similar to those of other developed capitalist countries.

Combining these perspectives, it is hard to avoid the conclusion that, in fact, Canada's primary concern in its role in Africa is the search for economic advantage. That explains the ambiguities in policy: foreign aid is tied to Canadian exports, because a major part of its purpose is to build markets for those exports; trade policy follows conventional self-interest, because that is its mandate; foreign investment is encouraged, because it will benefit Canadian corporations; and South African ties are encouraged, because they are profitable.

This is not to say that Canada's *only* concern in Africa is economic advantage; there are enough humanitarians in government to avoid such a simple position, and a certain constituency in the country that supports Third World social justice sufficiently to give government humanitarianism a political justification. But "hard-nosed" men in the Department of Industry, Trade and Commerce, and "realists" in the External Affairs Department see to it that humanitarianism doesn't hinder unduly the search for economic advantage. Canada will implement generalized preferences for less-developed countries, but not on the main Third World industrial goods the country imports. Ottawa will condemn continued South African control of Namibia, but will not impede Canadian corporate investments there. CIDA will stress rural development, but will not cease tying aid, though that is essential to facilitate such broader-based growth. The Prime Minister's office will talk of commitments to international equality, but will not have Canada support significantly higher world coffee prices.

What does this search for economic advantage reflect? In part it reflects the special interest and privileged access to government of Canada's large corporations — those that buy the low cost imports from Africa, sell profitable exports through aid, and draw the returns from direct investment there. Such firms have significant informal influence on our government, especially in African countries, where our embassies serve Canadian businessmen with special attention. This influence is all the more effective because opposing groups have little organized, continuing voice in Canada, despite the efforts of Oxfam, the YWCA, various academic groups and returned CUSO volunteers. In part, too, however, Canada's role in Africa may reflect broad government economic strategy. Ottawa seems to be attempting to widen Canadian trade links, and to encourage the growth of Canadian multinational corporations — all to lessen the preeminence of Canadian ties to the U.S. economy.[32] Africa, the Caribbean and Latin America represent soft markets for such efforts, as well as profitable bases from which Canadian multinational corporations can grow.

The result is that Canada becomes a kind of quiet, second-string partner of the U.K., France and the U.S. in building up in Africa new patterns of dependence which leave poor African countries increasingly dependent on developed country technology, on primary product sales in developed country markets, and on direct investment inflows. These patterns, as noted above, shape the internal dominance in African states of wealthy local classes that seek to maintain such dependent ties.

The alternative to that new-style colonialism is what Third World countries now talk of as a New Economic Order. Their rhetoric focuses mostly on commodity price increases at the moment, but the key implications of their strategy are much more co-operation among poorer countries, much more self-reliance in technology and investment, and therefore much less dependence on developed capitalist economies. To mean much for the poor majorities of the world, the strategy must also imply profound income and asset redistribution within less-developed countries. This can only be made possible by breaking the control of those wealthy local classes strengthened by the international dependence relationship.

How could Canada's role in Africa adjust to favour that alternative? Some relatively simple changes in policy could be made. First, Canada could reshape its aid programme, particularly by untying it from Canadian exports, pumping more of it through multilateral channels like the U.N., and concentrating bilateral aid in countries following egalitarian development strategies. Trade policy reform could be even more important, especially a more positive response to producer cartels and commodity agreements, and reforms giving fuller Canadian market access to Third World manufactured exports (made possible by government adjustment assistance to low-wage Canadian producers, such as Quebec textile workers). The government could also cease its indiscriminate efforts to promote Canadian direct investment abroad; like the Danish government, Ottawa could assist only those particular Canadian firms establishing projects very clearly of benefit to the poor majorities of less-developed countries.[33] Canada could also institutionalize ways to help

197

poorer nations bargain better with Canadian companies abroad, and establish means by which such countries could avoid relying so much on the multinationals. For instance, Ottawa could establish a Canadian marketing agency to provide poorer countries with easier entry to Canadian marketing channels, and use the International Development Research Centre to help build up alternate means of technology transfer to less-developed nations. Finally, Ottawa could accelerate change in Southern Africa, by eliminating trade preferences for South Africa, shifting Canadian trade commissioners out of that country, and discouraging ties between Canadian business and the South African economy.

Foreign policy roles, like political stances generally, usually reflect some basic socio-economic forces at work in a political economy. It is somewhat unreal to paint possible reforms in Canada's role in Africa in abstraction from the issue of what forces might support such a changed role. A constituency is emerging in Canada with a more sophisticated understanding of the problems of Third World poverty and a realization that more "foreign aid" is not the answer to these problems. But that constituency remains very small. Moreover, it seems clear that much lessened influence for Canada's large corporations is a prerequisite for change, and, given that the search for economic advantage in Africa may respond to U.S. ties at home, a reformulated strategy for Canada toward the U.S. may also be necessary. Ironically, then, it is by identifying social forces which will cut back special corporate influence inside Canada, and generate a changed Canadian strategy toward the United States, that one may be most likely to identify the social forces through which a change in Canada's role in Africa will be generated. If such forces are committed to social justice and human dignity at home, they may take a *serious* commitment to those concerns into the Canadian-African relationship.

Notes

1. All statistics on trade in the chapter are calculated from Statistics Canada publications, by year, from 1968 to 1974, issued under the following titles: *Imports by Country; Imports by Commodity; Exports by Country; Exports by Commodity.*

2. Allan MacEachen, "Canada and Africa", Speech to the Conference of the Canadian Association of African Studies, Toronto, February 19th, 1975, pp. 2-4.

3. K. V. Ram, "Canadian Missions in Africa: A Survey", Paper presented to the 1975 Conference of the Canadian Association of African Studies, York University, p. 1.

4. See W. G. Huff, "Canadian Bilateral Aid: Canadian content and Balance-of-Payments Cost," *Journal of World Trade Law*, Vol. 7, No. 5, (Sept.-Oct. 1973), pp. 587-595.

5. Ghana, Kenya, Nigeria, Sierra Leone, Tanzania, Zambia, Cameroun, Zaire, Gabon, Guinea, Ivory Coast, Liberia, Mauritania, Senegal.

6. Statistics Canada, *Quarterly Estimates of the Canadian Balance of International Payments*, 1973-1974.

7. G. Bailey, "Canadian Bilateral Aid as a Promoter of Exports," 1974. (Unpublished paper for the School of International Affairs, Carleton University.)

8. See such critics as Pierre Jalée, *The Pillage of the Third World*, 1968; A. G. Frank, *Capitalism and Underdevelopment in Latin America*, 1967; H. Magdoff, *The Age of Imperialism,* 1966; A. Amin, *Neo-Colonialism in West Africa*, 1973.

9. MacEachen, *op. cit.*, pp. 1-2.

10. See W. W. Rostow, "The Take-Off into Self-sustained Growth," in A. N. Agarwala and S. P. Singh, eds., *The Economics of Underdevelopment*, 1958.

11. I. Adelman & C. Morris, *Economic Growth and Social Equity in Developing Countries*, 1973. See also H. Chenery *et. al., Redistribution With Growth,* 1974, chap. 1.

12. See the argument developed in Adelman & Morris, *op. cit.,* chap. 4 and 5.

13. For details of this project and its effects, see J. Loxley and J. S. Saul, "Multinationals, Workers and the Parastatals in Tanzania," *Review of African Political Economy,* Vol. I, No. 2 (1975), p. 74.

14. The most comprehensive outline of such a strategy in the Africa context can be found in International Labour Office, *Employment, Incomes and Equality: A Strategy for Increasing Productive Employment in Kenya*, Geneva, 1972.

15. Government of Tanzania, "Co-operation Against Pover-

ty", Presentation to the Conference of Non-Aligned States, Lusaka, Zambia, 1970.

16. G. K. Helleiner, "Canadian Commercial Relationships with the Third World", in L. Freeman, ed., *Unequal Partners: Development in the Seventies — Where Does Canada Stand?*, 1970, p. 14.

17. This paragraph draws on data and analysis from G. K. Helleiner, "Manufactued Exports from Less Developed Countries and Industrial Adjustment in Canada", mimeo, 1974.

18. For an introduction to the debate, see: N. Girvan, "Multinational Corporations and Dependent Underdevelopment in Mineral-Export economies," *Social and Economic Studies,* Dec. 1970; G. L. Reuber, *Private Foreign Investment in Development*, 1973; J. Rweyemamu, "The Political Economy of Foreign Private Investment in the Underdeveloped Countries," *The African Review*, March 1971; P. Streeten, "The Multinational Enterprise and the Theory of Development Policy," *World Development*, Vol. 1, No. 10 (October 1973).

19. A case study of the operations of multinational corporations in the Kenyan soap industry shows this effect. See: S. W. Langdon, "Multinational Corporations, Taste Transfer and Underdevelopment: A Case Study from Kenya," *Review of African Political Economy*, 1975.

20. Discussed in more detail in: S.W. Langdon, "Canadians, too, can act like Imperialists . . .", *Saturday Night,* Jan. 1974.

21. See F. Perroux and R. Demonts, "Large Firm — Small Nation," *Presence Africaine*, 1962; D. Seers, "Big Companies and Small Countries," *Kyklos,* 16:4, 1963.

22. One example in Kenya saw a Danish horticulture export company bargain out a ban on competing company activity for 8 years, plus a 25 year exemption from new taxes. See: J. Carlsen, "Danish Private Investment in Kenya," Institute for Development Research (Copenhagen, 1973); pp. 35, 44, 53.

23. Profits may be repatriated surreptitiously by subsidiaries through paying higher than market prices for parent imports or charging lower than market prices for exports to the parent. See: S. Lall, "Transfer-Pricing by Multinational

Manufacturing Firms," *Oxford Bulletin of Economics and Statistics*, Aug. 1973.

24. G. Legge, C. Pratt, R. Williams and H. Winsor, *The Black Paper: An Alternative Policy for Canada Towards Southern Africa*, 1970, p. 1.

25. See United Kingdom, *Rhodesia: Report of the Commission on Rhodesian Opinion under the Chairmanship of the Right Honourable the Lord Pearce*, May, 1972.

26. Study and Action Committee of the World Relationships Committee of the YWCA, *Investment in Oppression*, 1973, pp. 27-30.

27. Much U.S. investment abroad is guaranteed against expropriation by American government agencies, and partially financed by credit from the government's Export-Import Bank. The U.S. government now refuses such support to investors in Namibia, and seeks to persuade its companies not to invest there. See *ibid.*, p. 38.

28. Legge, Pratt, Williams & Winsor, *op. cit.*, p. 11.

29. Study and Action Committee, *op. cit.*, p. 39.

30. See the Ottawa *Citizen*, June 22, 1973—June 29, 1973.

31. Study and Action Committee, *op. cit.*, p. 41.

32. See, for instance, Alastair Gillespie, later the Minister of Industry, Trade and Commerce, arguing for such development of Canadian multinationals in D. Godfrey, ed., *Gordon to Watkins to You*, 1970.

33. The Danish government operates an Industrialization Fund for Developing Countries; it will provide loan or share-capital for Danish firms investing in poorer countries, if the projects meet various development criteria — such as generating rural employment in particularly underdeveloped parts of the poor country. The Fund does not, however, appear to keep a close enough watch on the projects in which it becomes involved, with the result that some projects established with its support also take exploitative advantage of less-developed countries. See Carlsen, *op. cit.*, pp. 35 ff. Interestingly, however, Carlsen's critical study was part of a programme to monitor Danish investment in poorer countries, set up by the government-funded Institute for Development Research in Copenhagen. Such a programme could also be initiated by the Canadian government.

CHAPTER 9

CANADIAN POLICY
AND THE
DEVELOPMENT OF
LATIN AMERICA *

Stephen J. Randall

Nothing could have thrust Canadians into more direct awareness of Latin America than the harsh realities of the military overthrow of Chilean President Salvador Allende in September of 1973. The Trudeau Government, especially Mitchell Sharp, then Secretary of State for External Affairs, appears to have been surprised by the intensity of the concern among Canadians over Chilean civil liberties and the plight of its refugees. Yet that public response, from the churches, labour organizations, civil liberties groups, and professional associations underscores the changes of the past decade that have taken place in the Canadian perception of Latin America and the Third World.

A growing public awareness and a fundamental alteration in foreign policy are, however, rather different phenomena. It could be argued with some conviction that a country of marginal economic, political and military power such as Canada, which is nevertheless viewed as part of the industrialized modern world, has little role to play in a geographic area long considered an American sphere of influence. Given the generally pro-United States position of foreign policy since 1945, one is confronted with the rather fundamental question whether Canada can achieve anything more than a collaborative role vis-a-vis the U.S. in Latin America. If there is room for an independent Canadian

*Author's note: For the purposes of this chapter Latin America is defined as the Spanish and Portuguese speaking countries of South and Central America.

role, in what area does it lie and what efforts have Canadian governments made in the recent past to tap that potential? A brief examination of the current state of Latin America places our role in perspective and suggests where there may exist some latitude for a truly progressive, small-scale Canadian contribution in the future during the vital decades in which the developed and developing nations may move closer to a power equilibrium.

I

Although few would question the sophistication of the cultural and intellectual traditions of Latin America, in that area which we have loosely termed "progress" the region continues to hover on the brink of modernization. Some sectors have developed more rapidly than others, and the gap between rich and poor continues to widen under the half-hearted and often ill-devised efforts to redistribute wealth. With 300 million people, ranging from Brazil's 102 million to the 2 million of Panama, Latin America represents 8 percent of the world total. Its population doubled between 1930 and the 1960's and will double again before the turn of the century. The density of population, long a problem, has become acute with the continued shift from rural to urban. In the thirty years it took the Latin American population to double, the urban population tripled; the segment showing the most marked growth has been the poverty-ridden areas of the cities, where an estimated 20 percent of all Latin Americans now reside. The statistics suggest that this marginal group is increasing at the approximate rate of 15 percent a year and if not checked will represent an insurmountable dilemma for human development. Statistics pertaining to population density are misleading; in terms of total area, density appears to be low, but when considered in terms of actual settlement patterns the concentration of population is apparent. In 1971 Central America had a density of 34.2 per hectare (2.47 acres), and South America 13.9 per hectare as compared with Canada's 2.3. Central American countries remain primarily rural in population, but further south the picture changes. Uruguay and Venezuela with 80.8 percent and 78.4 percent urban respectively have higher concentrations in cities than Canada (73.6 percent). Other countries are not far behind; Chile is over 68 percent; Mexico is almost 60 percent; Brazil, with its vast plains and unsettled jungle areas is 56 percent urban and

203

boasts two cities over 9 million inhabitants. Colombia is 53 percent urban.[1]

Some control over population growth is of course essential if development objectives in the areas of health, housing, and employment are to be realized. For Venezuela, for example, to reduce unemployment to 5 percent, given its current population growth (which is slow compared to the continent as a whole) would necessitate adding 1.65 million new jobs by 1985 combined with an economic growth rate of 6.8 percent per year. Mexico also needs to create 600,000 new jobs each year simply to maintain its current growth rate, but that in itself will do nothing to alleviate its estimated housing shortage of 3.5 million units, illiteracy rate of 20 percent and maldistribution of medical services. The prospects for such growth in the region as a whole are gloomy. The manufacturing sector has in the past failed to create the number of jobs anticipated and in fact accounts for a decreasing proportion of total employment, although service industries remain one of the rapid growth areas.

Health problems are one of the most serious by-products of over-population and poverty. Especially tragic is the high infant mortality rate. In the first half of the 1960's, deaths for those under five years of age accounted for 42 percent of total deaths compared with 7 percent in Europe in the same period. Infant deaths in the 1950's and 1960's ranged from Brazil's high of 107.6 per 1,000 births (1959) to Venezuela's low of 46.9 (1969), as compared with Canada's 19.3 (1969). A 1973 Pan American Health Organization study comparing ten countries indicated that nutritional deficiency was the most important factor in these deaths and that the problem is more acute in rural than in urban areas.

Industrialization has made important gains in the past half century, yet agriculture remains the sector which most closely touches the lives of Latin Americans.[2] In 1970 the agricultural sector contributed two thirds of the total product in Latin America as a whole, and one third in Chile, Argentina, and Uruguay. Agriculture has, however, failed to achieve its potential either because of inefficiency of labour and management or because of the desperate need for land reform.

The inability of agriculture to absorb the expanding population is reflected in the annual urban migration of thousands of landless agricultural workers in search of employment and attracted by promises of higher wages. The higher average incomes characteristic of the urban dweller are reflected as well in the generally inequitable distribution of incomes. A 1966 study by the Economic commission for Latin America revealed that the highest 20 percent of the population received an average income twelve times that of the bottom 50 percent compared with the United States where the highest 20 percent earn five times that of the lowest 50 percent.

Even the most authoritarian and conservative Latin American regimes have come to accept some form of agrarian reform as essential. The typical campesino (rural dweller) subsists on a tiny plot of land (minifundia) of a few acres. In Latin America as a whole, 75 to 80 percent of all farmers have farms smaller than twelve acres in size, constituting collectively less than 10 percent of arable land, leaving a small percentage of landowners in control of more than 70 percent of the productive land (the phenomenon of latifundia, legally defined as holdings of more than 80 basic irrigated hectares). Ecuador provides a striking example of this; in the 1960's some 100,000 farms constituted only 1 percent of the available agricultural land.

The need to meet the crisis of the countryside, as well as to alleviate the pressures on the cities, has led most countries to attempt some form of agrarian reform in the past generation, from the more radical approach of Chile, Peru, Mexico and Bolivia to the cautious progressivism of Colombia. It is generally agreed that if land reform is to be purposeful it has to be on a large scale and to be implemented with sufficient speed to mitigate opposition from traditional landed elites. The less than complete success realized by various reform programs stems not so much from a lack of sincerity on the part of those initiating the reform as from political opposition, the absence of strong peasant organizations to provide local support, and technical, legal, and administrative difficulties related especially to the crucial issue of compensation for expropriation.

Chile under Allende provides one of the most pertinent examples, largely because the Allende Government adhered very closely to the model for effective agrarian reform.[3] When Allende assumed office, Chile already possessed a decade old legal and political commitment to reform derived from the Presidencies of Jorge Alessandri and Eduardo Frei. In fact, Chile had created an Agricultural Colonization Bank as early as the 1920s; but colonization proved to be a poor substitute for substantial reform. Under pressure from campesino organizations as well as Alliance for Progress agencies, Alessandri supported the establishment in 1962 of an Agrarian Reform Corporation (CORA) and an Institute for the Development of Agriculture and Livestock. The 1962 legislation was highly ineffective at least partly because it failed to challenge the power of the large landowners. Since Chilean law provided that no land could come under CORA until full compensation had been paid, wholesale redistribution was almost impossible. Frei and the Christian Democrats went further, identifying the objective of reform as the establishment of individual family farms. 1967 legislation strengthened the government's power to expropriate for social progress and to pay compensation for a thirty year period. Although the pace of redistribution was not sufficiently rapid to satisfy all political factions, there is little doubt that Frei's government made substantial progress over that of his predecessor. By mid-1970 approximately 20,000 families had been resettled, mostly in the better agricultural areas of the Central Valley, although this was short of the projected 100,000 families.

What most distinguished Allende's agricultural reform from that of the Christian Democrats was the commitment to breaking the economic and political power of the old landed elites as a necessary prerequisite to reform. Although Allende's Minister of Agriculture, Jacques Chonochol, worked essentially within the limits of the 1967 agrarian legislation, it was this commitment to reform that made possible the subsequent achievements. Still hampered by political opposition and legal delays, the Allende Government nevertheless expropriated and brought under the direction of the reform administration almost 20 percent of the nation's agricultural land. This compares favourably with the less revolutionary accomplishments of Ecuador and Colombia where only 5 to 10 percent of the agricultural land has been directly affected by the reform administration. Whether or not agrarian reform was responsible, and in spite of serious subsequent problems related to agricultural productivity, the fact remains that 1972 marked the highest availability of food per capita in Chilean history.

In the economic sector as a whole, several Latin American countries have in the past generation moved haltingly, but with some determination, toward a more substantial control over the process of industrialization and natural resource development. Sparked by the example of Bolivia and Mexico in the 1930s and Peru in the 1960s, Canada's major trading partner in South America, Venezuela, in the summer of 1975 passed an oil nationalization law which will ultimately bring the industry fully under state control. Emboldened by the wealth derived from petroleum and its membership in OPEC the Christian Democratic government of President Andrés Pérez has also made overtures for the leadership of the continent, agreeing to underwrite a number of development projects in Central America and attempting to create SELA (Economic System for Latin America). Resource control is an area where Canadians have a good deal in common with Latin America, especially in terms of relations with the United States. This shared experience combined with an element of Latin American nationalism may serve to loosen the hold of United States' interests and expand Canadian involvement. Yet that same nationalism may operate to threaten Canadian investment, especially long-established firms such as The Royal Bank of Canada and Brascan, and this threat alone may push Canada into a collaborative position vis-a-vis the United States in attempting to contain the thrust of nationalist economic policies abroad.

II

This then is the Latin America with which Canada must come to terms, and it is by no means certain that Canadian interests can be fully reconciled with the effective social and economic development of Latin America. The challenge which confronts Canadian policy is a Latin America which needs development and the revolutionary redistribution of wealth, where the force of nationalism has been used and abused by both left and right on the political spectrum, where the collective voice of the developing world has become more strident and more insistent in its demand upon the peoples of the developed international community. Thus far the Canadian performance has fallen substantially short of making Canadian policy the "cutting edge of the left".

The recent flurry of Canadian business interest in Latin America should not obscure the fact that in terms of our overall objectives in foreign policy Latin America has and will continue to occupy a position of marginal importance, as much as many of us would like to see it otherwise. Our traditional orientation toward Europe, the Commonwealth, francophone areas and the United States has been supplemented in the past generation by enhanced relations with Pacific perimeter countries and the Middle East. It is within the context of this general expansion of Canadian involvement abroad that Canadian interests have strengthened ties with Latin America.[4]

Diplomatically, Canadian involvement in Latin America dates from Canada's emergence from its own formal colonial status in the 1930s and World War Two years, when there was mutual benefit for Canada and several of the major Latin American powers to expand relations. Brazil and Argentina, partly to offset United States power, evinced new interest in Canada in this period, although formal commercial ties had existed with both countries since 1911. Canada did exchange ministers with the two nations and with Chile, Cuba, Venezuela, Mexico and Peru before the end of 1946, but United States opposition to Canadian entry into the Pan American Union and Mackenzie King's reluctance to become embroiled in a region dominated by the United States tended at this juncture to retard the development of a fuller relationship.[5] Where there was government initiative, it tended to be in the area of trade. James MacKinnon, Minister of Trade and Commerce during the war, led commercial missions to Latin America in 1941 and 1946, the latter leading to the conclusion of most-favoured-nation agreements with Colombia and Mexico, although Colombia in fact never ratified the agreement.

Outside government circles, interest in Latin American affairs remained marginal in the 1940s. The major exception to this lack of public interest in Latin America was and has been French Canada where there is much more substantial cultural affinity for the region. During the war years nationalist elements viewed the Latin American connection as a potential counterweight against both Great Britain and the United States. One manifestation of this sentiment was the formation in 1940 of the Union des Latins d'Amérique, with the Rector of the University of Montreal as honorary president and supported by the Roman Catholic Church, among other groups.

For more than a decade after 1946, the official enthusiasm of the war years trailed off. There were continued efforts to expand commercial relations, but such highly publicized initiatives as the C. D. Howe mission in 1953 had only marginal results. Canadian political leaders in the late 1940s and the 1950s, including Louis St. Laurent, Vincent Massey, and Lester Pearson, tended to be unsympathetic to expanding the Canadian role in the inter-American system and opposed to membership in the Pan American Union, a posture which received the support of the English language press. Ironically, the United States now courted the Canadian connection. John Foster Dulles, speaking in Toronto in 1948, openly recommended Canadian membership in the Pan American Union, but like John F. Kennedy's similar suggestion more than a decade later, this recommendation was not well received.[6]

The late 1950s and the early 1960s, until the Cuban revolution and later the missile crisis intervened to cloud Canadian perspectives, marked a new high point in official interest in Latin America. John Diefenbaker's first Secretary of State for External Affairs, Sidney Smith, and his successor, Howard Green, both selected Latin America as a neglected area of Canadian policy where they could leave their personal imprint. Smith led a mission to Brazil, Peru, and Mexico in late 1958; under Green's direction External Affairs established a Latin American Division in 1960. By the end of the following year Canada had opened formal diplomatic relations with all nations in the hemisphere. As a non-member of the Organization of American States (OAS), Canada managed as well to maintain its diplomatic and commercial relations with Cuba at a time that the United States and most member states were breaking relations and imposing economic sanctions. Our Cuban policy derived to a degree from the anti-American orientation of the Diefenbaker government, which followed the British lead in maintaining formal ties with Castro's Cuba. That policy also made good business sense from the perspective of Canadian interests in Cuba which stood to profit from continued relations at a time that United States firms and investments were being expropriated.

Interest was high in the early 1960s in the question of Canadian membership in the OAS. In 1961 Canada sent a delegate to the Quito meeting of the OAS and an official observer mission to the Punta del Este meeting that institutionalized the principles of the Alliance for Progress. Yet Canada continued to hold back from a specific commitment partly because of anxiety over the implications of membership for relations with the United States and partly because of doubts concerning the effectiveness of the OAS itself. Public opinion was highly fragmented, with opposition again coming from the leaders of the English language press such as the *Globe and Mail*, and from some businessmen reluctant to be further identified with the United States in their efforts to break into Latin American markets. On the other hand, *Time* (Canada), *Le Devoir*, The Canadian Chamber of Commerce and the Canadian Labour Congress expressed support for Canadian membership.[7]

Paul Martin's advocacy of membership throughout the 1960s heightened some expectations in External Affairs, but it seems to have been very much a solo flight with little if any endorsement within cabinet circles. Lester Pearson seems to have believed that American predominance in Latin America left little latitude for Canadian action, and his successor, Pierre Trudeau, articulated an equally unenthusiastic attitude toward the idea of OAS membership during the 1968 Liberal Party leadership campaign in his vague references to the possibility of greater Canadian involvement if Canada were ensured reasonable independence from the United States in decision-making.[8] The fact remains, of course, that once in office Trudeau did initiate what he hoped would be a significant reappraisal of Canadian foreign policy. Initially at least, that reappraisal involved financial belt-tightening with the result that in 1969 External Affairs closed three embassies in Latin America.

III

There was also, however, a more positive dimension to the reappraisal which was published in 1970 as a White Paper, *Foreign Policy For Canadians*. In 1972, four years after a large scale ministerial mission toured Latin America, and after almost three decades of debate, this country became one of the first nonmember states to be granted permanent observer status to the OAS.[9] External Affairs contends that the Canadian Government adopted this position in order to underline interest in inter-American relations and "to stress that this interest is not merely an extension of Canada's relations with the United States." Observer status excludes Canada from voting either in the Permanent Council or the General Assembly, but it does enable participation in some OAS deliberations, including the various

informal rounds of Foreign Ministers' meetings and two particular entities, the Inter-American Economic and Social Council and the Inter-American Council for Education, Science and
Culture. In addition, Canada is active in eight inter-American
institutes, some of which it has recently joined. A Canadian currently heads the geography committee of the Pan American Institute of Geography and History, centred in Mexico City, and
Arthur Blanchette, Director of the Historical Division, External
Affairs, is on the Board of the Institute. Canada is also a
member of the Statistical Institute (since 1943); the Inter-
American Centre for Tax Administrators; the Centre for Latin
American Monetary Studies; the Postal Union of the Americas
and Spain (since 1931); the Pan American Health Organization
(since 1871), which is the regional agency of the World Health
Organization; the Inter-American Institute of Agricultural
Sciences; and the Inter American Development Bank (BID).
From 1942 until we withdrew in 1955, Canada also belonged to
the Mexico-based Inter-American Conference on Social Security. Canada is not active, however, in the Inter-American
Children's Institute (Montevideo) or the Inter-American Commission of Women (Washington). Nor does it contribute to the
Indian Institute, in large part because of the apparent absence of
any meaningful interest in the organization among native Canadian groups.[10]

Canada's position in inter-American relations is perhaps not
as ambiguous as its observer status in the OAS implies. Although
the Latin American states recognize the fact that Canada is involved with parallel problems vis-a-vis the United States in the
area of resource controls, foreign investment, and national identity in general, Canada is nevertheless, by virtue of its wealth
and foreign aid programme, considered part of the developed
world dominated by the United States. Since the OAS represents
essentially two groups, the United States and the Latin
American states, were Canada to become a member, it would
become too closely identified with the United States. This is one
of the factors which has kept Canada out of the organization;
another has been the concern over the military dimension of the
OAS. According to the charter of the OAS, member nations are
required to sign the Rio Treaty of Mutual Assistance, which
pre-dates the creation of the OAS at the 1948 Bogota Conference.
Most of the large Latin American nations do not view the

defence aspect of the OAS as especially important, but from the point of view of the United States and several of the less powerful Latin American countries, the concept of security is a guarantee of military aid in the event of aggression, not only from outside the continent but also from one's neighbours. As long as collective security remains an integral function of the OAS (or perhaps more accurately as a front for unilateral action by the United States in sensitive areas), it is unlikely that Canada will consider membership.[11]

In a sense the military issue is a red herring. Economic and social questions comprise the real issues in the OAS. The Tenth Inter-American Conference in Caracas in 1954, for example, emphasized the economic, cultural and social development of the region, and except for the diversion of the Cuban revolution and "subversive" activities in the hemisphere in the 1960's that concern has only intensified, in spite of the fizzling out of the Kennedy-inspired Alliance for Progress. Most important in this respect was the Latin American meeting in Bogota in November, 1973, which provided the basis for the New Dialogue agenda considered at the Foreign Ministers' meeting at Tlatelolco (Mexico City) in March, 1974 and Washington eight weeks later. Centred out for discussion have been subjects of persistent concern in Latin American countries: the structure of international commerce and the monetary system; economic development; international corporations; the Panama Canal question; technology transfer. Most of these issues have cropped up with predictability over the past half century but have never been resolved to the satisfaction of either the United States or Latin America.[12]

In the area of trade, Latin America has pressed unsuccessfully for major tariff reductions to facilitate exports to the United States; at the same time the region maintains highly protective levels on imports. Secretary of State Kissinger asserted at Tlatelolco and Washington that the United States would not increase its tariff restrictions; but there have been no concessions of a general nature, and they are not likely to come in a period of deepening international economic difficulties. Yet, at the time of writing, early in 1975, twenty of the Latin American and Caribbean members of the OAS condemned the American Foreign Trade Act of 1974 for excluding members of the Organization of Petroleum Exporting Countries from the new tariff preferences contained in the Act, and there are similar attacks on the 1975 Act.

Since the failure of the OAS members present at the November, 1974 Quito meeting to succeed in lifting the Cuban embargo, the United States has shifted its position, placing Canada in a more comfortable position. The American policy in 1975 was the result of several factors: the hostile Latin American response to the failure of the Quito sessions and what some considered were "coercive and discriminatory" provisions in the 1975 United States Trade Act; the United States desire to place a damper on the growing influence of Venezuela and Peru in Latin America; and the friction in United States-Canadian relations resulting from the prohibition of America multinationals trading with Cuba. Consequently, in contrast to the Quito meeting in 1974 where the United States failed to send Henry Kissinger and where its delegates abstained from voting, in July 1975 at San José, Costa Rica, the United States delegation cast an influential favourable ballot. The following month the White House announced that it was lifting the ban on trade with Cuba by the foreign subsidiaries of American based multinationals.

The American measures have improved the Canadian position. Before mid-1975, the Trudeau government was caught between nationalists desiring greater control over United States firms operating in Canada, and the traditional continentalism of the Liberal Party. The lifting of the embargo and the potential for a normalization of Cuba's role in the hemisphere places Canada in a more stable position than it has been in since 1959 in its relations with Cuba. Yet, ironically, what Canadian influence on the decision may have existed was indirect. As an observer of OAS transactions Canada could lend no more than moral support to the deliberations at Quito and San José.[13]

Within the context of Canada's decision to seek observer status in the OAS, the Canadian government has also expanded in other areas of inter-American relations. The 1968 ministerial mission to nine Latin American countries contributed to the completion of the Latin American segment of the 1970 White Paper, *Foreign Policy for Canadians*; ironically, it did not envisage any major expansion of Canadian relations with the area, but did recommend a fuller role in technical assistance. The White Paper took a rather traditional line on the OAS and Canadian membership in BID (the Inter-American Development

Bank). Oxfam of Canada expressed the sentiments of many groups interested in the developing world when it criticized the excessively negative tone of the White Paper in a brief to the House of Commons Standing Committee on External Affairs and National Defence in January 1971. The Oxfam report expressed concern with the narrow definition of Canada's international role in terms of Canadian economic growth as opposed to an orientation more in keeping with the rhetoric of social justice.[14] Oxfam's objections have not been met in the past four years. The coolness of the official Canadian reception of the Allende government in Chile stands in stark contrast to the enthusiasm with which the government has supported business interests in Latin America.

Since the 1960s Canada has expanded its bilateral and multilateral development assistance in an effort to create new markets for Canadian goods. Even before Canada joined BID in the spring of 1972, most of its funds intended for Latin America were channeled through the Washington-based organization. Prior to membership, Canada committed some $74 million administered by the Bank under the supervision of the Canadian International Development Agency in the form of low interest, long-term development loans tied to the purchase of Canadian goods and services. When Canada joined the Bank, it agreed to transfer the funds obtained from the repayment of the earlier loans to the Fund for Special Operations.[15] The Fund for Special Operations is concerned primarily with providing more flexible terms for economic and infrastructure projects such as land settlement, housing, sanitation and education in the least developed of the member countries. The fact that these loans are repayable in the lending currency (invariably dollars) and usually lead to the purchase of goods and services in the developed nations takes the loans out of the realm of selfless aid. In addition, membership in BID gives Canada access to information that enhances the chances for Canadian firms, especially consulting firms, to obtain contracts related to the use of loan funds. That BID is by no means a non-political organization is reflected in the fact that after relative inactivity in Chile during the Allende years, eight months after the military coup the non-Latin American nations in BID, including Canada, agreed to refinance the Chilean external debt; Chile also received a $22-million loan for agricultural development.[16]

In addition to the multilateral funds allocated to Latin America through BID, the World Bank, and United Nations organizations, Canada has expanded its bilateral assistance programme. In 1973 Canada committed $8.1 million in bilateral assistance to Latin America in the form of grants. It disbursed $4.2 million of that assistance. It also disbursed $9.7 million in loans committed in 1972, although there were no new loans in 1973. The 1973 disbursements to Latin America represent 4.3 percent of total bilateral aid in comparison with 46.6 percent for Asia, 17.5 percent for Francophone Africa, 15.1 percent for Commonwealth Africa, and 5 percent for non-governmental organizations. Canadian policy stipulates that 80 percent of bilateral aid must be tied to Canadian goods and services and that of the goods purchased under the tied portion of the loan 66⅔ percent must be Canadian produced.[17] The same terms apply to special funds for bilateral assistance such as the one set up in the spring of 1974 to extend aid to the least developed Latin American nations. In the fall of 1974 Canada committed $150,000 of the fund to Honduras for a study that will determine the optimum location for lumber-processing facilities in Olancho Province. The goods and services connected with the study and subsequent development will be purchased in Canada.

The low priority of Latin America in Canadian foreign aid is at least in part the result of the very different development needs of the region when compared with Asia and Africa. This is reflected in the small number of CIDA advisers present in Latin America. As recently as 1971 there were no CIDA technical experts in Latin American countries compared with 37 in Asia and 286 in French and Commonwealth Africa. In 1973 there were 15 CIDA advisers in Latin America.

On the fringe of Canadian policy, in the sense that they receive some funding through CIDA, are the various non-government organizations which have long been involved in Latin America. By 1973 there were more than twenty such organizations assisted by CIDA, including Oxfam; the YMCA; the Boy Scouts; The United Church; CUSO; Canadian Executive Services Overseas; special programmes such as that organized by the Coady International Institute at St. Francis Xavier University; and the Canadian Catholic Organization for Development and Peace, which in turn supports individual Catholic agencies. Approximately 15 percent of CIDA's non-government organization funds are allocated to Central and South America, although expenditures have increased only marginally in the past six years in both areas, in part because of the absence of initiative from some of the groups concerned. The Roman Catholic Church and Catholic orders have made the largest commitment; in 1972 alone there were some two thousand Canadians in Latin America under their auspices, almost one third of all the Canadian teachers, missionaries, and advisers active in the area under the various non-government organizations.

Canadian direct aid to Latin America in the past several years has become increasingly technical and professional, largely at the insistence of the host countries and agencies, in a movement away from the type of voluntarism characteristic of the early days of CUSO, in part at least in response to critics who portray foreign aid as little more than paternalism.[18]

One organization which has recently made a unique contribution to Canada's approach to foreign aid is the International Development Research Centre (IDRC). Its creation in 1970 by an act of Parliament may be viewed as an official act of foreign policy; however, it operates relatively free of government interference, and IDRC officials consider the organization an independent body. Unlike CIDA and the Export Development Corporation (EDC), the basic motivation of IDRC is not to promote Canadian trade or development tied to Canadian economic interests. One of the moving spirits behind IDRC in 1969, Irving Brecher, who was at that time head of the Centre for Developing Area Studies at McGill University, noted that one of the main purposes of the organization was to focus on research. Organizers wished to avoid the political and administrative problems experienced by OAS and U.N. agencies and to deal with "the whole question of the transfer and adaptation of advances in science and technology to the less developed countries". With an international Board of Governors, which identifies the policy priorities, and with a scientist, David Hopper, as President, the IDRC has been relatively well-equipped to achieve some of its objectives. As it has evolved in the past four years the objective which has gained primacy has been to "assist the developing regions to build up the research capabilities, the innovative skills, and the institutions required to solve . . ." the problems of the developing world.[19]

Because Latin America is better equipped than some

developing regions to provide its own researchers and facilities, the first priority of the IDRC has been met to some extent. Consequently, the IDRC, in contrast to the Rockefeller and Ford agricultural research centres in Latin America, has concentrated not on transferring foreign specialists and technology but on encouraging indigenous research and innovative projects. In addition to its head office in Ottawa, IDRC has established a regional office in Bogota (as well as Dakar and Singapore) in order to make policy more responsive to local needs. Ranked by region in terms of total IDRC expenditures or approval expenditures, as of March 31, 1974 Asia had received 31.6 per cent, Africa 29.4 per cent, the Caribbean and Latin America 12.8 per cent, involving a budget of $22.6 million for 1973-74. In the Caribbean and Latin America allocations have been in the area of agriculture, food and nutrition sciences, population and health sciences, and social sciences and human resources, in that order.

Agriculture has been one of IDRC's main concerns in Latin America. The problems of the agricultural sector have given IDRC the opportunity to co-operate with Latin American agencies for experimentation in small farm development. Originating in Mexico, the emphasis on the individual small farmer has expanded southward. In Colombia, for example, the Instituto Colombiano Agropecuario (ICA) in 1971 turned its extension division over to IDRC for an experiment with small independent farmers on 400,000 acres of land in the Andean foothills near the town of Caqueza, east of Bogota. The project was designed to bring about higher crop yields, improve livestock, provide credit facilities for implements and fertilizers and to improve marketing. In 1973 an additional $716,000 was approved for phase 2 of the project, the development of an integrated rural development research and training centre. Interest stimulated by the pilot Caqueza project led the Colombian Government to expand the programme under its own auspices.

The IDRC has been involved in several other research projects which concern Latin America, including the Cassava/swine project concentrated at the International Centre for Tropical Agriculture (CIAT) in Cali, Colombia, and the experiments of the International Centre for the Improvement of Maize and Wheat

(CIMMYT) in Mexico. Both projects have necessitated considerable co-operation between Latin American and Canadian scientists and contributions from the Universities of Guelph, Manitoba, and McGill's Macdonald College. In sum, IDRC has made a contribution where Canada has a great deal to offer in the way of technical knowledge and in an area of vital concern in a world where food products are so inequitably distributed.

IV

As a nation with a traditionally agricultural and extractive economy, Canada has relied heavily upon foreign trade. In 1973, for example, Canadian exports were 25.2 per cent and imports 25.8 per cent of GNP, higher than the United Kingdom, West Germany, France, Japan, or the United States.[20] Although Latin America has for a generation been identified as a promising market for Canadian goods, trade with the region remains a source of unrealized hopes and ambitions. Yet Latin America continues to receive constant attention from a trade conscious government, especially as the economy continues to suffer the malaise of "stagflation". There are now some thirty trade commissioners in Latin America, and in the fall of 1974 the Minister of Industry, Trade and Commerce, Alastair Gillespie, led another of the business-government trade missions that have become a fairly common occurrence in Canadian-Latin American relations since 1940.

The October 1974 mission concentrated on Brazil and was designed in the interest of long-term Canadian prospects, providing an opportunity for senior level discussion within the political and business sectors. The long-range objective, in part, accounts for the relatively minor sale of several million dollars worth of Canadian equipment and material that resulted from the mission; yet some businessmen and government officials appear confident of their ability to take advantage of Brazil's current high growth rate and its policy of "selective" nationalism; that is, Brazil welcomes foreign investment as long as the Brazilian state determines the conditions and the priorities.

Officially, the Export Development Corporation is the most important agency promoting trade with Latin America and other areas, although CIDA also extends lines of credit which make it possible for a recipient country to import goods and services without having to obtain scarce foreign exchange. Created in 1969, the EDC absorbed the functions of the Exports Credit

Insurance Corporation established in 1945. With twelve directors, seven from the public service and five from private industry, the EDC has since 1971 had three basic functions: to provide export credits and insurance for consumer goods and capital equipment; long-term financing for major projects abroad; and foreign investment insurance. When the Trudeau Government called an election in May 1974, a bill was before Parliament to increase EDC's long-term lending ceiling from $1.5 billion to $4.25 billion for the corporation account. Since the bill died with Parliament, for the last six months of 1974 EDC was virtually without funds, and the effects of this absence of crucial trade financing have been felt in 1975.[21]

There has been some concern among Canadian protectionists that this type of financing of capital investment in Latin America will create interests competitive with Canadian producers; it remains a question that has not been fully answered. When a member of the Senate Banking Committee queried the President of EDC in 1971, the latter replied: "there is no doubt that it would appear at first blush that it is perhaps creating competition for the Canadian, but if we do not do it, someone else will and their manufacturers will have more business and exports . . ." Another allegation has been that EDC is more sympathetic to large firms than to the small businessman.[22]

In Canada's total trade picture, with approximately 5 per cent of Canadian trade in 1974 (4 per cent of exports; 6 per cent of imports), Latin America is fifth, behind the U.S., Western Europe, the U.K., and Asia. In absolute but not relative terms Canadian trade with the region has expanded considerably in the past 20 years. Exports, for example, rose from $108 million in 1959 to $351 million in 1970 to more than $1.4 billion in 1974 (including all South and Central American countries and the Antilles). Canadian exports have been primarily finished and semi-finished industrial goods, especially since the conclusion of the 1965 Auto Pact with the United States. In 1970 exports of motor vehicles and parts were the most important Canadian export commodity to Latin America, followed by newsprint, wheat and wheat flour, steel, aircraft equipment, aluminum, and general machinery, a pattern which has continued through 1974. Three-quarters of Canadian imports in terms of value are petroleum products, accounting for Venezuela's high prominence in Canadian trade. After crude and refined petroleum products, Canada's primary imports from Latin America have been coffee, fresh fruit and vegetables, textiles, metal bearing ores, and canned meats, products which are responsible for generating much of Latin America's foreign exchange earnings.[23]

Significant for the future of inter-American commercial relations has been the Latin American effort in the past generation to strengthen regional ties by establishing regional trade organizations. The Central American Common Market and the Andean Group (1969) have been more successful than the larger Latin American Free Trade Association (LAFTA) in establishing common tariffs and facilitating internal trade. Although it appears highly unlikely that LAFTA will succeed in establishing a real free trade area, the strengthened regional groupings have complicated the commercial picture for Canada and made it necessary for some firms to locate in Latin America in order to circumvent tariff walls.[24] It is a striking fact that Canada has a generally favourable balance of trade with most individual Latin American countries, with the major exception of Venezuela, because of Canadian dependence on Venezuela petroleum. In contrast, Canada has an unfavourable balance of trade with the Central American Common Market. Commodity balance of trade data suggest, then, that there is some compatibility between the trade interests of Canada and Latin America, but it is this potential market for exports that continues to attract Canadian business interests.

Both federal and provincial governments have increased their commercial and investment contacts with Latin America in the past six years. Ontario has been the most aggressive, and there is considerable feeling in the western provinces that federal efforts have been too Ontario oriented, with the result that the industry ministers from the four western provinces are now initiating their own trade missions. Quebec and Alberta have already sent a trade mission to Brazil recently, and more will likely follow.[25]

The private organization most active in economic promotion and with increasingly close ties to External Affairs is the Canadian Association for Latin America (CALA), which has a membership of some ninety active firms and individuals. CALA got under way in 1969, promoted initially by Grant Glassco and subsequently by Robert Winters, with the support of leading Canadian businessmen anxious to expand trade.[26] Under the current direction of Michael Lubbock, a British businessman formerly active in Peruvian railroads, CALA has sponsored a series of active conferences which have included prominent Latin American political and economic leaders. In 1972 the Developing Aid Committee of the Canadian Association for Latin America (CALA) established working relations with CIDA and IDRC and the Canadian Council for International Co-operation, leading to the establishment of a special advisory committee in the Canadian Hunger Foundation to promote technology transfer. In keeping with its "internationalist" perspective, CALA has also joined the Inter-American Council for Commerce and Production, which is the principal organization linking the private enterprise sectors of the United States and Latin America. In the past few years, CALA has received assistance from External Affairs for organizing information seminars across Canada. It was also active, largely with Brascan initiative, in establishing a Toronto-based Brazil-Canada information centre, and a Mexico-Canada Bilateral Businessmen's Committee.

The road to more meaningful commercial relations with Latin America remains poorly marked. Latin American priorities in the area of regional organization, resource controls, foreign exchange restrictions, tariffs, and national flag preference in shipping policy, will continue to frustrate Canadian businessmen for some time to come. But if Canada is sincere in promoting Latin American development, it will have to accept the legitimacy of the priorities the Latin American nations have themselves identified.[27]

V

Well before the establishment of diplomatic relations with Latin America, Canadian and Canadian-based firms in the areas of petroleum, banking, insurance, agricultural machinery, and utilities, among others, had made a substantial investment in Latin America. In the 1930s the value of investment by Canadian-incorporated companies was small even in comparison with firms incorporated in minor European countries; this has expanded to the point where in 1970 there were over fifty "Canadian" companies active in the area.[28] Canadian and British banks were pioneers in establishing local branch banks in the Caribbean and South America at the turn of the century, initially in response to the needs of Canadian fishing interests and subsequently in an industrial context. In several countries, such as Colombia, the Royal Bank of Canada was sporadically the largest foreign bank from 1914 until the Second World War. Since 1940 competition from domestic banks supported by nationalist legislation and from major British and American banks, has pushed Canadian banking into a secondary capacity, but the Royal Bank remains strong in Brazil, Colombia, Argentina, and Venezuela. The presence of Canadian banks underlines the Canadian role. Royal, for example, provides market information and local credit facilities for Canadian businesses attempting to establish abroad. Royal's International Division in Montreal provides financing, sometimes in cooperation with the EDC, for Canadian exporters. In terms of personnel policy, the general trend has been toward a decline in expatriates and the promotion of nationals, often under pressure from local governments. In Argentina and Colombia, for example, in Royal Bank's operations there are two expatriates out of 355 employees and 13 out of 234 respectively.[29]

Before the Second World War there were also ties between the Royal Bank and two of the "Canadian" petroleum interests involved in South America, the International Petroleum Company and the Andean National Corporation, IPC, with head office in Toronto until the early 1950s, operated in Peru and Colombia until expropriation and the expiry of concessions respectively curtailed activities. IPC was a subsidiary of Imperial Oil, which in turn is controlled by Standard Oil of New Jersey. In Colombia in the inter-war years, the American Department of State handled all questions of a diplomatic nature for the companies. The Andean National Corporation, the pipeline company which serviced IPC's Colombian fields, was controlled by Cordillera Investments of Montreal, a wholly-owned subsidiary of IPC. To strengthen the Canadian identity of the company, several prominent Canadians, among them the President of the Royal Bank, were "elected" to the Board; but actual control in the 1920's was in the hands of Captain J. Flanagan, an American connected with Jersey Standard. The same type of situation has prevailed with other Canadian-based firms active in Latin America, including Alcan and Inco, which attempt to capitalize on their Canadian identity while, in the case of Alcan, directing Latin American operations from New York.[30]

Of the $860 million in Canadian direct investment in Latin

America, $648 million is in Brazil followed by Mexico and Argentina. Canada is the third largest foreign investor in Brazil, ranking a distant third behind the United States and West Germany. Canadian DFI in Brazil in 1973 was 7.9 per cent of the total compared with 37.5 per cent for the U.S. and 11.4 per cent for Germany. These statistics obscure the fact that the largest Canadian-incorporated firm operating abroad is a major force in Brazil. Since it was established in 1912, Brascan (formerly the Brazilian Traction, Light and Power Co.), has become the largest single foreign investor in Brazil, with $142 million compared with Volkswagen's $119 million. As the *Last Post* revealed in its March 1973 treatment of Brascan, only a minority of the corporation's shares are held in Canada or by Canadians, although the executive has been predominantly Canadian, and the company has had close links with prominent Liberal politicians. The complexion of Brascan in Brazil has altered substantially since its initial venture into street railways, most of the diversification coming since the 1960s when it sold its telephone interests. Some $21 million from that sale went into the purchase of Labatt stock; but the company also diversified in Brazil. Among its operations are an investment bank in Rio; an agricultural research organization in Recife; part interest in Brink's in Sao Paulo; 45 per cent interest in a nylon manufacturing plant, Celanese do Brasil; 50 per cent interest along with its affiliate, Labatt's, in a brewery and bottler of soft drinks in Rio and Belo Horizonte; a 100 per cent interest in a Rio brokerage company, along with other investments in food packaging, rail cars, tires, motor vehicle chassis, textiles, and hotels. Its most significant operation remains Light Servicos de Electricidade, S.A., more commonly known as The Light. Since its creation out of Sao Paulo Light in 1956, it has been Brascan's largest subsidiary in Brazil and the fourth largest company in the country. Its book value was approximately $640 million in 1972, accounting for 65 per cent of Brascan's profits.[31]

Canadian policy-makers have found Brazil's industrial boom of the past decade decidedly more attractive than the political and social problems that have accompanied it. Amnesty International reported over one thousand cases of severe political torture in Brazil in 1972, and although the current government of General Ernesto Geisel has paid lip service to the ideal of liberalization, there has been little affirmative action to justify the rhetoric. In the meantime, Canadian commercial missions have descended on Brazil in an effort to capitalize on the economic boom, even while signs of its impermanence begin to appear.

Canadian policy in final analysis, then, appears to have fallen substantially short of the Trudeau government's stated objective of being the "cutting edge of the Left", at least where Latin America is concerned. Our foreign aid has on the whole evinced some improvement, moving away from its earlier voluntaristic paternalism. The same might be said of the scientific work of the International Development Research Centre, but IDRC can only indirectly be considered an actual instrument of Canadian policy. The main thrust of Canadian policy remains commercial and economic expansion in the interests of the Canadian business community and allegedly the economy as a whole. Such a policy is premised on two assumptions: that, as the Minister of Industry, Trade and Commerce recently commented, the transnational firm is the best vehicle for developing technology and trade; and, that simply by promoting Latin American trade along traditional lines, Canada is actually doing something to promote "development". To perpetuate Latin American dependence on extractive-export industries is self-defeating when contrasted with the type of economic diversification requisite to create sound economies. Canadian efforts to sell unnecessary "hardware" to Latin America, for example, underline the failure of both federal and provincial governments either to understand or empathize with Latin American needs. The proposed sale of a Candu reactor to Argentina is a specific instance in which Canadian efforts will do little to promote social, economic, and political equilibrium of that nation. Nor is there unanimous agreement with the statement by the Minister of Industry, Trade and Commerce in support of the transnational firm. It may be a convenient vehicle for trade promotion and technology transfer; whether it is also the best vehicle for achieving meaningful economic and social progress remains, however, a controversial question.[32]

Unfortunately, the Canadian response to the Allende administration in Chile from 1970 until the coup in 1973 suggests that when confronted with a fundamental alternative, Canadian policy-makers will opt for a collaborative position vis-a-vis the United States. Canadian reception of Allende was cool. It included a refusal to support the extension of new credits, either bilaterally or multilaterally, although old programmes were not discontinued. There was an uneasy feeling among some officials in External Affairs that relations with Allende were somehow incompatible with Canada's role in NATO. One official identified Canada's main "interest" in Chile as specifically Bata Shoes and generally the protection of free enterprise capitalism. There was also a willingness to accept the rationalizations of the Chilean junta that an armed, parallel government was emerging in Chile behind an emasculated Allende administration. The Canadian position in Chile did much to undermine the good relations created among progressive forces in the 1960s when Canada managed to steer policy toward Cuba somewhat independently of the United States. If there is a contradiction between Canadian policy toward Cuba and that toward Chile, that contradiction emphasizes the failure of the Liberal Trudeau government to reconcile the reformist rhetoric of its foreign policy toward the developing areas with its more fundamental adherence to continentalism and international capitalism.

The reality is that several hundred million Latin Americans are growing increasingly aware of a standard of living higher than that of the hillside slums where so many of them dwell. As a participant at a 1971 CALA meeting observed, these people constitute "an explosive nucleus of discontent and disruptions". One can understand why a government, politically responsible to the Canadian electorate, would in a period of economic uncertainty continue to emphasize the potential commercial benefits of our relationship with Latin America. There is little evidence, however, that such a policy will make any contribution to the cause of social progress. It is premised on that vital ingredient of all foreign policies — self-interested nationalism.

Notes

1. For a general introduction to the literature on population growth see the 1973 Annotated Bibliography published by the Smithsonian Institution's International Program for Population Analysis. Data in this section is drawn from: OAS Instituto Interamericano de Estadistica, *América en Cifras* (1974); *Statistical Abstract of Latin America for 1971* (1972); Pan American Health Organization, *Child*

Mortality in the Americas (1973); *The Latinamericanist*, Vol. IX (May 5, 1974). Some of the data on Brazil are from the *Financial Post,* November 9, 1974. Useful on urbanization is R. M. Morse, ed., *The Urban Development of Latin America, 1750-1920* (1971), and L. Cardenas, ed., *Urbanization of Latin America* (1967).

2. A well-documented study dealing with agrarian reform is Peter Dorner, ed., *Land Reform in Latin America: Issues and Cases* (1971), published for the Land Tenure Center at the University of Wisconsin. Also useful is J. R. Thome, "The Process of Land Reform in Latin America", - *Wisconsin Law Review, Vol. 1* (1968).

3. On Chilean land reform see the following: Land Tenure Center, University of Wisconsin, *Chile's Agricultural Economy: A Bibliography* (1974); Solon Barraclough and A. Affonso, *A Critical Appraisal of the Chilean Agrarian Reform,* Occasional paper, Vienna Institute for Development (1973); Jacques Chonchol, "Land Reform in Chile", *Canadian Forum* (November-December, 1970); Richard Feinberg, *The Triumph of Allende* (1972).

4. The best introduction to Canadian policy in Latin America are the brief sections in the Canada in World Affairs Series published by the Canadian Institute of International Affairs, on which I have drawn liberally for this section. For the years of the Trudeau Government, Peter Dobell, *Canada's Search for New Roles* (1972) makes occasional reference to Latin America. For a full scale treatment of Canadian-Latin American relations we will have to await J. C. Ogelsby's soon to be published account of the past one hundred years. Useful articles include the following: J. Ogelsby, "Canada and the Pan American Union: Twenty Years On", *International Journal,* Vol. 24 (1968-69); D. R. Murray, "Canada's First Diplomatic Missions in Latin America", *Journal of Inter-American Studies and World Affairs,* Vol. 16 (May, 1974); J. Slater, "The Decline of the OAS", *International Journal,* Vol. 24 (1968-69); John Harbron, "The Growing Pressures on Canada to Seek Hemispheric Identity", *International Perspectives* (May-June, 1974); Harbron, "Ending a Historic Isolation", *International Perspectives* (May-June, 1972); Ian Lumsden, "The Free World of Canada and Latin America", in

Stephen Clarkson, ed., *An Independent Foreign Policy for Canada?* (1968). Also useful is an unpublished background paper prepared by the Department of External Affairs, "Canada and Latin America" (1973).

5. Prime Minister Mackenzie King's attitude is reflected in a statement to the House of Commons, *Debates,* August 4, 1944, p. 5912.

6. *Globe and Mail,* March 9, 1948.

7. For the debate over Canadian membership in the OAS see John Harbron, *Canada and the OAS* (1963).

8. For Paul Martin's position in the early 1960's, see House of Commons, *Debates,* January 24, 1963, p. 3073. On Trudeau's statement during the 1968 campaign see *Globe and Mail,* April 5, 1968.

9. Interview with Ambassador Pick, Canadian Permanent Observer to the OAS, November 27, 1974. Interview with M. Guy Choquette, Associate Director, Latin American Division, November 5, 1974.

10. *Handbook on the OAS* (1972); External Affairs, "Canada and Latin America".

11. Interview with Ambassador Pick.

12. U.S. Congress, Senate, Report of Senator Mike Mansfield on the Tlatelolco Conference, Mexico City, to the Senate Foreign Relations Committee, March, 1974; OAS, Comunicado, *Reunion de Ministros de Relaciones Exteriores, Washington, 18 de abril de 1974.*

13. Interview with Ambassador Pick; *Le Devoir,* August 22, 1975.

14. Canada, House of Commons, Standing Committee on External Affairs and National Defence, *Proceedings* (1970-71).

15. External Affairs, "Canada and Latin America".

16. BID, *News Release,* March 30, 1974.

17. Material on BID is drawn from Colin Bradford and Caroline Pestieau, *Canada and Latin America* (1972); E.A., "Canada and Latin America"; CIDA, *Annual Aid Review,* Memorandum to the Development Assistance Committee, Organization for Economic Cooperation and Development (September, 1974); CIDA, *Annual Report,* various years.

227

18. CIDA, *Annual Report, 1971-72*. On Canadian aid in general see Clyde Sanger, *Half a Loaf* (1969).

19. House of Commons, Standing Committee on External Affairs and National Defence, December, 1969. Material on IDRC is from an interview with Messrs. W. Plumptre and Clyde Sanger, October 22, 1974; IDRC *Annual Reports;* David Hopper, "Research Policy", Address at Bogota, March 19, 1973.

20. Address of Alastair Gillespie to CALA, June 17, 1974.

21. Bradford and Pestieau provide a good analysis of EDC and CIDA trade and investment promotion. See also the July, 1973 issue of *Canada Commerce,* which focuses on Latin America.

22. Canada, Senate Banking Committee, *Hearings,* March, 1971; interview with an official of the Canadian Export Association, October 21, 1974.

23. *Canada Commerce* (February and May 1974); Department of Industry, Trade and Commerce, *Trade of Canada,* various issues. Bradford and Pestieau provide a full analysis of Canadian-Latin American trade before 1970. UN, *Yearbook of International Trade Statistics, 1972-73;* Inter-American Development Bank, *Economic and Social Progress of Latin America* (1973); *Financial Post,* November 9, 1974.

24. Bradford and Pestieau, pp. 206ff; M. Wionczek, "Multinational corporations and the Andean Common Market", *Canadian Forum* (September, 1971).

25. Note 23 for sources; for the provincial position see the *Financial Post,* November 9, 1974; *Montreal Star,* November 18, 1974.

26. CALA, *News Release,* March 22, 1973

27. CALA *News,* November, 1972; *Canada Commerce,* May, 1974; *Financial Post,* November 9, 1974; interview with official of the Canadian Export Association.

28. J. C. M. Ogelsby, "Relaciones Canadienses Latinoamericanas", *Estudios Internacionales* (abril-junio, 1972). Pestieau; Statistics Canada, 1970 Report, "Canada's International Investment Position, 1926-1967". M. Bernstein, ed., *Foreign Investment in Latin America* (1966).

29. Interview with Mr. L. L. Street, Area Executive, Latin America and Caribbean, Royal Bank of Canada, October 29, 1974; correspondence with officials of The Royal Bank; Clifford Ince, *The Royal Bank of Canada, A Chronology: 1864-1969* (1969).
30. S. Randall, ''The International Corporation and American Foreign Policy'', *Canadian Journal of History,* Vol. IX (August, 1974).
31. Department of Industry, Trade and Commerce, "List of Companies Incorporated in Canada and Holding Direct Investments in Latin America'' (unpublished, August, 1973).
32. H. Johnson, "The Multinational Corporation as a Development Agent", *Columbia Journal of World Business* (May-June, 1972); J. Levin, *The Export Economies* (1960).

CHAPTER 10

CANADA'S RELATIONS
WITH CHINA
SINCE 1968

Maureen Appel Molot

Introduction

On October 13, 1970, after twenty months of negotiations, Canada established diplomatic relations with the People's Republic of China. Until recently, the issue of Canada's relations with Peking assumed a prominence in the overall picture of Canadian foreign policy that for the most part it did not warrant. From time to time between 1949 and 1969 the Canadian government publicly debated the pros and cons of a change in its position of non-recognition, although as government spokesmen noted in their speeches on the subject, what was involved was the recognition of a government, not the approval of a regime. Moreover, as a result of official references to the strong, negative American stance on recognition of Mao's regime, non-recognition in Canada had come to symbolize to many foreign policy analysts the domination of Canadian policy by American interests.[1] During and following the Stockholm sessions on recognition, commentators dissected the Canadian bargaining position, the likelihood of Canadian success, and reasons for delays between meetings, the price Canada paid for recognition and the implications of the Canadian breakthrough.[2] Finally, in the first four years after recognition, Canadians experienced a kind of euphoria about China through the exchange of a variety of missions, the exploration of trade opportunities and the discovery of the esteem with which a Canadian doctor, Norman Bethune, is viewed by the Chinese.

Since 1974 the Canadian perspective on Sino-Canadian relations has become more congruent with the actual importance of the People's Republic to Canada in diplomatic and economic terms: a recent analysis of Canadian foreign policy goals and the states whose activities affect the achievement of these objectives ranks China as a marginal actor;[3] furthermore, although Canadian exports to China have been impressive and are of particular consequence to the western provinces, future Canadian exports to China of agricultural, mineral and processed commodities will have to compete against the products of other nations, most notably those of the United States and, in the case of processed goods, Japan as well. The need for a candid evaluation of the possibilities for trade and other links between Canada and China has been underlined by the hard diplomatic realities of the forced postponement of a trip by the Vancouver symphony orchestra to China in the fall of 1974 and the request by the Canadian government for withdrawal of a Chinese diplomat in the spring of 1975.[4] This essay will examine the factors leading up to the 1968 decision to seek mutual recognition with the People's Republic of China, the period of negotiations over recognition from February 1969 to October 1970, relations between the two countries since the establishment of diplomatic ties, and will assess the future direction of the relationship.

It is generally agreed that the Canadian Government was moving toward recognition of the new Chinese government and support for its membership in the United Nations when the Korean War broke out.[5] Thereafter, from 1950 to the mid-1960s, Canada's policy toward the People's Republic of China was enmeshed in the complexities of the China question, which included diplomatic recognition of a government recently in power, the admission of that regime to the United Nations, the status of Taiwan, and government sensitivity to American views on the recognition issue. During this period, Canadian spokesmen sometimes confused the separate issues of recognition and U.N. admission, a confusion which perhaps sprung from their hope that the initial revision of Peking's diplomatic status would originate in the U.N. On occasion, they indicated their intent to work for Peking's membership in the world organization before any consideration of recognition. [6] From time to time senior members of the Canadian government flirted with the recognition question and suggested that the problem would have to be re-examined in the future, but their interest was blunted by such events as attacks by Chinese forces on the offshore islands or the war with India and by American opposition to any change in the Canadian position.

While official diplomatic contacts were impossible because of the Cold War context in which the issue was seen, Canada maintained commercial links with China. These became of great importance to Canada when the Conservative government concluded a large wheat deal with Peking in 1961.[7] Almost immediately China became an important and continuing customer for a product Conservative and later Liberal governments were always anxious to sell, and sentiments supporting closer contacts with the People's Republic of China began to emerge. As Cold War issues receded and were replaced by a concern to diversify Canada's economic relationships, pressure to regularize Sino-Canadian contacts grew. When the last "U.N. first" Canadian effort failed in 1966,[8] government thinking edged toward an attempt to improve relations with China through a bilateral approach. The outbreak of the Great Proletarian Cultural Revolution, however, delayed any immediate move in this direction.

Negotiations Over Recognition

The thrust of Canada's China policy changed notably with the selection of Pierre Elliott Trudeau as leader of the Liberal Party in April 1968. Although the movement toward recognition had begun during the Pearson administration, senior Department of External Affairs officials have suggested it was Trudeau's determination to push the issue that made the difference. Trudeau had visited China in 1949 and in 1960 and assumed office with a commitment to recognize the People's Republic of China. During the election campaign Trudeau declared that if elected his government would move

> to recognize the People's Republic of China Government as soon as possible and to enable that government to occupy the seat of China in the United Nations, taking into account that there is a separate government in Taiwan.[9]

Acting on his election promise, Trudeau instructed the Department of External Affairs to review Canada's China policy and to assess the consequences of recognition from a variety of perspectives in the summer of 1968. The Department document which resulted from this review discussed Canada's general interests in the Far East and many of the specific factors which had impeded recognition. Of these, the status of Taiwan received most attention and perhaps reflected the greatest alteration in the Canadian position. As recently as the 1966 United Nations debate on the admission of China, Canada had advocated the representation of the governments of both Peking and Taipeh in the General Assembly.[10] The Trudeau government intended to recognize only one government of China, the one which exercised effective control of the country: if Canada recognized the government in Peking, she would withdraw recognition from the government in Taipeh. In the event that Canada was the first Western nation to begin recognition talks with Peking, Canadian officials expected the Chinese to try to use Canada as a test case for acceptance in the West of their claim to Taiwan by making it the prerequisite for recognition. Canada was not prepared to accept Peking's position that Taiwan was an inseparable part of China and it was this demand, the briefing book predicted, that would prolong the discussions over recognition.

Other issues discussed by the review included the admission of the People's Republic of China to the United Nations, the impact of recognition on Sino-Canadian trade, outstanding Canadian claims against the People's Republic of China for compensation for the Ming Sung ships, and the old Canadian Embassy in Nanking, and the potential treatment of Canadian diplomats in Peking. Canada's position on the admission of Peking to the United Nations had evolved parallel to her stand on recognition: if Canada recognized the Peking government, she would support membership for that government in the United Nations and would withdraw support for the then present incumbent of the China seat. In its evaluation of the impact of recognition on trade, the review was rather cautious. Large wheat sales to China had been negotiated without recognition and assessments of other trade possibilities at that time suggested, despite the enthusiasm of Canadian businessmen for trade with China, that exports of non-grain products to Taiwan would exceed those to Peking. (Canadian exports to China since 1970 have proven this judgment incorrect.)

The review also noted that the Canadian interest in China reflected the government's awareness of Canada as a Pacific nation and its responsiveness to the interest of the Western provinces in expanding Canadian ties across the Pacific. This theme was reaffirmed eighteen months later in the Trudeau Government's foreign policy white paper which described the

Canadian decision to seek diplomatic relations with the People's Republic of China as an action reflective of the changing Canadian policy emphasis and "linked with the Government's desire to give more emphasis to Pacific affairs generally".[11]

One other topic covered by the External Affairs briefing paper is worthy of comment because it reflected a concern of many involved in the preparation of the review, the possibility that the Chinese might not be ready to resume international contact. China was emerging from the Cultural Revolution in 1968 and appeared to External Affairs Department analysts to be interested in pursuing new diplomatic ties. William Saywell has suggested that Peking's perception of threats to its national security prompted a shift in Chinese foreign policy and in its attitude to relations with the Western world. China's distrust of the Soviet Union, her concern about Soviet-American détente and her feeling that Moscow had better access to the western press and to non-Communist governments led her to see diplomatic contacts and membership in the United Nations in a more positive light than at any time since 1956.[12] Thus, the briefing document suggested, when Canada made overtures to Peking, the Chinese were expected to be receptive.

While the Canadian government was evaluating the recognition question it was also conferring on the subject with interested governments. Of these, the government of the United States was obviously the most important and the one upon whose reactions to the proposed Canadian move on recognition there was the most speculation. It was perhaps fortuitous that discussions with Washington began during the 1968 United States presidential election campaign, for it was reasonable to assume that a new administration, whatever its party, might be more receptive to the Canadian position than the outgoing Johnson one. State Department officials, who in those months had to anticipate the policy of a new administration toward China, reacted somewhat more mildly to the Canadian feelings on recognition than they might have at a time when there was less pressure on them to remain flexible.[13] Even before the Nixon administration assumed office, it appeared that American policy toward the People's Republic of China would undergo a major shift.[14]

The most frequently cited American reaction to the Canadian announcement on 10 February 1969 of an approach to the

Chinese on recognition is the statement issued by Robert Mc-Closkey, the U.S. State Department's Press Officer, which noted the Department was

> very much concerned over the possible implications of such moves for the position of the Government of the Republic of Nationalist China which is a responsible and co-operative member of the international community and with which the Government of Canada maintains diplomatic relations.[15]

There were no American references, as there had been in the past, to the aggressiveness of Peking, nor were there any formal or informal declarations or threats against Canada. Some American legislators may have opposed the Canadian action, but the administration, despite its concern over the future of Taiwan, may have begun to realize that the U.S. position of antipathy to international discourse with the People's Republic of China was rapidly being undermined. During the fall and winter of 1968-69, the Canadian Government listened to a variety of American objections to its plan to recognize China, but informed Washington that it intended to proceed. When Prime Minister Trudeau visited Washington in March 1969, he and President Nixon may have discussed the Canadian recognition decision. In his statements to the press, the Prime Minister emphasized both Canada-U.S. comity and Canadian determination to pursue policies different from those of the United States. Canada did not accept the United States' view of the People's Republic of China and felt that a regime which contained one-quarter of the world's population could no longer be ignored.[16] Whatever the views expressed by the two leaders in their private talks, the question of China was not mentioned in the joint summary of their discussions.[17] The only public references to China during Trudeau's Washington trip were made by the Prime Minister during an address to the National Press Club.[18]

Among the other governments with which the recognition issue was raised were Belgium and Italy, who were also interested in beginning recognition talks with the People's Republic, and the United Kingdom and Japan. The former two countries encouraged and supported the Canadian initiative while the latter two expressed more negative opinions. The

British cautioned the Canadians on the basis of their own experiences with Peking, which included the mistreatment of British diplomats and journalists and British property. The Japanese acted to dissuade Canada from recognition, partially, it has been suggested, at the behest of the United States.[19] Japan also expressed some concern about the territorial claims of the Peking government, a concern which Canada attempted to assuage by making it clear that recognition of China did not mean recognition of all its territorial demands. In meetings with Japanese officials, External Affairs Minister Mitchell Sharp noted that the two governments viewed the question of recognition of Communist China in a somewhat different light and promised to keep them informed of progress on the recognition talks.[20]

During the review process, the decision was taken to have the Canadian embassy in Stockholm approach the Chinese. Stockholm was one of three locations mentioned in the External Affairs briefing book as a potential site for recognition talks and its eventual selection was based on a number of factors. The Canadian government needed a capital in which the People's Republic of China had representation and a country whose own relations with Peking were cordial. Moreover, it wanted a location where the activities of Canadian embassy officials would not receive too much publicity and where cipher communications with Ottawa were good. Stockholm satisfied these three criteria and had, as a bonus, an experienced Canadian diplomat in Arthur Andrew. The Canadian government felt that the Chinese should have some say on the locale of the discussions so that Stockholm remained an uncertain choice until the views of the Chinese were ascertained.

Ambassador Andrew received the Department of External Affairs working document in September 1968 but did not receive any instructions to initiate contacts with the Chinese until February 1969. On February 10th, 1969, Secretary of State for External Affairs Sharp announced in the House of Commons that the Canadian Embassy in Stockholm had been instructed to propose to the Chinese Embassy in that city the opening of talks on recognition and the exchange of ambassadors.[21] In April 1969, Mr. Sharp elaborated on the Government's decision:

> The question is not really "Why should Canada recognize Peking?" but "Why should Canada not seek diplomatic

relations with the world's most populous nation?'' In our view, the normal, logical and reasonable thing would be to have diplomatic relations with a country of such importance. We would have preferred to deal with the matter in the context of the United Nations. In the absence of such a solution, it is now our best judgement that whatever the uncertainties and disadvantages there may have been, these are unlikely to outweigh the arguments for trying to normalize our relations with the People's Republic of China.[22]

The first meeting between the Canadian ambassador and the Chinese *chargé* in Stockholm did not transpire as officials in Ottawa had anticipated. Mr. Andrew had been instructed to ask the Chinese whether or not they were interested in beginning talks on mutual recognition with Canada, and if so, where they would like the discussions to be held. But representatives of the People's Republic in Stockholm, who knew of External Affairs Minister Sharp's February 10th statement to the House of Commons and therefore were aware of the Canadian position, stated their conditions for recognition at the first meeting between the two sides. In effect, the negotiations over recognition began without any agreement to negotiate.

This scenario relieved the concern in Ottawa over the possibility of a Chinese rebuff of Canadian intentions. Canadian officials noted that Italy and Belgium made contacts with the Chinese on the question of recognition about the same time as Canada, but that their discussions did not really get going. Canadian discussions with Peking officials, on the other hand, proceeded slowly but never stopped. It is possible that the Canadian starting position was more acceptable to the Chinese than that of Canada's two NATO allies. There were other reasons, however, which made the People's Republic of China receptive to recognition talks with Canada: Canada's commercial relations with China had increased substantially since late 1960 when the latter began purchasing large quantities of Canadian wheat; a number of Canadian businessmen had visited China in th late 1950s and early 1960s and, impressed with the potential for exports to China, recommended Canadian recognition of the government in Peking; Canada recognized the Nationalist government in Taiwan but she had neither opened an embassy in Taipeh nor developed any strong commitment to Chiang Kai-

Shek's regime; finally the Chinese saw Canada not just as any Western nation but as one closely linked to the United States and one which would be a useful source of information for them about both the United States and the United Nations.

The Chinese stipulated their three conditions for recognition at their first meeting with the Canadian ambassador toward the end of February 1969. These were 1) recognition of the Peking regime as the only government of China; 2) support for that regime's claim to the Chinese seat at the United Nations; and 3) recognition of Taiwan as an inalienable part of China. The first two points were acceptable to Canadian authorities. The third Chinese demand was, of course, the difficult one and the issue on which the successful conclusion of the recognition talks in reality hinged. The Canadian government had already decided to recognize only one government of China; if Canada recognized the government in Peking she would withdraw recognition from any other regime which styled itself as the government of China. Moreover, if recognition talks proved successful, Canada would support the admission of the P.R.C. to the United Nations. In the 1970 General Assembly vote on the subject which took place one month after Canada formally recognized Peking, Canada favoured the transfer of the China seat to the People's Republic. Canada also supported the U.S.-sponsored resolution that the issue of the China seat was an "important" question that required a two-thirds majority, but indicated that future support for this resolution was uncertain.[23] One analyst has suggested that U.S. Secretary of State Rogers was advised privately in 1970 that the Canadian position on the "important" resolution was a transitional one to allow the United States time to adjust to the new situation and that in 1971 Canada would oppose this proposal.[24] In 1971, Canada voted for the Albanian resolution which called for the replacement of the Nationalist Chinese by a delegation from Peking and opposed the U.S.-sponsored procedural resolution.[25]

Canada also had interests she wanted protected by the recognition agreement. Canada insisted that the communique establishing diplomatic relations contain the provision that the parties would exchange ambassadors and open embassies in each other's capitals as quickly as possible and that Canadian diplomats in China would be treated in accordance with accepted international practices. Both of these Canadian demands resulted from difficulties other nations experienced with Peking; some recognized the People's Republic but were not able to send ambassadors to China, while the emissaries of others were subject to harassment during their postings in Peking. Canada also sought assurances from the Chinese during the negotiations that its outstanding claims against the Peking regime for the nationalization of the Ming Sung Ships and compensation for the old Canadian embassy in Nanking would be discussed after recognition.[26]

There was some feeling during 1969-70 that the Chinese saw their negotiations with Canada as a potential model for similar talks with other nations and were testing Canadian resolve. From October 1969 through mid-summer 1970, the two sides talked past each other on the matter of Taiwan, the Chinese questioning Canadian sincerity, the Canadians remaining adamant that any statement on territorial claims was inappropriate in a discussion of recognition. Secretary of State for External Affairs, Mitchell Sharp, indicated from time to time while the talks were underway that recognition of a country did not necessitate recognition of all its territorial claims; and that "it would be presumptuous of the Canadian Government" to pronounce upon the status of Taiwan one way or the other. To underline this view, the Minister drew the parallel on one occasion that Canada did not ask the Government of the People's Republic of China to endorse Canadian territorial claims.[27] The problem facing Canada was "to find an adequate means of expressing its own 'non-position' on Taiwan",[28] though if this could not be done Canada was prepared to fail in its recognition bid. However, despite the rhetoric and the gaps between meetings, necessitated by the obligation of the Chinese ambassador to consult Peking, the talks were never suspended, a fact which reaffirmed the Chinese interest in mutual recognition.

In August 1970 it became clear that both sides wanted a recognition agreement. The Canadian government proposed a two-fold approach to alleviate differences over Taiwan which the Peking government agreed to accept. In the official communique the Canadian government would "take note" of the position of the People's Republic of China that Taiwan was an "inalienable part" of its territory and would then issue its own clarifying statement in which the Canadian view of the Taiwan issue would be explained in more detail.[29] At a meeting on August 1st, the first and last paragraphs of the final recognition announcement were agreed upon and the phrasing of statements on Taiwan was discussed. This issue was considered further on September 18 when the Canadian clarifying statement was presented to the Chinese. On October 3rd, the negotiators agreed on the contents of the communique as a whole, subject to home government approval and began consideration of the technical details of recognition. The recognition agreement was formally signed by the two ambassadors, Margaret Meagher [30] and Wang Tung, in Stockholm on October 10th. Three days later External Affairs Minister Sharp announced to the House of Commons the successful conclusion of mutual recognition between Canada and the People's Republic of China.[31]

Relations Since Recognition

In the first three years after recognition many missions were exchanged between the two countries. China took advantage of her new diplomatic ties with Canada to show other nations that she had come out of the Cultural Revolution and was ready to pursue foreign contacts. For Canadians, and Canadian businessmen in particular, the establishment of relations with the People's Republic meant an opportunity for contacts with a fascinating country and potential market which had long been closed. The first Canadian ministerial mission to China, led by Industry, Trade and Commerce Minister Jean-Luc Pépin, left for China in June 1971, only eight months after the conclusion of recognition talks. Included in the delegation were officials from the Departments of Industry, Trade and Commerce, Agriculture, National Revenue, Energy, Mines and Resources and External Affairs, and spokesmen for economic and trade associations concerned with agriculture, forestry, pulp and paper, mining, manufacturing, banking, engineering, exporting and importing. Its purpose was to initiate links with Chinese ministers, officials and representatives of state trading corporations and to advise the Chinese on the range of products Canada could supply.[32] Pépin returned to Canada with a number of commitments from Peking, among the most important of which from the Canadian perspective was that China would continue to consider Canada first as a source of wheat when import needs arose.[33] During their discussions the Chinese indicated to

Pépin, furthermore, their willingness to host a large Canadian trade fair, to consider the Canadian bid for an air route to China and to undertake periodic consultations with Canada on trade matters. Moreover, China's foreign trade minister accepted Pépin's invitation to visit Canada with a Chinese trade delegation and did so in August 1972. The success of the Pépin mission and the receipt of the Chinese ministerial mission fourteen months later[34] were indications of the initial importance with which China viewed her ties with Canada.

Other Canadian ministerial and non-ministerial missions to China took place in 1972 and 1973. In August 1972, External Affairs Minister Sharp travelled to Peking to open the Canadian trade fair in that city, the largest such exposition Canada had ever held abroad, and to hold talks with Chinese leaders.[35] 1973 saw Energy, Mines and Resources Minister Donald Macdonald head a delegation of mining and petroleum experts[36] and Minister of State for Science and Technology Jeanne Sauvé lead a scientific mission to China.[37] They were followed in October of 1973 by Prime Minister Trudeau, whose trip to China was made at the invitation of Premier Chou En-Lai. During his stay in Peking, the Prime Minister broadened the range of contacts he and his officials had with their Chinese counterparts and signed a trade agreement between the two countries. Understandings and arrangements between the two sides in the fields of trade, medicine, science and technology, cultural affairs, academic and other exchanges and consular affairs, were discussed by Chinese and Canadian officials. After the Prime Minister's visit, and as a direct result of it, Canada and China signed an exchange of notes constituting an understanding on consular and related matters and on the reunification of families. Because of the Prime Minister's long-standing interest in China, his visit contributed in a symbolic way to the consolidation of Sino-Canadian relations. At the banquets the two Prime Ministers hosted for each other, and each praised the other in warm tones.[38] Prime Minister Trudeau digressed from his prepared text to recall an earlier visit to China:

> . . . Thirteen years ago I sat in this Great Hall thinking some day we should recognize this great nation. I saw at a distance and with admiration the leaders of China . . . and for me it is a great pleasure to be host to some of these leaders.

241

Two nights earlier Prime Minister Chou had remarked, "Today we are very glad to entertain our old friend here again" and had used a Chinese term for "old friend" which implied empathy and understanding of China and the Chinese.

In the first half of 1974 a number of Canadian scientific and technical missions went to China to pursue understandings reached with the Chinese during the various ministerial meetings of the previous years. For example, a medical team went to China in April 1974 to study acupuncture and a group of consulting engineers visited China in June 1974 to explain to the Chinese the role of their profession in capital construction projects. Since then, the number of missions exchanged has lessened. A variety of bureaucratic and diplomatic factors underlie the fall-off in the pace of delegations. The high level of diplomatic interactions of the previous few years strained bureaucratic resources on both sides because of the time required to plan for and to receive missions. The dispatch and receipt of missions also was costly to the Chinese in foreign exchange. Moreover, a continuation of the high level of Canadian contacts with China would have been at the cost of Canada's relations with other parts of the world. It was this evaluation of priorities that led Canada to postpone, for the moment at least, the opening of a consular office in Shanghai or Canton, even though Canada was the first Western country to sign a consular understanding with China, which provided for the right of consular access. China, too, has been increasing the number of countries with which she maintains diplomatic ties and is desirous of expanding her economic contacts with Japan and the European Community. This inevitably means that the People's Republic will devote less attention to Canada.

The economic aspect has been and continues to be the most important facet of Sino-Canadian ties. Between the conclusion of the first wheat sale to China in 1961 and recognition in 1970, Canada exported over $100 million of grain annually to the P.R.C., with the exception of 1967.[39] In those years, the non-grain component of Sino-Canadian trade rarely accounted for more than one to two percent of total Canadian exports to China. Moreover, although Canadian politicians vacillated over diplomatic recognition of Peking, they were almost unanimous in their support for continuing and expanding the trading relationship.

TABLE I
CANADA'S TRADE WITH THE PEOPLE'S REPUBLIC OF CHINA
(P.R.C.), 1961-1974
(millions of Canadian dollars)

Year	Exports	Imports	Exports to P.R.C. as a % of total Canadian Exports	Imports from P.R.C. as a % of total Canadian Imports	Grain Exports to P.R.C.	Non-Grain Exports to P.R.C.	Grain Exports as % of total Exports to P.R.C.
1961	125.5	3.2	2.2	0.05	122.7	2.8	97.7
1962	147.4	4.5	2.3	0.07	147.2	0.2	99.9
1963	104.7	5.2	1.5	0.1	104.4	0.3	99.7
1964	136.3	9.4	1.7	0.1	136.1	0.2	99.9
1965	105.1	14.5	1.2	0.2	104.7	0.4	99.6
1966	184.9	20.6	1.8	0.2	182.8	2.1	98.9
1967	91.3	25.1	0.8	0.2	89.2	2.1	97.7
1968	163.2	23.4	1.2	0.2	157.8	5.4	96.7
1969	122.4	27.4	0.8	0.2	119.8	2.6	97.9
1970	142.0	19.0	0.9	0.1	121.6	20.4	85.6
1971	204.1	23.3	1.2	0.2	190.7	13.4	93.4
1972	258.6	48.4	1.3	0.3	227.3	31.3	87.9
1973	287.7	52.9	1.2	0.2	186.8	100.9	64.9
1974	434.2	60.9	1.4	0.2	334.0	100.2	76.9

Statistics Canada, *Trade of Canada: Imports by Countries and Exports by Countries* (Ottawa: Information Canada, published annually).

Pre- and immediate post-recognition assessments of the impact of diplomatic links on trade were cautious. Shortly after the conclusion of recognition talks, Industry, Trade and Commerce Minister Pépin noted that while Canada had not recognized China in order to increase exports, Canada would take "whatever commercial advantage it could" out of the new relationship.[40] In fact, two weeks after the announcement of recognition, Canada and China concluded the largest one-year wheat transaction up to that time,[41] and substantial annual wheat sales to China have continued. On two occasions, the June 1971 and August 1972 visits to China by Pépin and Sharp, respectively, the Chinese indicated their long-term interest in Canadian wheat.[42] These promises to Canada, when coupled with conscious reluctance to purchase Australian grain,[43] suggested that China was linking politics with economics in her imports of foodstuffs and that initially, at least, Canada would stand to benefit economically from her decision to recognize Peking. The establishment of diplomatic relations has also facilitated the diversification of Canadian exports to China, exploration of the potential market in China for Canadian products and an increase in Canadian imports from China. While Sino-Canadian trade remains a small part of the total Canadian trade picture, and indeed, of Canadian trade with nations of the Pacific, the Canadian government expended considerable effort in the years following recognition to increase the level of economic interaction between the two countries.

Upon his return from China in July 1971, Industry, Trade and Commerce Minister Pépin established a China task force within his department to co-ordinate and plan departmental activities with respect to China. Because China was the only country on which the Department of Industry, Trade and Commerce had a task force, the unit had some symbolic value in the eyes of both countries. At the outset, the task force canvassed the divisions of IT&C to assess the potential for the export of manufactured and resource goods to China, answered questions from corporations desirous of doing business with China and investigated subjects such as visas and the role of state trading companies, with a bearing on Sino-Canadian commerce. The group was responsible for preparation of the briefing book used by the Canadian participants in the December 1970 trade consultations in Peking, and also was heavily involved in the arrangements for the Canadian trade fair in Peking in August-September 1972.

The Canadian Trade Exhibition in Peking, to which the Chinese committed themselves during Pépin's visit, was a large and costly effort by the Canadian government to indicate to the Chinese the variety of products Canada had for export.[44] More than two hundred Canadian companies participated in the exposition. From the Canadian perspective, the most difficult problem between Ottawa and Peking in the negotiations over the fair was the participation of U.S. subsidiaries. In the 1950s and

1960s Sino-Canadian trade was hampered by American opposition to all commerce with China and the responsibility American parent companies had to assume under American law for the trade of their subsidiaries with the People's Republic. Chinese antipathy to the U.S. trade controls translated into a continuing reluctance to make purchases from Canadian subsidiaries of American corporations. As late as the spring of 1971, the Chinese had invited only a few Canadian subsidiaries with a relatively small percentage of known U.S. ownership and no wholly-owned subsidiaries to attend the semi-annual Canton Trade Fair and they had not expressed any interest in procuring Canadian exports containing a significant percentage of U.S.-made components.[45] Pépin spent considerable time during his visit to Peking discussing the issue of subsidiaries, but the only concession he got from the Chinese was that they would examine trade deals with subsidiaries on a "case-by-case basis".[46] The Chinese attitude worried Canadian trade officials because with the exception of agricultural commodities and some raw materials, most of the items Canada wanted to export to China, particularly manufactured goods, were produced by companies controlled in the United States.

The question of participation by American-owned subsidiaries in the Peking Fair was on the agenda of the first bilateral trade meeting and was discussed again in February 1972 when Canadian officials went to Peking to continue arrangements for the trade exhibition. Canadian officials countered the Chinese insistence on wholly-owned Canadian companies at the fair by alleging that Canada was a special case with respect to corporate ownership, that a trade fair without the participation of subsidiaries would not accurately display the breadth of Canadian industry and that the Chinese had to accept Canada as a free market economy in which corporate ownership changed, just as Canada accepted the Chinese mode of commerce, the state trading corporation. Whether the Chinese were persuaded by these arguments or were swayed by the relaxation in February 1972 of the U.S. trade embargo against China to the level of restrictions imposed on American exports to the communist nations of Eastern Europe and the Soviet Union,[47] they agreed to permit trade fair participation by any firm which was recognized by Canada as a Canadian company. Chinese authorities left the actual choice of participating corporations to the Department of Industry, Trade and Commerce. In the end, some forty U.S.-controlled companies exhibited at the Peking show and, although the Chinese hedged in February on the likelihood of purchases from subsidiaries, a number of participating subsidiaries returned to Canada with contracts for sales to China.

Since the Peking fair, Canadian firms have continued to exhibit their products at the semi-annual Canton fair and some thirty-four companies representing various sectors of the electronics industry participated in the Canadian Electrical and Scientific Instruments Exhibition in Shanghai, April 16-24, 1974. The exchange of trade missions in specific fields, such as oil and gas, mining, electrical power, ports and harbours and railway technology[48] has also enabled many Canadian companies to explore the Chinese market and talk with officials of state trading corporations about Chinese import needs. The results of Canadian participation in all the Chinese trade fairs, but particularly the Peking exposition, and the various missions have been evaluated by the Department of Industry, Trade and Commerce as part of its efforts to develop a trade strategy with respect to China. IT&C authorities have suggested that knowledge of what the Chinese do *not* want to buy from Canada is as important as an awareness of their purchase interests.

Yet another aspect of the attempt to augment Sino-Canadian trade was the institution of regular, bilateral consultations between Canada and China on trade requirements and trade problems. Agreement to undertake periodic discussions on trade matters came during Pépin's June 1971 visit to Peking. The first two annual trade consultations were informal in the sense that no formal agreement to hold these talks was concluded until October 1973. The inaugural sessions under the preliminary arrangement were held in Peking December 1971 when officials of both sides discussed the development of mutual trade, the import requirements and export capabilities of each side and plans for forthcoming trade fairs.[49] A second set of meetings was held in Ottawa in December 1972. During his stay in Peking, the Prime Minister signed a three-year Trade Agreement between Canada and the People's Republic of China which provided for the reciprocal granting of most-favoured nation status, easier access for Canadian businessmen to Chinese markets, and the establishment of a Joint Trade Committee to oversee the implementation of the trade agreement. This accord formalized the annual bilateral consultations on trade matters and permitted special meetings to discuss questions of mutual interest. The first meeting of the Joint Trade Committee was held in Peking in December 1973, the second in Ottawa in February 1975[50] rather than in December 1974 to accommodate the Chinese who indicated they would not be ready for a year-end session. The third meeting of the Committee will be held in China early in 1976.

The meetings are the most important forum in which bilateral trade matters are discussed. Officials of both countries review bilateral trade relations, determine and schedule exhibitions and mission exchanges for the following calendar year and examine specific problems which do or may impede the expansion of economic ties. Among the matters considered at these joint sessions have been Canada's bilingual labelling regulations, which are posing a problem for the Chinese in terms of packaging items for export to Canada, the composition of Canadian exports to China and the Canadian desire to sell more manufactured items, China's dissatisfaction with her trade deficit with Canada, Chinese textile exports, difficulties encountered by Canadian businessmen in China and the growing Chinese interest in purchasing manufactured goods directly from American parent companies rather than the Canadian subsidiaries with which they had dealt previously. Although most of these issues do not lend themselves to an easy solution and are likely to remain on the agenda of the Joint Trade Committee for years to come, participants on the Canadian side felt that the meetings did contribute to a better understanding of the intricacies of Sino-Canadian commerce. Canadian bureaucrats also look to the committee sessions as an opportunity to assess China's import priorities for the coming year.

What have been the economic results of the first five years of formal Sino-Canadian ties? Mutual exports have increased fairly steadily.[51] On the Canadian side, exports have become more diversified, reflecting the efforts made by government and industry to sell a greater variety of Canadian products to China. In 1971, wheat accounted for 93.4 per cent of Canadian exports to the People's Republic. Since then grain sales have comprised 87.9 per cent, 64.9 and 76.9 percent of Canadian exports to China in 1972, 1973 and 1974, respectively. Among the non-grain items purchased by the Chinese are ferrous and non-ferrous metal products, potash, and capital equipment in the telecommunications and electrical fields. A number of Chinese commitments to procure large technical manufactured products from Canada, for example, satellite communications stations, generators and jet engines,[52] have resulted from negotiations begun at the trade fairs or during missions.

Although Sino-Canadian commerce has grown, there are frustrations on both sides. On the Canadian side, Industry, Trade and Commerce officials talk hopefully of still greater diversification of Canadian exports to China, but recognize that one of the factors weighing against more varied sales is the sums the Chinese are spending on Canadian wheat. The trade imbalance between the countries may pose a second problem. If a state trading company is interested in an item produced both in Canada and France, for example, a decision might be made to buy the French product because of China's large deficit with Canada. Canadian officials also expressed some unhappiness that China has not yet purchased a turn-key plant[53] from Canada, even though Prime Minister Trudeau was told by the Chinese that "when they decide to purchase a complete synthetic rubber producing plant they would consider Canada first" and Polysar has been trying to conclude an agreement since 1973. In fact, however, compared to other industrialized nations, the structure of Canadian industry often prevents the offer of a complete plant from a single industrial source. Although the Department of Industry, Trade and Commerce has established a section to seek and co-ordinate complete plant opportunities abroad, Canadian firms have not pursued the sale of turn-key operations in China as actively as the Department has hoped. Other issues affecting both the sale of turn-key plants and export diversification in general are the Chinese preferences for fixed price contracts and their reluctance to use consulting engineers who are independent rather than integrated into a one-company project. Canadians for their part, are hesitant to bid on contracts which do not contain escalation clauses and consider consulting engineers who draw on the resources of different companies to mount projects, an integral part of the industrial process.

Canadian participants in the bilateral trade talks expressed some frustration, too, with their efforts to convince the Chinese of the value of some advance indications of their anticipated import requirements. This information, which has been forthcoming in only a sporadic and vague way, could be used by IT&C officials to alert interested Canadian firms of Chinese intentions so as to enable these firms to plan their production levels accordingly. The differences in domestic economic decision-making and operations between the two countries have resulted from time to time in Canadian inability to fill Chinese orders for commodities such as sulphur and potash. Finally, a few officials indicated some concern about the nature of technical exchanges with China which they felt were very one-sided; with little benefit for Canada. This sentiment was echoed by executives of corporations in resource-based industries who worried that Chinese delegations would examine their plants and processing and then try to imitate them without any advantage to Canadian firms. As a result of their participation in trade fairs and their negotiations with visiting delegations, Canadian businessmen, many of whom initially held visions of almost unlimited markets in China, have developed a more realistic appraisal of the potential for sales to the Chinese. Some Canadian firms, particularly large companies who can afford it, will continue to pursue the Chinese market in the hope of future sales, while others have turned to markets less uncertain than that of the People's Republic.

From the Chinese perspective, the biggest cause for dissatisfaction with Sino-Canadian trade is its asymmetry. Although Chinese exports to Canada have trebled since 1970, they have not increased at a rate close to either Canadian exports to the People's Republic or Taiwanese exports to Canada. The Chinese recognize that their economic structure makes it difficult for them to adapt to the demands of the Canadian market and that they must compete with products manufactured in Taiwan and South Korea. Chinese leaders are aware of the problems of exporting to the West and have instructed their officials to learn what items potential buyers want. To this end, the Chinese sent a large mission to Canada in December-January 1973-74 to study packaging, labelling and health and other requirements peculiar to the Canadian market. Even Premier Chou En-Lai was aware of the rather poor quality of some Chinese manufactured goods. Canadian officials recall an incident in which the Premier pulled out a rolled up and very stretched underwear sleeve to illustrate to his officials the need to improve the calibre of their products.

At sessions of the Joint Trade Committee Chinese officials have complained that Canada is not adhering to the most favoured nation section of the Sino-Canadian trade agreement with respect to imports of Chinese textiles. The issue of textile imports in fact antedates the establishment of Sino-Canadian diplomatic contacts. Canadian textile producers have long been concerned about competition from Chinese imports and have accused the Canadian government of whittling away at the domestic textile market in order to sell wheat to China.[54] Under the 1963 wheat agreement between Canada and China, Chinese exports to Canada of "sensitive" items, including textiles, were limited to $7 million annually. Although the size of this voluntary quota upset Canadian producers, the Chinese did not fill it.[55] In the years immediately following recognition, Chinese appreciation of Canadian sensitivity to textile imports remained and they continued to agree to a voluntary quota on such exports to Canada which, again, they did not fully use. In 1974, no voluntary quota was accepted. However, by 1974, the nature of the problem of textile imports from the People's Republic had changed somewhat and Chinese textiles were no longer seen as a major threat to the Canadian domestic market. In fact, in 1974, the Chinese under-fulfilled the levels of textile exports agreed to in 1973. Between 1972 and 1974, the number of Chinese textile export items under restraint had decreased to two: towels and trousers. Items such as cotton fabrics, cotton yarn, sheets, blouses, mens' and boys' gloves and workclothes were dropped from the restraint list because, for reasons of price or style, they had become less competitive in the Canadian market, or because a Canadian textile and clothing board investigation suggested that these exports did not threaten injury to Canadian producers. If Chinese textile products become more competitive, the issue of textile imports may reappear on the agenda of Sino-Canadian relations. The Chinese are anxious to ship textiles to Canada and feel this is one area in which their exports to Canada can expand. For her part, Canada will be under conflicting pressures to augment her imports from China on the one hand, and to protect Canadian producers on the other.

A continuing problem, which is also discussed regularly at

joint trade meetings, is that of valuing Chinese products. Because their economy permits the Chinese to export items with great price flexibility, Canadian tariff authorities have on occasion been reluctant to accept Chinese declarations of value. The two Canadian departments involved, Revenue Canada and Industry, Trade and Commerce, have differing perspectives on the importation of Chinese goods, the former being concerned that regulations governing the evaluation of imports and the imposition of duty are applied consistently, the latter that evaluation disputes and additions of duty to Chinese products harm efforts to promote increased trade. To the extent that these questions of quotas and dumping arise, something that is happening with sufficient frequency to cause concern, Sino-Canadian trade relations are impeded.

Before discussing some other aspects of post-1970 Sino-Canadian relations a brief comment on Canada's trade with Taiwan in this period may be of interest. Taiwan naturally severed diplomatic ties with Canada immediately following Ottawa's recognition of Peking. However, the rupture of political ties has not adversely affected trade between the two countries.[56] During recognition talks Canada indicated to representatives of the People's Republic that her trade with Taiwan would continue.[57] Taiwanese textile, electronics and food exports to Canada have increased markedly over the past few years and Taiwan participated in an international trade fair, in Vancouver in 1971.[58] Canadian exports to Taiwan have not grown, as dramatically, in part because of the difficulties of identifying trade opportunities without Canadian government assistance. The only official trade links between Canada and Taiwan stem from the need, from time to time, to negotiate textile quotas. The Canadian Export Association and the Toronto Dominion Bank[59] are among Canadian institutions which have expressed interest in developing Canada's commercial contacts with Taiwan. With the current sense of realism about Sino-Canadian trade and lessening corporate concern about blacklisting by the People's Republic of firms which trade with Taiwan, Canada's economic relations with the island may expand.

While he was in Peking in 1973, Prime Minister Trudeau signed an understanding on consular and immigration matters with China. The consular accord permits each side to establish a consulate-general in the other country, the Chinese in Van-

TABLE II
CANADA'S TRADE WITH TAIWAN, 1961-1974
(thousands of Canadian dollars)

	Exports	Imports
1961	2,219	1,856
1962	4,387	2,910
1963	3,759	5,875
1964	6,178	9,063
1965	6,577	9,333
1966	8,410	13,089
1967	12,267	23,569
1968	16,893	34,379
1969	12,631	42,456
1970	18,315	51,936
1971	13,947	80,706
1972	24,476	126,186
1973	33,704	163,771
1974	41,469	193,756

Source: Statistics Canada, *Trade of Canada: Exports by Countries and Imports by Countries* (Ottawa: Information Canada, published annually).

couver, the Canadians in either Canton or Shanghai. It also simplifies visa procedures and allows the Canadian government access to its citizens in China. The Chinese, who had wanted to widen their representation in Canada to include an official presence on the west coast since shortly after the conclusion of mutual recognition, opened their consulate in Vancouver in November, 1974.[60] The functions of the office will include liaison with Vancouver's large Chinese population, trade promotion and assistance to Chinese seamen who dock in Vancouver aboard Chinese ships. Because Canadian officials can monitor political occurrences and commercial activity in China from existing offices in Hong Kong and Peking, Canada did not attach high priority to a second office in China and has no plans at present to take advantage of this provision of the consular agreement.

From the Canadian perspective, the most important contents of the consular understanding were those relating to reunification of families. The Canadian embassy in Peking can now process applications made by Canadians on behalf of their families in China. To the end of 1974 approximately 350 Chinese immigrants had arrived in Canada. Immigration officials expected the over 6500 remaining applications to be processed during 1975 and the first half of 1976. Each application is considered by the Department of Manpower and Immigration to account for an average of 2½ people, so that the total number of Chinese citizens desirous of coming to Canada may be as high as 15,000. Precise numbers are not known. The bulk of the applications were submitted following final agreement on the reunification programme during the Prime Minister's visit to China. This programme will not be affected by changes proposed in Canadian immigration laws in the fall of 1974 because most of the applications were received prior to the announcement of the immigration policy review.[61] Canadian officials expressed guarded satisfaction with the functioning of this segment of the consular accord and suggested that the Chinese had been generally cooperative in the administration of the agreement. Their criticism lay with the slow pace at which applications were handled by the Chinese bureaucracy prior to their receipt for evaluation by Canadian immigration authorities. Now that the immigration agreement has been in force for some time, however, the Chinese may respond to Canadian requests for greater control over the process.

One of the matters of dispute between Canada and the People's Republic of China was the settlement of outstanding Canadian claims against China for losses resulting from nationalization and other seizures of Canadian properties after October 1, 1949. These included the "Ming Sung" claim, an official government claim with respect to the former embassy in Nanking and an unascertained number of private claims. The Ming Sung claim was settled by an exchange of notes between Ottawa and Peking in June 1973. The claim arose out of a 1946 loan obtained by the Ming Sung Industrial Company from three Canadian banks to finance construction of nine ships by two Canadian companies. The loan was guaranteed by the Canadian government. The ships were built and delivered to the Chinese company in 1949. Later in that year, the Ming Sung Company was nationalized by the new People's Republic and therefore prevented from repaying the loan. Pursuant to the terms of the guarantee, the Canadian government had to pay the Canadian banks. Under the claims settlement, the Chinese government agreed to repay the Canadian government the full amount of $14,469,183.06.[62] In December 1974, the Canadian government called for information from Canadians about any possible claims they might have against the People's Republic for transmission to Chinese authorities. Because there had been no accord between the two countries on a formal claims agreement, there was no guarantee that the claimants would collect compensation; nonetheless, the Canadian government was acting on an understanding that the Chinese would look into any private claims Canadians might submit.[63] Settlement of these outstanding claims would remove a potentially minor impediment to trade[64] and, more importantly, would signify, symbolically if not practically, China's willingness to adhere to one part of the accepted code of international conduct.

A direct Sino-Canadian air link has been a possibility since Industry, Trade and Commerce Minister Pépin's visit to China in 1971, when Premier Chou En-Lai endorsed Canada's bid for such a route. Negotiations began in May 1972 in Peking and were concluded in Ottawa in October of the same year.[65] Canadian Cabinet approval of the air agreement and the designation of Canadian Pacific Airlines as the Canadian carrier followed in March 1973.[66] The formal Civil Air Transport Agreement between Canada and the People's Republic of China and a technical protocol on the operations of the agreed air services were signed in Ottawa on June 11, 1973.[67] Original expectations were that CP Air would begin service to China sometime in mid-1974, and this was later revised to October 1974. However flights had still not begun by December 1975. The delay arose initially from the need to negotiate transit and refueling arrangements with the Japanese, who were unwilling to grant these conditions to CP Air before the inauguration of their own Tokyo-Peking service,[68] and later because of a fare dispute with the Chinese.[69] The Chinese took advantage of the hiatus to reopen the negotiations on onward flight rights which, under the Sino-Canadian air transport agreement, were to be arranged after the commencement of flights between the countries.[70] It is possible that these logistical disagreements are masking Chinese reassessment of the value of an air link with Canada and doubts about China's ability to cope bureaucratically with an influx of air traffic. Until the differences on traffic rights and fare are settled direct air connections between Canada and China will remain in abeyance.

Through exchanges in the fields of education, culture and sports agreed upon in principle during Sharp and Trudeau's visits to China, Sino-Canadian relations have extended beyond the confines of trade and related areas. The breadth of these exchange accords was seen as another early indication of Canada's special relationship with China. Many of the agreements have come to fruition: a programme of student exchanges enabled the first group of Chinese students to arrive in Canada in April 1973 and their Canadian counterparts to enter China in November of that year;[71] an exchange of professors began in late 1974; an exhibition of Chinese archaeological relics unearthed since 1949 was held at the Royal Ontario Museum in Toronto in the fall of 1974;[72] and an exhibition of Canadian paintings, the first from any Western country, was on view in Peking and Shanghai in the spring of 1975.[73] Other arrangements, such as the performance of a Canadian orchestra in China, have yet to materialize. The negotiation of all the exchange agreements was prolonged and difficult. The cultural side of Sino-Canadian ties is more intimately connected to the internal political climate in the People's Republic than is trade and the Chinese are extremely sensitive to foreign influences in the cultural realm. The anti-Confucius campaign in progress in China during 1974, for example, affected China's cultural contacts with the West in general and with Canada in particular, and resulted in the postponement of the Vancouver symphony's trip to China. This campaign rendered the visit of an orchestra which would perform the works of composers such as Schubert and Beethoven, who were themselves under criticism from Chinese authorities, unacceptable. Moreover, the Canadian paintings selected for display in China were chosen with great care by the Chinese, who indicated a definite preference for pre-twentieth century art. Because cultural links are heavily influenced by ideological considerations and intra-party rivalries within China and, because, as a result, officials in the cultural agency, unlike their colleagues in the state trading corporations, do not have the final authority on cultural arrangements, Sino-Canadian cultural relations are difficult to plan and will likely be limited in number.

Canada's contacts with the People's Republic in international forums such as the United Nations can be characterized as having more form than substance. During the first year of Peking's membership in the U.N., the Chinese delegation consciously consulted Canada and other experienced middle-rank members like Austria on procedural questions. More recently, the Canadian delegation at the U.N. has included China among the countries with which it holds talks prior to the opening of the General Assembly session. The first of these formal meetings to discuss agenda items was held in 1974. From the Canadian perspective the discussion was not very successful: Canadian officials hoped to engage their Chinese counterparts in a dialogue over current issues while the Chinese used the meeting for a formal presentation of their views. Another meeting between the two delegations was expected before the 1975 General Assembly convened but the consultation did not materialize because of difficulties encountered in scheduling talks between the two heads of missions. It is hoped that the bilateral talks at the U.N. will resume in 1976.

The two nations have also held discussions relating to Law of the Sea matters. When China joined the U.N. Seabed Committee, which was responsible for the preparations for the third Law of the Sea Conference, she quickly invited Canada to hold consultations to review issues connected with the conference. These talks were held during sessions of the Seabed Committee. Meetings between the two countries on Law of the Sea problems were also held at various times in Peking. Moreover, during his visit to China, the Prime Minister explained Canada's legislation on the Arctic to the Chinese. On many maritime questions the views of the two governments are similar, reflecting their positions as coastal states. However, in their bilateral discussions Canada has usually had more information to transmit to Peking than she had received in return. There have been no real negotiations between the two countries nor any interest in working towards a common position on Law of the Sea matters.

Although Sino-Canadian contacts on maritime questions have been more extensive than on most international issues, in general Canada does not see her international diplomatic relations with Peking as being of significance beyond the formal exchange of views.

Speculation about the Future of Sino-Canadian Relations
In the first few years following recognition, there was a special tone to the Canadian relationship with the People's Republic of China. Peking indicated a definite intention to purchase Canadian wheat, signed a consular accord with Canada and agreed to a number of Sino-Canadian cultural exchanges. Canada sent numerous missions to China and significantly increased her exports to that country. The special relationship served a purpose for both sides. China used the conclusion of recognition talks with Canada and her acceptance of the Canadian "take note" formula on Taiwan to demonstrate to the world that she had come out of the Cultural Revolution and was ready to resume international contact. Subsequently, a number of countries adopted the Canadian formula for granting recognition to Peking. To China, Canada was not just any western nation, but one which, because of location and history, would be a valuable source of information about the United States. China also saw Canada as a safe, reliable Western state with which she could try out a consular agreement. Canadian industry could provide technical expertise to China. Finally, the Chinese were grateful to Canada for helping to defeat the United States' procedural resolution, which proposed that Peking's admission to the U.N. be considered an "important" question, and for supporting Chinese membership in the world organization. From the Canadian side, Sino-Canadian relations enhanced the political viability of the "third option" and the Trudeau government's stress on developing ties with Pacific rim countries. Canada's exports to the People's Republic grew dramatically, to the benefit particularly of the Western provinces which produce and ship the wheat, potash and wood products to China.

Since 1974, the intensity of Sino-Canadian links has lessened, although the warm tone of the relationship will probably persist to the end of the decade. In strictly diplomatic terms, Sino-Canadian relations are likely to be limited. China appears to have only a minor role to play in the issues and arenas designated as important to Canadian foreign policy objectives. The two countries will continue to confer at the United Nations, but China's growing experience in international forums, her lack of interest in many international problems of concern to Canada and her ideological approach to interstate relations suggest that Sino-Canadian diplomatic ties will remain at the level of formal exchanges of views. Moreover, as Peking slowly increases her diplomatic contacts with the United States, Canada's importance as a post for observing Washington decreases.

The economic side will continue to be the most important facet of Sino-Canadian ties. If, as experts suggest, China will need to import grain at least until the end of the seventies,[74] then the largest component of current Canadian exports to the People's Republic is guaranteed a market. However, Canada is anxious to diversify her exports to China. Prospects here may be less influenced by political considerations than was China's stated preference for Canadian wheat. The Canadian and Chinese economies are essentially competitive rather than complementary.[75] Canada has a wide range of technical items to sell to China, but there is not much she can import from the People's Republic. The variety and quality of Chinese exports have limited appeal in the Canadian market. Nevertheless, Canadians may find that in order to increase their exports to China, they will have to accept more Chinese imports and assist the Chinese in accommodating to Canadian markets, even though efforts by the Department of Industry, Trade and Commerce in this direction may provoke some opposition from domestic interests. Moreover, Canadian technological products will have to compete for sales with similar goods manufactured in West Germany, Japan and the United States. John Burns, the *Globe and Mail* correspondent in Peking, wrote during the 1974 Canadian Electrical and Scientific Instruments exhibition in Shanghai in which Canadian firms participated

> (the) Chinese are remarkably conservative in their trading patterns and they will hardly be won away from the notion that the best sources for high-technology equipment are the established leaders in the field — Japan, Britain, West Germany and the United States. Canada . . . can never aspire to more than a minor slice of the pie . . .[76]

At the same time, there are some kinds of technology in which the Chinese are showing increasing interest and which Canadians have noted expertise, such as oil drilling and railway equipment.

Many Canadian businessmen are now less enamoured of commerce with the Chinese than they were initially after the establishment of diplomatic ties. They have found doing business with the People's Republic frustrating and time-consuming. Some Department of Industry, Trade and Commerce officials echoed this attitude, adding that time spent exploring possible markets in the People's Republic has meant that other more potentially successful export opportunities have not been probed. Continued expansion of Sino-Canadian trade will also depend on the view adopted by the Chinese leadership on foreign trade. Important segments of that elite appear ambivalent as to whether an increase in foreign trade, with a concomitant increase in dependence on imported goods and technology, might imply some departure from the basic party principle of self-reliance. In short, Canada's future relations with the People's Republic of China depend on the international priorities of China's leaders and on Canada's ability to convince the Chinese that their ties with Canada are of value. Whatever the level of future Sino-Canadian contacts, Canadians will approach the relationship with a greater sense of realism than they exhibited from 1970 to 1974.

Notes

1. Among the fairest assessments of American influence in the determination of Canada's China policy is the essay by John W. Holmes, "Canada and China: The Dilemmas of a Middle Power" in A.M. Halpern, ed., *Policies Toward China: Views from Six Continents* (Published for the Council on Foreign Relations by McGraw-Hill Book Company, 1965), pp. 103-122. See also Peter C. Dobell, *Canada's Search for New Roles: Foreign Policy in the Trudeau Era* (London: Oxford University Press, 1972), p. 150, James Eayrs, *Canada in World Affairs, October 1955 to June 1957* (Toronto: Oxford University Press, 1959), pp. 78-82; John D. Harbron, *Canada Recognizes China: The Trudeau Round 1968-1973* (Canadian Institute of International Affairs, Behind the Headlines, Vol. XXXIII, No. 5, October 1974), pp. 6-7; F.Q. Quo and Akira Ichikawa, "Sino-

Canadian Relations: A New Chapter", *Asian Survey*, Vol. 12, No. 5 (May 1972), pp. 386-398; and Chester Ronning, *A Memoir of China in Revolution: From the Boxer Rebellion to the People's Republic* (New York: Pantheon Books, 1974), pp. 182-186.

2. For example, John W. Holmes, "Canada and the Pacific", *Pacific Affairs*, Vol. XLIV, No. 1 (Spring 1971), pp. 12-13; Quo and Ichikawa, *op. cit.*, pp. 391-398; D.C. Thomson and R.F. Swanson, *Canadian Foreign Policy: Options and Perspectives* (Toronto: McGraw-Hill Ryerson Limited, 1971), pp. 114-116; and a multitude of articles in major Canadian papers between the fall of 1968 and the fall of 1970.

3. Harald von Riekhoff, "An Analysis of Canadian Foreign Policy Objectives", forthcoming in a volume of essays on Canadian foreign policy, edited by Paul Painchaud.

4. *Globe and Mail*, April 29 and May 3, 1975; *Ottawa Journal*, April 30, May 2 and June 10, 1975. Articles in the press suggested that the withdrawal request was made for "security reasons". The government refused to comment on the reason for the requested departure. The timing of this episode was rather suspicious and may have been stage-managed by the Americans to discourage recognition of Peking by the Philippines. The diplomat was alleged to be channeling funds to Philippine revolutionaries.

5. See, for example, John Holmes, "Canada and China", *op. cit.*, p. 104 and Maureen Appel, "Canadian Attitudes to Communist China" (unpublished M.A. Thesis, McGill University, August 1964), pp. 22 and 25.

6. See for example, External Affairs Minister Pearson's statement to the House of Commons, Standing Committee on External Affairs, April 24, 1956 to the effect that the "recognition of China is a question which is really up to the U.N. . . . both go together" or the strategy enunciated by Prime Minister Diefenbaker to the House of Commons that China should first be admitted to the United Nations after which Canada would consider the question of recognition. House of Commons, *Debates*, April 26, 1961, p. 4028.

7. Annually after 1961, with the exception of 1967, Canada sold more than $100 million worth of grain to China. See

Table 1. For a discussion of the incentives and disincentives to Canadian trade with China in the days prior to recognition see Henry S. Albinski and F. Conrad Raabe, "Canada's Chinese Trade in Political Perspective" in A. Stahnke, ed., *China's Trade with the West: A Political and Economic Analysis* (New York: Praeger Publishing Inc., 1972), pp. 89-133.

8. Canada's role in the 1966 U.N. debate on the seating of the People's Republic of China is discussed in "Chinese Representation in the United Nations", *External Affairs*, Vol. XVIII, No. 12 (December 1966), pp. 538-544 and in a statement made by Prime Minister Pearson to the House of Commons, November 24, 1966. *Debates*, pp. 10274-7.

9. Office of the Prime Minister, Press Release, May 29, 1968.

10. "Chinese Representation in the United Nations", *op. cit.,* pp. 542-543.

11. *Foreign Policy for Canadians*, Six volumes (Ottawa: Information Canada, 1970), Volume 1, p. 33.

12. "Reflections of a new China hand", *International Journal*, Vol XXIX, No. 3 (Summer 1974), pp. 329-341.

13. F. Conrad Raabe, "The China Issue in Canada: Politics and Foreign Policy" (unpublished Ph.D. dissertation, Pennsylvania State University, 1970), p. 264.

14. Harbron, *op. cit.*, p. 9.

15. *Globe and Mail*, February 12, 1969.

16. *New York Times*, March 26, 1969.

17. "Joint Summary of Discussions of President Nixon and Prime Minister Trudeau, March 25, 1969", *External Affairs*, Vol. XXI, No. 6 (June 1969), pp. 231-234.

18. Address of Prime Minister Trudeau to the National Press Club, March 25, 1969. Reprinted in Roger Frank Swanson, editor, *Canadian-American Summit Diplomacy*, 1923-1973 (Toronto: McClelland and Stewart, 1975), pp. 274-283. It should be noted that none of the reporters who questioned the Prime Minister mentioned the Canadian decision to recognize China. All the references to China were made by the Prime Minister.

19. Raabe, *op. cit.*, p. 269.

20. "We are fully aware that the Government of Canada and the Government of Japan view the question of recognition of Communist China in a somewhat different light — and

we recognize that our interests may well be different. We have, however, kept in close contact with the Japanese Government as our plans developed and have listened carefully to what they had to say. We shall continue to do so and we hope they understand the reasoning which has led us to this step." Address by the Secretary of State for External Affairs, the Honourable Mitchell Sharp, to the Foreign Correspondents' Club, Tokyo, on April 15, 1969. Reprinted in *External Affairs*, Vol. XXI, No. 5 (May 1969) p. 198.

21. *Debates*, February 10, 1969, p. 5307.

22. Address by the Secretary of State for External Affairs, the Honourable Mitchell Sharp, to the Foreign Correspondents' Club, Tokyo, on April 15, 1969. Reprinted in *External Affairs*, Vol. XXI, No. 5 (May 1969), pp. 197-198.

23. *International Canada*, November 1970, p. 233.

24. Peter Dobell, *op. cit.*, p. 106.

25. *International Canada*, July-August 1971, p. 169, September 1971, p. 182 and October 1971, pp. 197-198. See also Marion A. MacPherson, "Looking at the 20-Year Debate over China's Voice at the U.N.", *International Perspectives*, January-February 1972, pp. 3-6.

In reply to a question in 1975 about the possibility of the Canadian government supporting the re-entry of Taiwan as a member of the United Nations, Mitchell Sharp, the Acting Secretary of State for External Affairs told the House of Commons:

> . . . Canada has always followed a one-China policy. We have no intention whatever of upsetting that position. We believe the government of China is the government at Peking. The question of Taiwan is one to be decided by the Chinese people and not by us.

Debates, June 16, 1975, p. 6778.

26. "Canadian Recognition of the People's Republic of China", *External Affairs*, Vol. XXII, No. 12 (December 1970), p. 417.

27. Address by the Secretary of State for External Affairs, the Honourable Mitchell Sharp to the Foreign Correspondents' Club, Tokyo, on April 15, 1969. Reprinted in *External Affairs*, Vol. XXI, No. 5 (May 1969), p. 198 and House of Commons, *Debates*, July 21, 1969, p. 11384.

28. "Canadian Recognition of the People's Republic of China", *op. cit.*, p. 416.

29. See the statement made by the Secretary of State for External Affairs to the House of Commons announcing the establishment of Canadian diplomatic relations with the Chinese People's Republic. *Debates*, October 13, 1970, p. 49-50. In his clarifying statement on the issue of Taiwan, the Secretary of State for External Affairs repeated the views noted in the previous paragraph.

30. Margaret Meagher succeeded Arthur Andrew as Canadian Ambassador to Sweden in July 1969, and conducted the balance of the negotiations with the Chinese.

31. This paragraph is based on information contained in "Canadian Recognition of the People's Republic of China", *External Affairs*, Vol. XXII, No. 12 (December 1970),p. 417. For the text of the joint communique announcing mutual recognition, see House of Commons, *Debates*, October 13, 1970, p. 49. The Communique was reprinted in *External Affairs*, Vol. XXII, No. 11 (November 1970),p. 378.

32. For a report on Pépin's mission see *International Canada*, July-August, 1971, pp. 164-165.

33. *Globe and Mail*, July 5, 1971.

34. Canadian officials considered the dispatch of a Chinese ministerial mission to Canada in the summer of 1972, less than two years after recognition, to have been very fast by Chinese standards. Foreign Trade Minister Pai Hsiang-kuo's visit to Canada is described in *International Canada*, July-August, 1972, pp. 113-114.

35. Comments on Mr. Sharp's visit to China can be found in *International Canada,* July-August, 1972, pp. 111-113 and October 1972, pp. 192-194.

36. *Ibid.*, April 1973, p. 134.

37. *Ibid.*, September 1973, p. 247. There have also been two provincial missions to China, one led by Ontario Revenue Minister Allan Grossman in March 1972, the other led by British Columbia Premier David Barrett in November 1974. Both missions examined trade opportunities. See *International Canada*, March 1972 and November 1974 respectively.

38. The speeches by the Prime Ministers are noted in Harbron, *op. cit.*, pp. 1-2.
39. See Table 1. For more detailed discussions of Sino-Canadian economic relations, see Albinski and Raabe, *op. cit.*, Henry S. Albinski, "Foreign Policy Considerations Affecting Trade with the People's Republic of China: Canadian and Australian Experience", *Law and Policy in International Business*, Vol. 5, No. 3, pp. 805-835; Tung-Pi Chen, "Legal Aspects of Canadian Trade with the People's Republic of China", *Law and Contemporary Problems*, Vol. 38, No. 2 (Summer-Autumn 1973), pp. 201-229; Claude E. Forget, *China's External Trade: A Canadian Perspective* (Montreal: Private Planning Association of Canada, 1971); and Samuel P.S. Ho and Ralph W. Huenemann, *Canada's Trade with China: Patterns and Prospects* (Montreal: Private Planning Association of Canada, 1972).
40. *Globe and Mail*, November 5, 1970.
41. On October 27, Otto Lang, the Minister responsible for the Wheat Board, announced the sale of a minimum of 98 million bushels of wheat valued at more than $160 million to China. *International Canada*, October 1970, pp. 21-7. See Table 1 for figures indicating the value of Canadian wheat exports to China on an annual basis.
42. *Globe and Mail*, July 5, 1971 and *Globe and Mail*, August 21, 1972.
43. Albinski quotes the Chinese Minister for Foreign Trade, Pai Hsaing-kuo as having told an Australian Labour Party delegation to China: "China used to buy more wheat from Australia than from Canada. But last year Canada established diplomatic relations with China. Canada abides by the 5 principles of mutual respect for territorial integrity and sovereignty, etc." *Op. cit.*, p. 815 and *passim*. In testimony before the Standing Senate Committee on Foreign Affairs, Industry, Trade and Commerce Minister Pépin said: "I do not think that one can always divide politics and trade too clearly... The Chinese do not divide the two, so we had better not either". Quoted in Ho and Huenemann, *op. cit.*, p. 3.
44. Industry, Trade and Commerce Minister Pépin stated that the fair would ". . . enable us to demonstrate Canadian

capabilities in the production and supply of a wide range of sophisticated manufactured products, semi-processed and basic industrial materials, agricultural and advanced engineering services. We will also be able to identify, for future development, Chinese interests and import requirements and hope to become better acquainted with Chinese trade officials, state trading corporations, producers and end users and to obtain a better understanding of the Chinese trading system". *International Canada*, July-August 1972, p. 113.

45. *Globe and Mail*, December 12, 1971 and Chen, *op. cit.*, p. 211.

46. *Proceedings of the Standing Senate Committee on Foreign Affairs,* No. 17, September 22, 1971, p. 18.

47. Chen, *op. cit.*, p. 212. Forget's monograph contains a detailed history of regulations adopted by the United States to prevent trade with China.

48. The Canadian ports and harbours mission went to China in late October 1975. The Canadian railway technology mission to China in November 1975 returned the visit made by a Chinese team to Canada in the spring of 1975. Canadian officials felt the Chinese were quite interested in Canadian equipment and experience and were hopeful that some sales might result.

49. *International Canada*, December 1971, p. 248.

50. *Ibid.*, February 1975, pp. 46-47.

51. See Table 1.

52. The purchases of a satellite station from RCA, the generator sets from Orenda Ltd. and the jet engines from United Aircraft of Canada Limited were noted in *International Canada* of July-August 1972, p. 114, February 1973, pp. 61-2 and November 1973, p. 307, respectively.

53. A turn-key plant is one designed, built and equipped by foreign technicians and is turned over to the purchaser ready to operate. In 1973-4, the Chinese bought a dozen of these ready-to-operate plants from Japan.

54. The Executive Director of the Canadian Apparel and Textile Manufacturers' Association stated in 1963:

> . . . For years now, Canadian governments have been giving away part of our textile market in order to sell wheat. With each new deal, there is a little bit given away.

One little bit doesn't hurt, but when it happens 20 times, the pinch is pretty severe.
Financial Post, August 8, 1963.

Prior to 1964, the importation of Chinese textiles was controlled by imposing dumping duties. See Ho and Huenemann, *op. cit.,* p. 43. For a discussion of MFN status under the Sino-Canadian trade agreement, see Chen, *op. cit.*, pp. 202-204.

55. Ho and Huenemann, *op. cit.*, p. 44-5.
56. See Table II.
57. See statement of External Affairs Minister Mitchell Sharp to the House of Commons, *Debates*, October 29, 1971, p. 9153.

Canada has remained consistent in her refusal to have any diplomatic contacts with Taiwan. In October 1975 the Government announced that an official delegation from Taiwan would not be allowed to enter Canada because the government has recognized the People's Republic of China as the official government of China. Canada no longer accepts official government passports issued by Taiwan. The issue arose because of the possibility that officials from the Taiwanese city of Taichung, which was "twinned" with the city of Winnipeg in the late 1960's, would want to visit Canada following the visit to Taiwan of a delegation from Winnipeg. *Ottawa Journal*, October 2, 1975.

58. Quo and Ichikawa, *op. cit.*, p. 396.
59. The bank opened a branch office in Taipeh in February 1975. The Bank of China as a result has ceased all trading with the Toronto Dominion Bank, *Ottawa Journal*, September 4, 1975.
60. *Globe and Mail*, October 29, 1974.
61. Statement by Manpower and Immigration Minister Robert Andras to the House of Commons, *Debates*, October 22, 1974, pp. 603-4.
62. Department of External Affairs, Press Release, June, 1973.
63. Ottawa *Citizen*, December 18, 1974.
64. Chen, *op. cit.*, p. 208.
65. *International Canada*, October 1973, p. 194.
66. House of Commons, *Debates*, March 9, 1973, p. 2065.
67. *International Canada*, June 1973, p. 196.
68. *Globe and Mail*, September 14, 1974.

69. *Ibid*, October 9, 1974.
70. *Ibid.*, October 24, 1974.
71. *International Canada*, April 1973, p. 140, September 1973, p. 247, October 1973, p. 265 and November 1973, p. 315.
72. *Ibid.*, March 1974, p. 64.
73. *Globe and Mail*, April 9, 1974.
74. Robert M. Field, "Chinese Agriculture in the Seventies: Production, Consumption and Trade", *Asian Survey*, Vol. XIII, No. 10, October 1973, p. 913.
75. N.D. Modak, "China and the Pacific Rim Community", *Executive*, Vol. 15, April 1973, pp. 22 and 24.
76. Victor H. Li, "Ups and Downs of Trade with China", *Columbia Journal of Transnational Law*, Vol. 13, No. 3, 1974, p. 377.

CHAPTER 11

CANADA'S ECONOMIC TIES WITH JAPAN

Keith A. J. Hay

Introduction

Thirty years ago, an observer would have been hard pressed to predict the economic developments in either Canada or Japan to 1975, or even less likely their interaction. Canada emerged from the War with a fledgling manufacturing sector, and during the 1950s experienced a resource investment boom that was to lay the basis for vast new streams of commodity exports to complement the traditional agricultural basics. Japan, faltering in the late 1940s, flourished at the beginning of the 1950s by supplying needed hardware for the Korean War. Still, it was not until the mid 1950s that the Japanese became truly capable of re-entering the world market as customers for their domestic needs and salesmen of the products of their reviving industries.

In the two decades since 1955, Canadian-Japanese economic relations have taken on substance through trade, complemented since the mid-1960s by international capital transactions, and more recently by a surge in tourism. Canadian exports to Japan were worth $91 million in 1955, and should be valued at over $2.0 billion in 1975. Imports from Japan registered $37 million in 1955, and will surpass $1.5 billion in 1975. Even allowing for inflation and exchange adjustments since 1971, these magnitudes are startling. They conceal changes in the mix of items that have occurred on both sides, broadening the base and reducing the fluctuations of merchandise trade, while spreading the benefits of international commerce more widely to consumers and producers on both sides of the Pacific. Growth in this commerce has been somewhat cyclical, mirroring the business cycles of Canada and Japan, and has not been without its thorny issues of tariffs, market access and supply constraints. Nevertheless, the importance to each country of this trade partnership has vastly increased in the post-war period. Canada is one of Japan's top ten suppliers, and Japan displaced Britain as Canada's number two international market in 1973.

International capital transactions between Canada and Japan are modest, and remain at an early stage of development compared to the trade history. Until recently, restraint in these transactions has been virtually all exercised by Japan. Using its Law Concerning Foreign Investment (Law No. 163, 1960 as amended), Japan parried all but the most earnest attempts of foreigners to buy into her economy. Exceptions were allowed only for those holding the rights to sophisticated technology, for instance electronic computers, which otherwise could not be acquired. Thus the Japanese economy prospered behind a tariff which secured high rates of return for local investors, while avoiding the foreign branch-plant syndrome. Pressure from the Americans to relax these barriers mounted during the late 1960s, and became overwhelming in the early 1970s. By this time Japan's trade successes had resulted in the accumulation of huge foreign currency reserves. Obviously, Japanese industry could compete at home and abroad; foreign firms must be allowed into Japan. By 1973, foreign capital entered Japan under substantially liberalized conditions, but few Canadian firms were interested in these opportunities. Canada's stake in Japan still depends on no more than a score of highly visible corporations and a smattering of medium-size joint ventures. Concomitant with the dissolution of barriers to the inflow of capital came liberalizing of Japanese external investment controls. Embarrassed by exchange reserves which finally ran over the $20 billion level in 1972, the Japanese Finance Ministry urged corporations to look overseas. A flurry of capital transactions occurred, some of which were directed towards Canada. After 1960 some minor investments had been sanctioned for Japanese companies, principally in loan or bond form, to Canadian mining and forestry operations. This trickle of funds totalled only some $150 million by 1968, but this amount was doubled in the next five years, mainly through more equity participation in the metallic minerals and forest product industries of Western Canada, complemented by small investments in manufacturing and assembly of such items as wire, textiles, television sets, and automobiles. When offices and service centres for dozens of Japanese corporations strung out from Vancouver to Halifax are added to the total, investment came to some $425 million by 1975. This amount is approximately one-hundredth of the value of American involvement in Canada, and less than one-quarter of British or even German capital holdings here. Nor is the Japanese commitment of capital for Canadian use likely to rise very rapidly in the immediate future. Reverses in the Japanese balance of payments since late 1973 have reduced available funds; Canada's new Foreign Investment Review Agency, policy on energy and non-renewable resource exports, and shifting provincial government strategies, have created uncertainties for prospective trans-Pacific investors.

The most recent developments in the economic ties between Canada and Japan have come in the area of tourism. Japanese have a view of Canada as a giant land of forests and lakes, preserving all the natural beauties so threatened by environmental depredation of their home islands. A recent survey showed Japanese ranked Canada among their first three vacation choices on these criteria. There were 52,000 visitors from Japan in 1973, and forecast data project 85,000 in 1975 spending more than $40 million, as the proportion of visitors spending more than twenty-four hours in Canada grows. These tourist earnings are expected to triple by 1980 with increasing Japanese affluence and a strong taste for consuming international travel.

From these quick sketches, it is evident that trade is the fulcrum of the Japanese-Canadian economic relationship, and even though the short-term prospects are restrained, the way ahead beyond 1978 suggests both a deepening and broadening of commercial prosperity for both partners.

Trade in the Seventies

In two years, between 1972 and 1974, Canada's exports to Japan soared from $959 million to a new record of $2.2 billion. Canadian purchases from Japan rose from $1.0 billion to $1.4 billion, switching a small $112 million bilateral deficit to a substantial $793 million surplus favourable to Canada. Among Canada's trade partners, this trade with Japan continued to be the most dynamic element. Its impact has been felt in every province of Canada, both by generation of income and employment and through the purchase of high-quality Japanese consumer and producer goods.

270

On the other hand, the effect of a global slowdown in the pace of economic activity, and a slackening in world trade has retarded Canada-Japan development. The OPEC offensive of late 1973 knocked off stride the only partially recovered Japanese economy. Thus, for two years, Japan has been in the grip of a recession of widening and deepening proportions. In an effort to stave off potential material shortages, Japan built up her inventories of fuels, metals, and forest products in 1973-1974. But, with failure of a demand revival to emerge at home, and with only automobile and electrical product exports holding firm, Japan found her stocks overflowing by mid-1974. At present, in 1975, inventory-sales ratios are gradually resuming manageable levels and, with a whiff of economic upturn on the wind, the volume of Canada's exports to Japan may be expected to pick up once more.

Japan has been in the grip of the worst national economic recession since recovery after World War Two. Although early forecasts suggested an upturn might appear during the spring of 1975, there are only now apparent some signs of actual recovery. The Miki government, newly installed at the end of 1974, was faced with a particularly virulent variety of the world-wide stagflation disease. On the one hand the economy was severely depressed, with a number of major industries such as petrochemicals, textiles and shipbuilding running at between two-thirds and three-quarters capacity and with no sign of quickening demand. On the other hand, the "Spring Labour Offensive" of 1974 had brought wage settlements of up to 30 percent per annum following upon and further pushing up record-breaking rises in consumer prices.

Led by the Finance Ministry and the Economic Planning Agency, the Miki Cabinet resolved to quell inflation by severely reducing the rate of growth of the money supply, raising discount rates, razoring increases from the Government's budget, and announcing that the new "Spring Labour Offensive" must be limited to a 15 percent increase for fiscal 1975. These measures successfully impeded the virus of inflation as shown by dramatic reduction in the rate of increase of the consumer price index, and stabilization of wholesale prices. Unfortunately, the economic medicine to produce this result has been so strong that it has left the level of prosperity and industrial activity very weak. It has proved very difficult to revive the flagging economy while hewing to a long-range objective of achieving an inflation rate below that of interest paid on bank deposits as of March 31st, 1977.

Japan's GNP rose slightly in the second quarter of 1975, after two successive previous quarters of decline. The effect was to leave the economy, in June, 1975, virtually at the same GNP level that had been reached in September, 1974. Consumer spending and business capital expenditure remained dull and, up to mid-year of 1975, the economy was being sustained principally by export earnings, government spending and a mild recovery in housing starts. However, not even this modest achievement could be sustained. After July, export-earnings turned down and the balance-of-payments turned sour. By September 1975, both exports and imports were very depressed, with export earnings showing the worst decline in 17 years, and imports in August, 1975, down by 13.6 percent from 1974 levels. Japan's grip on the U.S. market appeared to be badly shaken as sales fell by more than 30 percent — the worst setback since 1949. Only Britain, China, and U.S.S.R. continued to increase their imports from Japan in the third quarter of 1975.

Similarly, imports sagged. Canadian sales were cut along with purchases from all of the Western World — some 11.5 percent in total. Only China, selling oil and raw silk, ran counter to this import trimming trend. Canadian sales were slightly sustained by a recovery of Japanese foodstuff demand.

The combination of a stultified economy, rising unemployment and new setbacks in the trade account led the Miki government to overhaul its economic policies, and announce a fourth and much more stimulative program for economic recovery on September 17th, 1975.

Canada's prospects for trade with Japan are closely associated with the relative success or failure of these latest pump-priming measures. Without some economic counterthrust, the Japanese economy was headed for economic growth of only 0.6 to 0.7 percent in fiscal 1975, with all the obvious implications for her trading position. The September program was aimed at deflecting the economy to a much higher growth path so that the overall result for fiscal 1975 would indeed be 2.2 percent growth, with no increase in the inflation rate. To achieve this, the Miki government introduced a supplementary budget with spending estimates of $6.7 billion which was expected to create about $10 billion of new aggregate demand, in an effort to push the economy to a 6 percent growth rate in the last half of fiscal 1975.

Among other key points, the new recovery program contains important items that should eventually bear upon the recovery of a number of Canadian metallic mineral and forest-product export items, while expanding the need for Canadian coking coal. The Miki government plans to spend $4.2 billion on public works, road and rail construction, flood prevention, and additional loans to housing. More than $310 million will promote the use of pollution abatement devices by small business, and a further $190 million will be used by the Export-Import Bank to promote exports of plant and equipment and also to secure imports of such primary products as copper ores and blister. The Budget also contains provisions to ease the lot of the unemployed and those small businessmen hurt by bankruptcies of large corporations. Finally, the bank rate was reduced by 1.0 percent to 6.5 percent in October.

It will be some time before the success of this attempt to rekindle industrial activity in Japan can be judged. The program may be "too little and too late", especially since it avoids direct stimulation of private consumption and investment. Indeed, public works needs may result in supply bottlenecks and give rise to a new round of price surges. What is clear from all this is the new view of the Miki government that a trajectory of 6 percent per annum annual real growth is important if unemployment is to be avoided up to 1985. This view should certainly revive the flow of Canadian commodity exports from the lethargy of 1975 and so feed back positively into the Canadian economy.

The fight against inflation is viewed as paramount if Japan is to maintain her share of world trade. Recent studies have indicated that, even allowing for productivity gains, Japanese unit labour costs would rise 5 percent per annum, regardless of a less inflation-prone environment.

Both Canada and Japan maintain floating exchange rates which are keyed to the American dollar, and administered in a technical manner by their respective central banks. Thus, a strengthening of the U.S. dollar will most likely leave the functional exchange rate between Canada and Japan unmoved, other things being equal. Differing inflation rates between Canada and Japan can thus erode the competitive position of the higher inflater in the respective export markets, both vis-a-vis domestic competitors and third country suppliers. Certainly, there has been some anxiety over these outcomes for Canadian forest-product exports to Japan, and for imports of home entertainment equipment from Japan. A failure by Japan to control her inflation may accelerate the recent slide in exports of steel and all other capital goods, machinery and equipment. The critical question must be, therefore, can the Miki government gain its objective of single digit inflation by the end of March, 1976? Large Japanese labour unions have agreed to restrain their wage demands in 1976 if the government can bring the rise in the consumer price index into the 6-8 percent range. Although inflation had receded from the 24 percent peak rate of 1974 to around 10 percent in August, 1975, some major problems persist.

Central to Japanese consumer price psychology is the price of rice. The Miki government elevated the retail price of rice 18 percent in September 1975, following upon efforts to prop up farm incomes. Since April 1975, the prices of pork, beef, vegetables and fruits have all soared to new record levels. This has forced the government to re-open the Japanese market to meat imports, and, it has argued, to slash tariffs and grant preferences across a spectrum of meat, fish, fruit and dairy items. This move has also been explained as a gesture to less developed countries who have attacked Japan's agricultural trade policies at the Geneva GATT talks. Since rice prices are the key to which wage demands respond, it is clear that Japan must find a new way to make up the income deficiencies of its farmers by placing less reliance on a price-support system. Cash income subsidies to farmers would allow a further opening of the Japanese market to food imports and significantly benefit Canadian meat, grain and feed producers in competition with other offshore suppliers.

Summing up, the slowdown in Japanese economic activity that has lingered through 1974 and 1975 should gradually reverse itself in 1976. It is too early to say if recovery without severe inflation is possible for Japan in the last half of the seventies. It will be a double-edged problem. Too much fiscal and monetary stimulation will lead to roaring prices, retarded export performance and a short-lived spurt in imports before the brakes are jammed on again. The alternative to this type of every other year "stop-go" policy is conservative budgetary management. Too little stimulation will lack sufficient impetus to nudge the economy back onto a growth track. With luck, the Fall 1975 supplementary budget and additional fine tuning will allow a resumption of Japanese real growth at between 5 and 6 percent per annum up to 1980. In the past, it has been this growth performance that has provisioned and prompted major gains in Canadian-Japanese trade.

Trade and Japanese Industrial Development since 1955

A brief, but fairly accurate, way of typifying Japanese economic development over the past twenty years is to select the main motive force in each of a series of five-year periods. Between 1955 and 1960, it was labour force expansion that provided the main thrust to Japanese industrial development. This, then, was the period in which labour-intensive items dominated Canada's imports from Japan, featuring textiles, footwear, toys, paper goods, canned sea-foods and mandarin oranges. Japan's specialities in international trade reflect the basic structure of her industrial sector. As with most successful international traders, the commodities exported reflected Japan's comparative advantage in their production.

Indeed, so evident was the Japanese advantage in output of textiles and footwear, that North American producers of similar items felt threatened by a torrent of such goods. In response, cotton manufacturers in the United States approached Congress to curb imports. It should be noted in passing that the U.S. was and is the world's largest producer of textiles and, in 1955, exported three times as much yardage as was imported from all global sources, including the U.K., West Germany, Hong Kong and Japan.[1] Nevertheless, for 1956, Japanese textile producers, under extreme pressure from the U.S. textile industry and its congressional supporters, acquiesced in a voluntary export restraint on cotton fabrics, print cloths and blouses. From 1957 to 1961, these restraints (VER's) were formalized in agreements between the American and Japanese governments.[2]

It is important to recognize the general "spillover" effects of U.S. commercial policy in the Pacific upon the relations between Canada and Japan. Since sizing, style and distribution methods are very similar in Canada and the U.S., the Japanese exporter tends to produce items suitable for all of this giant North American market. When part, and in the case of the U.S., the preponderant part of this market is curbed or shut-off, then the natural tendency is to divert planned production to the remaining unobstructed market. Since the late 1950s, there have been numerous cases when U.S. quotas or VER's have faced Canada with a rising tide of diverted goods, leaving little or no option but to follow along similar policy paths to those already trod by the United States.

Commencing in 1960, Japan and Canada agreed upon VER's covering half-a-dozen cotton textile items, for example sheets, some miscellaneous fibres, certain rayons and other synthetics, plus plywood, stainless steel, flatware, and so on. These VER's were the first to be invoked in post-war Canadian commercial relations with any nation. By 1961, they had been extended to include nylon fabric, transistor radios, and tubes for radio and T.V. receivers. Certainly, as the 1960s progressed, a number of these VER's were terminated, but the prototype of agreement with Japan gave rise to similar limitations existing between Canada and seventeen other traders, ranging from Colombia to Macao and Romania by 1971.[3]

From 1960 to 1965, Japan entered into a further stage of industrial development. This half-decade featured the build-up of the heavy industry sector. Growth was thus spearheaded by capital accumulation, as vast investment was made in steel capacity, dockyards, petro-chemical complexes, metal and oil refineries, pulp and paper mills, and the like. Machinery and technology was purchased selectively from the United States and Europe with the aim of acquiring the most up-to-date methods of production and those giving greatest scope for continued innovation. It is not difficult to trace the impact on trade of these developments. Very soon Japan rose to prominence in shipbuilding and, subsequently, constructed more than half the world's total additional tonnage throughout the later sixties and early seventies.

The story has been the same for some other capital goods industries, which may not dominate world output, but which, nevertheless, have demonstrated a substantial, comparative advantage in production of such items as steel and ethylene. With this swing in advantage, the nature of Japan's export mix also shifted, so that, by 1965, producer goods made up the largest group of Canadian imports from Japan, rising from 26.8 percent of the total in 1960 to 36.0 percent by 1965, within which time iron and steel had climbed from 10.0 percent to 16.6 percent of our total imports. By contrast, consumer non-durables, which feature textiles and other labour-intensive items, had sunk from 43.5 percent to 29.9 percent in the same period.

As the heavy and chemical industries of Japan developed at a rapid pace in the first half of the 1960s, so did their needs for raw materials. Japan looked to her neighbours on the Pacific Rim to supply these inputs. Placing high importance on political stability and the ability to maintain uninterrupted supplies, Japan was naturally drawn to Australia, New Zealand and Canada as suppliers of minerals and fuels. By the early 1960s, Canada was exporting a high proportion of grains and forest products to Japan, a mix that was more or less typical of the other two major Commonwealth suppliers in the Pacific area.

In the early 1960s, Canada began developing an export trade to Japan of iron and copper ore, principally from British Columbia. By 1965, this commerce was valued at over $50 million, and other metallic minerals were also beginning to move; for example, zinc, lead, silver, molybdenum; and some fully and partly finished aluminum products, totalling in all some $30 million by 1965. M. Galway, in a publication for the Department of Energy, Mines and Resources, has argued that the growth of the British Columbia copper industry since 1965 can be attributed primarily to opportunities and investment provided by Japan.[4]

Canada's exports to Japan neatly dovetailed with the capital expansion phase of Japan's heavy industries, providing them with a reliable source of metallic and forest materials. Concurrently, Canada continued her long-term role as one of several Pacific Rim suppliers of grains and feeds to the bakery and farm industries in Japan.

The third quinquennium, from 1965 to 1970, can be viewed as one in which research, development and the advancement of technology were the main spurs to growth in Japan. This stage was reached because Japanese personal income had risen to a level at which an era of mass consumption of consumer durables could be sustained. There was then a rising domestic demand within Japan for personal transportation vehicles; home entertainment equipment; cookers, coolers and conditioners; and the other trappings of twentieth-century affluent living. For six years after the recession of 1965, Japanese industry ran at full blast, producing durable items, first for the local market and, increasingly, for export markets, principally in North America

277

and South East Asia, but gradually extending outward to Africa, South America and, finally, by 1970, reaching to Europe.

Years of high-level education, which has produced the most literate society in the world, paid off in very high rewards for Japan's industrial and bureaucratic elite during the last half of the 1960s. Having placed high priority on the training of scientists, technologists, engineers and mathematicians during the previous fifteen years, Japan had a highly skilled labour force to harness savings and technology to the cause of rapid industrial progress after 1965. Many of the processes and products were acquired from overseas either by royalty agreements, outright purchase arrangements, rights to regional world markets, embodiment in machinery and equipment, or through judicious allowance of technology-intensive foreign investments in Japan. At the same time, Japan used tariffs and certain non-tariff barriers to hedge off her domestic markets for autos, televisions, freezers and the like, in order to give her infant consumer durable goods industries a strong base in the 100-million consumer local market, before meeting international competition head on. By this means, Japanese producers received the benefits of large-scale production, developed selling organizations, and, as Abegglen terms it, acquired the "fruits of production experience."[5] All of this contributed to reducing unit costs of production in very short order, thus making the Japanese a formidable new force as competitors in world markets for consumer durables.

Besides the tariffs and Non-Tariff Barriers which existed in the late sixties, but have since been cut and partly dismantled, there existed more subtle obstacles to outsiders wishing to penetrate the Japanese domestic market for consumer goods. The first and natural difficulty was one simply of size. The market is big, but the unit commodities were and remain small by Western measures. There was, for instance, a large Japanese market in tiny cars with engines of 360 c.c., or about one-tenth the size of those in the standard North American automobile. Ten years later, the best selling Japanese automobiles at home and abroad are in the 1,200 c.c. engine class, about one-half the size of the smallest North American auto engine, for example, that of the Chevrolet Vega. This same size disparity is evident in televisions, Japan's 15" versus our 26" screen; refrigerators,

Japan's 6.8 cu.ft. versus our 15 cu.ft., furniture, and so on. The reasons are obvious. Japan is a very small country with a very high population density, resulting in high land prices, with a necessity to conserve travelling and living space. Furthermore, Japanese have been smaller in physical stature than North Americans. Thus, to enter the Japanese fashion market, for instance, it is necessary to develop specialized sizing to suit local requirements.[6] In general, North American manufacturers have considered the cost of "cutting their products down to size" — a metric size at that — too high for the rewards they might earn in the Japanese consumer market.

The other, often quoted, barrier to selling consumer items in Japan has been the distribution system. Again, space plays a role. Japanese distribute commodities frequently and in small batches, because of the limited access and storage potential of most retail outlets. This means that the importing-wholesaling-retailing chain is excessively long and costly. Indeed, import items often end up with a mark-up three or four times over the initial wholesale price. By this stage, the import is selling on "snob-appeal", or because of its very high price, rather than the usual consumer merit rating. Nevertheless, high prices discourage rapid consumption, or use of highly-prized imports, and limit their market growth. Over time, the distribution system has been modernized and streamlined.[7] In 1952, 99.1 percent of all Japanese retail establishments employed less than nine employees (95.4 percent used one or two); but, by 1968, this percentage was 96.8 percent, with 0.2 percent of establishments having fifty or more employees and doing almost 20 percent of all retail business. Since 1968, department stores, chain stores, and supermarkets have been claiming a steadily growing market share. Canadian producers of finished products, especially those destined for the consumer, have an expanded entrée to urban markets through the growth of these large stores, which often specialize in hard-to-find import items. Yet the competition is very great as many European and American producers scramble for a niche. In food items, for example, Canada is faced with the determined and sustained marketing efforts of Australia and New Zealand, who made Japan their number one export target after virtually losing the U.K. to the European Community.

Returning to Canada-Japan trade developments between 1965 and 1970, two points immediately emerge. Canadian exports amounted to $316.2 million in 1965 and were more than double this five years later. Imports went from $230 million to over $500 million in the same span. Furthermore, on both sides, there was a broadening and re-alignment of the mix of items traded. Starting in 1969, Canada commenced sales of uranium to Japan thus stimulating a Northern Ontario and Saskatchewan industry that had languished for ten years. Furthermore, expansion of Japan's iron and steel industry during the 1960s led to a widespread search for new coking coal sources outside the traditional suppliers in New South Wales, Australia. Initially, the interest centred on Queensland in North Eastern Australia, but by hard Work and careful selection of coal to suit Japanese specifications, scientists in the Canadian Mines Branch convinced steelmakers of Canadian coke potential. A small contract came into force in 1967 and other substantial deals followed in 1970 and the following three years. Meanwhile, by 1970, copper exports were five times as great as their 1965 level of $33.9 million. West Coast iron ore proved too costly for continued shipment in the small freighters demanded by local harbours, but other metals continued to expand. On the manufacturing side, Canada could usually manage no more than 3 or 4 percent of total exports, featuring a vast array of small items, many only sold intermittently, or perhaps in one spot sale Canadian exporters could not find the "staple" item that would sell day-in and day-out to the Japanese consumer. It should be noted that, in products such as meats, processed foods, fruits and liquor, where Canada might have expected just such a staple market, the Japanese emulated the European Economic Community by hedging the domestic market with an impenetrable thicket of tariffs, quotas, and other skilfully used non-tariff barriers (NTB's), for example, health regulations and liquor excise taxes.

On the other hand, the period from 1965 to 1970 saw the beginning of the Japanese consumer durable boom in Canada. Car and electrical appliance sales rose by a factor of five in this period, and many other items such as furniture, cameras, watches and sporting goods more than doubled their sales returns. By 1970, these durables accounted for some 45 percent of total imports, compared to 35 percent for producers goods and 20 percent for non-durables. The boom in consumer durables amply reflected Japan's ability to adapt and innovate technology in these fields, and blend these ideas into designs which found rapid consumer acceptance, not only at home but world-wide, while maintaining very competitive prices. Virtually every consumer in Canada, at some time, has appreciated such Japanese items. A survey carried out in 1971,[8] showed that Canadians had fewer prejudices against Japanese imports than their counterparts in the United States; less than half of Canadian respondents felt there was an adverse effect on the economy. In the United States, a similar survey found 75 percent of Americans with this view. About 85 percent of all replying to the Canadian sample were completely indifferent to the import origin of items they purchased, and only 6 percent were against Japanese items, compared to 4 percent who were anti-American. The other striking finding of this survey was that quality of product followed by price, style, brand and service, were the principal factors causing consumers to choose Japanese items, suggesting that, other things being equal, non-price competition has been a highly effective factor in establishing sizable Canadian market shares for Japanese products.

During the 1970s, the Japanese economy has been subject to a number of external dislocations. These commenced with the "Nixon Shokku" of August, 1971, in which the U.S. placed a 10 percent surcharge on all imports. Like Canada, Japan is highly dependent on the American market and perceived the surcharge as a serious setback. In 1972, following the Smithsonian Agreement, Japan revalued the yen by 16.6 percent; and again in 1973 the yen was effectively revalued by allowing it to float upwards. These currency re-alignments took place as a direct result of massive foreign exchange earnings by Japan between 1970 and 1973. Exports continued to grow very rapidly during this period, partly because, after 1971, Japan was continually faced with an excess capacity problem, a problem which has still not been resolved.

Shortages of food and feedstuffs reached apparent crisis proportions when the U.S. applied an export embargo to soybeans in June, 1973. This embargo came as a substantial shock to the Japanese who had been repeatedly reassured by the Americans that there was no need to look to alternative suppliers in Asia, including China, for soybeans. Since soya is a staple diet element, and the crushed bean becomes a food or feed, the Japanese are highly sensitive to supply interruptions in this commodity. Canada followed the U.S. very quickly and applied a similar export embargo on soybeans. These restraints only lasted for some three months, but three important points emerge from them:

    i) Export embargoes of key raw material and food items greatly upset confidence of buyers, causing them to reconsider their long-term supply arrangements.[9] This may mean that Japan will encourage food imports from new Asian, South American and European sources.

    ii) The soybean embargo gave weight to local Japanese interests who argued for an expanded domestic agricultural sector. Without protection from imports, Japanese agriculture would recede in importance even more quickly than has been observable in the last decade. However, since 1973, there has been a concerted effort to decrease Japanese dependence on food imports and strive for higher levels of agricultural self-sufficiency. On grounds of labour cost, scale, land shortages, and general factor endowment, this policy is uneconomic; nevertheless it may be pursued vigorously, at considerable cost to potential Canadian sales of feeds, grains and meats.

    iii) The soybean embargo was initially imposed by the U.S. Canada had no choice but to follow suit for fear that, otherwise, a massive international demand for this feed would have been deflected to the comparatively small Canadian market, so driving domestic consumers out, in the face of massive price increases.

Just as Canada had to follow U.S. negotiation of VER's to avoid a diversion of a massive flow of American-bound imports into Canadian ports, so too must we follow in applying Export Restraints for fear of a massive outflow of key resources. The important point to recognize is that American quantitative restraints on trade set parameters within which Canada is forced to manoeuvre. These commercial policies, decided in Washington, set certain basepoints around and between which Ottawa must adjust. It is important that Canadian policymakers make clear to their American and Japanese counterparts the interactive implications of such quantitative trade measures.

Fearful that expanded American grain sales to Russia would

squeeze them out of the market, Japan negotiated a long-term grain export agreement with the U.S. in Fall 1975, which should guarantee them supplies of food and feed grains for at least three years, and secure them against another soybean incident. Japan also intends to reach similar grain agreements with Canada and Australia, but these have yet to materialize.

For the Japanese, the soybean shock was shortly followed by the first of the OPEC moves to adjust oil prices. Since Japan derives three-quarters of its energy from oil, and more than 95 percent of this oil must be imported, principally from the Persian Gulf (especially Abu Dhabi), there was a particular vulnerability to the four-fold increase in oil prices. It has been estimated that, for every 1 percent increase in industrial output, Japan must consume 1.1 percent more oil. Furthermore, industrial use of oil is half as important again as private consumer use (60:40), whereas, in North America, this ratio is roughly reversed. Therefore, Japan has a relatively smaller private sector to squeeze upon to effect oil consumption savings, before actual cuts in industrial activity must occur. The oil bill soared from $10.4 billion in fiscal 1973-74 to $23.2 billion in fiscal 1974-75. In just two years, Japan swung from balance-of-payments surpluses of over $9 billion to a deficit of $13.4 billion at the end of the March, 1974, fiscal year. These swings in the external account were naturally coupled to a steep decline in the yen, from a high of approximately 265 to a constrained level of 300 to the U.S. dollar by mid-1974.

This is the background against which must be measured Japan's switch from being anxious to increase imports in 1971 and 1972, from being an avid capital exporter in the early 1970s, and from being a unilateral tariff cutter, to being highly concerned to re-balance its external payments and pay for oil, to hoping to assure future supplies of food and materials in a world fraught with embargoes and cartels, and to pressing for a multilateral improvement in trade access and freedom.

Commercial Policies: Canada-Japan

The main burden of Canada's commercial policy discussions with Japan is not so much concerned with the size and growth of our imports and exports but with the particular commodity-mix those exports represent.

As noted, Canada has applied VER's to certain Japanese textile products over the past fifteen years, but these are now of rather minor importance. From time to time, Japanese suppliers along with other international merchants have been the subject of "dumping" enquiries. Among other items, textiles, clothing, electrical machinery and television sets have all been scrutinized to see if their export prices correspond to factory gate fair market prices in Japan. Dumping has been found in some cases, but on other occasions Japanese sellers have been vindicated. Dumping and health hazard legislation are useful NTB's which have served to protect, in particular, Canadian electrical manufacturers who have seen their share of domestic markets falling. During 1975, some Japanese T.V. sets sold in Canada were recalled after sketchy evidence of health hazards was reported in the United States. A few months later, an anti-dumping tribunal found no evidence of dumping of colour T.V. sets, but recommended price hikes for these Japanese imports to avoid damaging their Canadian competitors in the future.

Canadians have repeatedly argued that Japan buys too few manufactured goods from Canada. The Honourable Jean-Luc Pépin, as Minister of Industry, Trade and Commerce, led a high-powered selling mission to Japan in early 1972. Since then, other federal and provincial ministers have made similar "tours-de-force". These missions have prompted buying groups from Japan to visit Canada and have stirred many of our own businessmen to take a careful look at the Japanese market. Nevertheless, the proportion of fully-finished goods sold to Japan by Canada has continued to slowly decline from 3 percent towards 2 percent of the total export value.[10]

There are some real difficulties in selling Canadian finished products to Japan. A survey of 150 Canadian exporters, in 1972, revealed a number of actual and conceptual difficulties encountered in this trade.[11] In 1971, Japan imported more than $2 billion of end-products, principally capital goods, but with a rising proportion of consumer items, mainly from the U.S., West Germany, the U.K., and other OECD nations. At that time, Canada's share of this market was less than $50 million. The problem seems to arise from difficulties on both the "demand side" (that is, in or entering Japan), and the "supply side" (that is, in Canadian supply capability or marketing). Roughly speaking, these classifications can be used as follows:

"Demand side" factors:

(1) *Japanese tariffs*. It should be noted that Japan unilaterally reduced tariffs on 1,865 items in late 1972.

(2) *Non-tariff barriers to trade,* such as,

i) *Distribution channels*. Within Japan these are very long, especially for furniture, wood products, soaps, sanitary fixtures, machine tools, textiles and foodstuffs, to name only a few obvious examples. As mentioned earlier, reorganization of retailing has and will ease this problem somewhat.

ii) *Health regulations and agricultural restrictions.* These, for instance, restrict purchases of Canadian apples due to possible moth infection. There are, however, many instances where Canadian food producers have changed or reduced additives, or otherwise conformed to Japanese consumer legislation and then found a ready market. This type of obstacle is not peculiar to Japan but may occur in Canada, the U.S. and other countries.

iii) *Specifications and grading*. Use of the metric system has caused awkward specification problems in finished metal products, machinery and lumber sales. Nevertheless, by dint of negotiation and superior marketing, the British Columbia Council of Forest Industries has made a very large inroad into the Japanese housing market. It must now convince Japanese officials to accept Canadian lumber grading standards. This is an example of aggressive and successful marketing.

iv) *Japanese labelling practice*. This demands that goods be especially denominated for that market, and because Canada produces few internationally recognizable brand name items, it is sometimes difficult to establish a market beachhead.

v) *"Administrative Guidance"* not to buy imports is occasionally cited by frustrated overseas salesmen, but documented cases are rare. Since 1971, Japan has been highly conscious of the need to import if she is to retain and establish new export markets. With revival of Japanese consumer demand in sight for 1976, and renewed possibility of external payments surpluses, Japan will be continuing to generally promote imports. The Ministry of International Trade and Industry is preparing an import-incentive programme even as this is written.

(3) *Transportation costs and distance from market*. The recent collapse of ocean freight rates, and break-up of the Pacific Ocean Freight Conference in particular, suggests that these costs will abate from the high levels reached during the "oil crisis". Japan is costly to visit, relative to similar costs incurred in North America, and selling visits may be many and lengthy. However, the trade benefits can be great.

(4) *The highly competitive Japanese market*. This is a factor for both domestic and other external producers. Canada faces tough competition from American, German, Scandinavian, Swiss, Dutch, British and French sellers of finished goods; and from Australia and New Zealand in foodstuffs.

(5) *Import substitution capacity*. Over the years, the Japanese have further developed this. Some of Canada's "money-spinners" of the 1960s, such as office machines, computer equipment, aircraft engines and spares, are no longer imported, but are produced in Japan.

The accompanying table is of interest in reviewing the actual impediments to trade specified by a survey group of Canadian manufacturers in 1972. This shows that tariffs and quotas used by Japan were *not* the major perceived obstacles to trade. In part, the language and social customs of Japan constrained Canadians, but the most important factors appeared to be quality competition, specification problems, supply constraints and *disinterest*.

On the "supply side", some of the problems encountered are as follows:

(1) *Lack of encouragement*. Canadian branches of multi-national enterprises may not be encouraged to export to Japan. On the other hand, there is evidence that a large business-machine manufacturer nominated its Canadian branch as a supplier to Japan as part of its global marketing strategy. This beneficial outcome seems more likely to occur in those multi-nationals where production has been rationalized and the Canadian plant *specializes* in various lines, rather than when the branch produces small quantities of every line item.[12]

(2) *Preference for head offices*. Japanese buyers would often rather do business with the head office of a multi--

TABLE I
PERCEIVED OBSTACLES TO CANADIAN FIRMS ACTUALLY OR POTENTIALLY EXPORTING TO JAPAN, 1972

Obstacles to Trade	Firm Had Experience in Japan	Firm Had No Experience in Japan	Total
High tariffs/quotas	8	4	12
Freight Costs	4	5	9
Health/Sanitation	2	—	2
Specifications	6	16	22
Social Customs	10	3	13
Japanese Government Regulations	6	3	9
Administrative Barriers	2	—	2
Anti-Import Attitudes	7	4	11
Competition - High Prices	8	9	17
- Quality	6	23	29
Parent Corporation in Japan Not Interested in Importing	1	—	1
Japanese Desire for Technology Not Commodity Itself	4	—	4
General Supply Constraints	7	14	21
Financial Problems	2	1	3
Not Interested	n.a.	20	20
Total	73	102	175

Source: K.A.J. Hay, *et. al., A Study of Practices, Problems and Potentials in Canada's Exports of Manufactures to Japan* (Ottawa, 1972), p. V-4. Further statistical information relevent to this chapter may be found in K.A.J. Hay and S.R. Hill, *Canada-Japan: The Export-Import Picture* (Ottawa, 1975).

national than with a Canadian branch. This approach allows them to avoid becoming entangled in a panoply of interconnected patent, royalty and marketing arrangements between Canada, Japan and the parent firm which is often in the U.S. or a European country.

(3) *Weak marketing effort.* Although Japanese missions buying in Canada have been impressed by technology, skilled labour, and quality-products, they are often surprised by Canadians' weak marketing effort at home and abroad.

(4) *Small capital base.* Some Canadian owned firms have a small capital base and only modest access to further funds. From time to time, such firms find themselves swamped by orders from the U.S. market, and can only consider Japan as a residual export market, rather than one in which to make a sustained effort.

Policy for the Seventies and Beyond

Through bargaining at the Multi-Lateral Trade Negotiations (MTN), Canada, in company with other nations, will obtain further access to the Japanese market over lower tariffs and through scrapped or expanded quotas. Nevertheless, as noted above, there are a number of other structural problems that must be overcome, particularly in the Canadian industrial sector, before very large increases in shipments of Canadian manufactures to Japan could be envisaged. Whatever the outcome of the trade negotiations, they will not, in the short run, appreciably change the fact that in trading with Japan, Canada's *comparative advantage* lies in the production of food, minerals, forest products and fuels.

Speaking to the Osaka Chamber of Commerce and Industry on June 24, 1975, Industry, Trade and Commerce Minister Gillespie noted, *inter alia*, two important objectives of Canadian industrial policy. These are, "developing efficient, internationally competitive industries" and "increasing the processing in Canada of our natural resources in order to maximize returns to Canada". At the same time, Mr. Gillespie noted that the Foreign Investment Review Act "is designed to review, not to inhibit or discourage, foreign investment to pursue our national objectives . . . and we certainly welcome Japanese investment".

Canada's desire to increase the extent of processing and fabrication of natural resources in our trade with Japan can fit very comfortably with the future growth projections of the

Japanese archipelago. Short of land, retreating from the edge of a pollution disaster, planning controlled, urban growth with a modest labour force increase, and, above all, needing to devise energy-conserving strategies, Japan is not as interested in refining, milling and processing raw materials to the semi-manufactured stage as she was a decade ago. With more growth in sight, Japan will need material supplies for her own finished-goods industries and for those established in her South East Asian vicinity. Canada is a natural partner to supply semi-finished products to Pacific Rim assembly plants. This strategy appears to fit reasonably well with Canada's preferred sector-by-sector approach to Multi-Lateral Trade Negotiations. There are, however, four points which should be borne in mind:

(1) Canada must prove herself a reliable supplier by ensuring an adequate transportation system to carry goods overseas, particularly through West Coast ports. At present, the transport system is particularly vulnerable to technical and manpower dislocations which impair reliability.[13]

(2) Mr. Gillespie's Osaka statement should help to ease Japanese fears about the Foreign Investment Review Agency. Further downstream processing in Canada for Japan should draw upon both Japanese technology and capital to blend with Canadian knowledge and control.

(3) Australia, New Zealand, U.S.S.R., Indonesia, Brazil, Iran and Chile will be strong competitors for processing sites.

(4) Because Japan has many sites and locations to choose from, Canada must expect strenuous negotiations and significant *quid pro quo's* to be given if Japan chooses to undertake further processing here. Thus, in the Multi-Lateral Trade Negotiations and in bi-lateral discussions, Canada must be willing to seek "deep, wide cuts in the tariff structure of other countries as well as our own, in an orderly fashion, and work hard for the dismantling of non-tariff barriers to trade".[14]

However, it is perhaps too optimistic and likely too costly to imagine Canada involved in a free-trade area arrangement with either Japan or the United States, as has been argued for by the Economic Council of Canada.[15] A Pacific Free Trade Area has a long tradition of academic support and much quantitative work was undertaken on this topic during the 1960s.[16] Now outdated, these estimates showed that Japan would benefit most from such an area, with Australia and Canada gaining least and the U.S. ranking in between. Since then, however, Japanese trade policy has become much more broadly based. Asia is a principal market for Japan and gives signs of long-term sustained growth. Furthermore, South America (particularly Brazil), and the Middle-East (Iran, Iraq, Saudi Arabia) are the current growth centres of the world and are set fair for sustained expansion through to the end of the century.[17] Japan sees these areas as the most dynamic in her trade matrix and the most likely to sustain her renewed growth trajectory. In these circumstances it is not likely that Japan would opt to join a group of maturing, slower growth OECD nations in a Free Trade Area. Further, the politics of oil and resource cartels argue against any official trading alignment between Japan, North America and Europe.

Neither Canada nor Japan can consider joining an exclusive trade club at this point in world development. While committed to freer trade, it is far better that improved access be granted to nations both rich and poor, and not restricted to some "super-EEC rich-men's club" within a free trade area bounded by a common (and high) tariff. The best route remains through widescale bargaining for improvements in multi-lateral trade freedom. Bearing in mind the special problems associated with global trade in energy and agriculture, Canada should be prepared to go beyond its current sector-by-sector approach to trade liberalization. To gain better access for higher levels of processed and finished goods, Canada has to contemplate extensive tariff cuts on manufacturing items, not just in our dealings with Japan but at all points of the compass. Clearly, this strategy will involve the gradual re-ordering of Canada's industrial sector, and this can be done neither overnight, nor without substantial adjustment assistance. It is widely understood, though often ignored, that consumer welfare gains are achieved through tariff cuts and by non-tariff barrier dislodgement. Relatively lower prices of imports can be enjoyed at the retail level, but liberalization also has the effect of lowering the costs of many inputs, for example, machines, specialized steel items, hardware, pipes, fixtures, and the like, thus improving the competitiveness of Canadian end-products which use these intermediate goods.

Tariff cutting may turn out to be much simpler and indeed rather less effective than coming to grips with National Trade Barriers. In an exchange of views, Canada and Japan have noted less than a dozen such barriers as serious irritants to either side. Given that GATT investigators have identified as many as eight hundred separate types of National Trade Barriers in use around the world, there is some hope for Canada and Japan finding common ground. In his Osaka speech, Minister Gillespie noted that Canada was creating industrial strategies for such industries as "forestry, steel, petrochemicals, aerospace, shipbuilding, electronics, automobiles, clothing and textiles, food processing and resources".[18] Elsewhere, the Minister noted that he hoped for industrial re-organization of a number of industries. This would reverse the trend toward branch plant proliferation in such industries as television construction, where the aim would be to cut the number of producers from ten down to three plants.[19] This is the approach necessary to the survival and strengthening of a number of Canadian industries, if economies of scale are to be reaped and international competitiveness improved. The sooner such sectors are identified, the better, for it will allow Canada to concentrate fully on those industrial segments which have the most to offer in the future. As the 1975 Canada-Japan Ministerial communique noted,

> . . . officials of the two countries should proceed as soon as possible to identify those areas of the Japanese and Canadian economies which held the greatest promise for increased and mutually beneficial economic co-operation. They agreed that the explorations would cover the manufacturing as well as the whole range of resource areas, and include such matters as expanded mutually beneficial investment, broader inter-corporate links including joint ventures, scientific and technological exchanges and conditions giving greater assurance of supply and of access to markets.[20]

Notes

1. The U.S. Department of Commerce figures for total cotton cloth (thousands of yards) imported are 133,252 and exported 437,493.
2. For details see J. Lynch, *Toward An Orderly Market*, (Tokyo, 1968), pp. 97-113.

24962

DATE DUE